# Lecture Notes in Computer Science    10730

*Commenced Publication in 1973*
Founding and Former Series Editors:
Gerhard Goos, Juris Hartmanis, and Jan van Leeuwen

## Editorial Board

More information about this series at http://www.springer.com/series/8183

Marina L. Gavrilova · C. J. Kenneth Tan
Nabendu Chaki · Khalid Saeed (Eds.)

# Transactions on Computational Science XXXI

Special Issue on Signal Processing
and Security in Distributed Systems

Springer

*Editors-in-Chief*

Marina L. Gavrilova
University of Calgary
Calgary, AB
Canada

C. J. Kenneth Tan
Sardina Systems OÜ
Tallinn
Estonia

*Guest Editors*

Nabendu Chaki
University of Calcutta
Calcutta
India

Khalid Saeed
Bialystok University of Technology
Bialystok
Poland

ISSN 0302-9743                    ISSN 1611-3349   (electronic)
Lecture Notes in Computer Science
ISSN 1866-4733                    ISSN 1866-4741   (electronic)
Transactions on Computational Science
ISBN 978-3-662-56498-1           ISBN 978-3-662-56499-8   (eBook)
https://doi.org/10.1007/978-3-662-56499-8

Library of Congress Control Number: 2018932201

Printed on acid-free paper

This Springer imprint is published by the registered company Springer-Verlag GmbH, DE
part of Springer Nature
The registered company address is: Heidelberger Platz 3, 14197 Berlin, Germany

# LNCS Transactions on Computational Science

Computational science, an emerging and increasingly vital field, is now widely recognized as an integral part of scientific and technical investigations, affecting researchers and practitioners in areas ranging from aerospace and automotive research to biochemistry, electronics, geosciences, mathematics, and physics. Computer systems research and the exploitation of applied research naturally complement each other. The increased complexity of many challenges in computational science demands the use of supercomputing, parallel processing, sophisticated algorithms, and advanced system software and architecture. It is therefore invaluable to have input by systems research experts in applied computational science research.

*Transactions on Computational Science* focuses on original high-quality research in the realm of computational science in parallel and distributed environments, also encompassing the underlying theoretical foundations and the applications of large-scale computation.

The journal offers practitioners and researchers the opportunity to share computational techniques and solutions in this area, to identify new issues, and to shape future directions for research, and it enables industrial users to apply leading-edge, large-scale, high-performance computational methods.

In addition to addressing various research and application issues, the journal aims to present material that is validated – crucial to the application and advancement of the research conducted in academic and industrial settings. In this spirit, the journal focuses on publications that present results and computational techniques that are verifiable.

## Scope

The scope of the journal includes, but is not limited to, the following computational methods and applications:

- Aeronautics and Aerospace
- Astrophysics
- Big Data Analytics
- Bioinformatics
- Biometric Technologies
- Climate and Weather Modeling
- Communication and Data Networks
- Compilers and Operating Systems
- Computer Graphics
- Computational Biology
- Computational Chemistry
- Computational Finance and Econometrics

- Computational Fluid Dynamics
- Computational Geometry
- Computational Number Theory
- Data Representation and Storage
- Data Mining and Data Warehousing
- Information and Online Security
- Grid Computing
- Hardware/Software Co-design
- High-Performance Computing
- Image and Video Processing
- Information Systems
- Information Retrieval
- Modeling and Simulations
- Mobile Computing
- Numerical and Scientific Computing
- Parallel and Distributed Computing
- Robotics and Navigation
- Supercomputing
- System-on-Chip Design and Engineering
- Virtual Reality and Cyberworlds
- Visualization

# Editorial

The *Transactions on Computational Science* journal is published as part of the Springer series *Lecture Notes in Computer Science*, and is devoted to a range of computational science issues, from theoretical aspects to application-dependent studies and the validation of emerging technologies.

The journal focuses on original high-quality research in the realm of computational science in parallel and distributed environments, encompassing the facilitating theoretical foundations and the applications of large-scale computations and massive data processing. Practitioners and researchers share computational techniques and solutions in the area, identify new issues, and shape future directions for research as well as enable industrial users to apply the techniques presented.

The current issue is devoted to research on *Signal Processing and Security in Distributed Systems* and is edited by Nabendu Chaki, Professor at the University of Calcutta, India, and Khalid Saeed, Professor at Bialystok University of Technology, Poland. This special issue comprises seven articles preceded by the guest editor's preface. The three best papers were invited following the 4th Doctoral Symposium on Applied Computation and Security Systems (ACSS), and four other contributions were accepted following an open call for papers. The authors for the selected papers are from Europe, North America, and India.

We would like to extend our sincere appreciation to the special issue guest editors, Nabendu Chaki and Khalid Saeed, for their dedication, diligence, and inspiration in preparing this special issue on a very relevant and important topic. We would also like to thank all of the authors for submitting their papers to the special issue and the associate editors and referees for their valuable work. We would like to express our gratitude to the LNCS editorial staff of Springer, who supported us at every stage of the project.

We do hope that the fine collection of papers presented in this special issue will be a valuable resource for *Transactions on Computational Science* readers and will stimulate further research into the vibrant area of computational science applications.

November 2017

Marina L. Gavrilova
C. J. Kenneth Tan

# Guest Editors' Preface

This special issue includes the extended versions of high-quality papers selected from the 4th Doctoral Symposium on Applied Computation and Security Systems (ACSS) held at the National Institute of Technology (NIT) Patna, India, during March 17–19, 2017. ACSS has been co-organized annually since 2014 by the University of Calcutta together with Ca Foscari University, Italy, and Bialystok University of Science and Technology in Poland.

The Doctoral Symposium on Applied Computation and Security Systems (ACSS) aims to facilitate PhD scholars enrolled at universities and research institutes around the world to present and discuss part of their research work with peers in their fields. Each contributed paper presented at ACSS must have at least one enrolled PhD student as the first author of the submission and his/her supervisor(s) as co-author(s). As indicated in the name of the symposium, security remains one of the primary focus areas for this annual meet.

A two-volume post-symposium book has been published by Springer in the AISC series since the inception of ACSS in 2014. The ACSS books are indexed by Scopus and Web of Sciences. In 2015, a new sub-series called ACSS was introduced under AISC and the post-symposium ACSS books are published in this sub-series. The papers selected for this special issue indicate the excellence that marks the success of ACSS in bringing PhD scholars into this forum for the exchange of ideas toward achieving greater scientific goals.

The first paper in this volume is "A ZigZag Pattern of Local Extremum Logarithm Difference for Illumination invariant and Heterogeneous Face Recognition" authored by Hiranmoy Roy and Debotosh Bhattacharjee. The authors propose a new method for face recognition and in the process they introduce Local Extremum Logarithm Difference (LELD) image representation, which is illumination-invariant. A novel methodology for matching of illumination-invariant and heterogeneous faces is proposed here. In this work, the authors build on the premise that since edges are invariant for different modalities, the focus for recognition would be on edges. A novel local zigzag binary pattern, called Zigzag Local Extremum Logarithm Difference (ZZPLELD) is proposed by the authors to capture the local variation of LELD. The proposed methodology is tested for different illumination variations, sketch photos, etc. Recognition of around 96% accuracy with multiple databases under varying illuminations establishes the efficacy of the work. The accuracy is even higher for the sketches viewed. A rank-1 accuracy of 99.69% is achieved for the NIR-VIS benchmark database.

In the second paper titled "Automatic Identification of Tala from Tabla Signal" by Rajib Sarkar, Ankita Singh, Anjishnu Mondal, and Sanjoy Kumar Saha, the authors present a scheme for identifying the *Tala* from the *Tabla* signal. Tabla is the mostly widely used percussion instrument in Indian classical music and it is played according to a *Tala*. Each tala is formed as a specific sequence of *Bol*s that repeats itself. In this paper, the authors have segmented *Bol*s using a Attack-Decay-Sustain-Release (ADSR) model. This leads to the generation of a transcript showing the *Bol* sequence for a given *Tabla* signal. A novel matching scheme is proposed to match the *Tala* templates and transcript for the given signal. Experimental verification using a large variety of datasets confirms the performance of the proposed methodology. The work may turn out to be pioneering research in developing a robust and automated system for analyzing and evaluating the performance of a learner.

The third paper in is titled "A Novel Approach of Retinal Disorder Diagnosing Using Optical Coherence Tomography Scanners" and is written by Maciej Szymkowski and Emil Saeed. In this work, the authors present a detailed study of OCT and OCT-related diseases. The authors conduct the work on the hypothesis that it is possible to create an image-based system for automatic diagnosis of various retinal diseases with high accuracy. OCT is a promising technology that provides a great amount of data in each sample. The novelty is the automatic identification of healthy images from pathological retinas. They propose a new algorithm and implement the same. The objective is to detect sick eyes suffering from diabetic retinopathy and certain types of age-related macular degeneration. Experiments validate that it is possible to automatically detect anomalies in the retinal structure. If the proposed technology is translated to the actual application scenario, this would help shorten the diagnostic pathway.

The fourth work titled "Algebraic and Logical Emulations of Quantum Circuits" is by Kenneth Wingate Regan, Amlan Chakrabarti, and Chaowen Guan. The paper contributes to the theory of quantum circuits with a number of original theoretical results. The focus is on complexity issues that are particularly relevant as the scalability problem is paramount for quantum circuits. The authors adopt a novel approach using algebraic and logical emulations. This provides an interesting setting to formally model complexity properties. The contribution is mostly theoretical, but a few experimental results provide evidence of their actual impact. We hope that readers will agree that this paper is one of the most thought-provoking articles in this special issue.

The fifth paper, "Advanced Monitoring-Based Intrusion Detection System for Distributed and Intelligent Energy Theft: DIET Attack in Advanced Metering Infrastructure," authored by Manali Chakraborty, presents a new attack type specific to smart power grids called Distributed and Intelligent Energy Theft (DIET) attack. The authors subsequently propose a two-tier intrusion detection system (IDS) to detect the DIET attack. The proposed solution also includes passive monitoring on the system to ensure an additional level of security. The idea is novel and supported by significant analysis of simulation results using standard simulation software. The results are interesting and impressive. The proposed IDS is also capable of detecting type-1 and type-2 attacks.

The sixth paper in this Special Issue titled "Combining Symbolic and Numerical Domains for Information Leakage Analysis" by Agostino Cortesi, Raju Halder, Pietro Ferrara, Matteo Zanioli deals with securing information flow. The proposal is based on an abstract interpretation framework comprising symbolic and numerical domains for information-flow analysis of software combining variable dependency analysis with numerical abstractions. The accuracy of the dependency variable sensitivity is enhanced by analyzing the abstract programs over a numerical abstract domain. Static analysis of information leakage with the tool Sample provides the proof of concepts for the proposed theory. The authors claim that the proposed approach yields improvement in accuracy and efficiency. A propositional formula domain based on a dependency variable was developed to realize the information flow for the abstract language. Besides, further abstract semantics are developed for both imperative and database query languages. The proposed theory is sound and able to analyze the information flow without any major constraint of the target language. An interesting experimental result is illustrated over a set of security benchmarks. The work is interesting, and the results are adequate to establish the claims.

The last article in this volume, "Minimizing Aliasing Effects Using Faster Super Resolution Technique on Text Images" by Soma Datta, Khalid Saeed and Nabendu Chaki, presents a novel resolution enhancement technique to reduce the aliasing effects from the text documented image maintaining low computational time. The proposed hybrid method provides better resolution for the most informative regions. The proposed method is verified on aliasing-affected text documented images. A distinct advantage of the proposed method over other conventional approaches is that it requires lower computational time to construct a high-resolution image from the respective low-resolution one. The proposed method offers much better smoothness value than the other existing methods.

We take this opportunity to express our heartfelt thanks and indebtedness to Prof. Marina Gavrilova, Editor-in-Chief of *Transactions on Computational Science*, for her continual guidance in making this Special Issue. We thank the journal's editorial staff for their support and hard work toward developing the volume. We are grateful to the authors for their high-quality contributions and cooperation in preparing this special issue. With a deep sense of gratitude, we appreciate the support from the ACSS Program Committee members and reviewers, especially from Prof. Agostino Cortesi and Prof. Rituparna Chaki for choosing the best of the submissions from ACSS 2018. They did an excellent job in encouraging authors to make significant extensions and advancements of the original works that were presented during the symposium. Our special thanks to the organizers of ACSS 2018 for their support in organizing the symposium. The culmination of their efforts at the grass-root level has led to this special issue.

This foreword will remain incomplete without a mention of the readers of this special issue of the *Transactions on Computational Science* journal. Many thanks to all of them!

November 2017                                                          Nabendu Chaki
                                                                      Khalid Saeed

# LNCS Transactions on Computational Science – Editorial Board

# Contents

# A ZigZag Pattern of Local Extremum Logarithm Difference for Illumination-Invariant and Heterogeneous Face Recognition

Hiranmoy Roy[1]([✉])[iD] and Debotosh Bhattacharjee[2]

[1] Department of Information Technology, RCC Institute of Information Technology,
Canal South Road, Beliaghata, Kolkata 700015, India
hiranmoy.roy@rcciit.org
[2] Department of Computer Science and Engineering, Jadavpur University,
Kolkata 700032, India
debotoshb@hotmail.com

**Abstract.** A novel methodology for matching of illumination-invariant and heterogeneous faces is proposed here. We present a novel image representation called local extremum logarithm difference ($LELD$). Theoretical analysis proves that $LELD$ is an illumination-invariant edge feature in coarse level. Since edges are invariant in different modalities, more importance is given on edges. Finally, a novel local zigzag binary pattern $LZZBP$ is presented to capture the local variation of $LELD$, and we call it a zigzag pattern of local extremum logarithm difference ($ZZPLELD$). For refinement of $ZZPLELD$, a model based weight value learning is suggested. We tested the proposed methodology on different illumination variations, sketch-photo and NIR-VIS benchmark databases. Rank-1 recognition of 96.93% on CMU-PIE database and 95.81% on Extended Yale B database under varying illumination, show that $ZZPLELD$ is an efficient method for illumination invariant face recognition. In the case of viewed sketches, the rank-1 recognition accuracy of 98.05% is achieved on CUFSF database. In the case of NIR-VIS matching, the rank-1 accuracy of 99.69% is achieved and which is superior to other state-of-the-art methods.

**Keywords:** Illumination-reflectance model
Modality-invariant feature · Illumination-invariant feature
Local extremum logarithm difference · Local zigzag binary pattern
Heterogeneous face recognition

## 1 Introduction

Biometric authentication is becoming a ubiquitous component of any modern systems, such as mobile phone, smart TV, computer, etc. There is a set of unique biometric features, such as fingerprints, faces, retinas, DNA samples, ears, etc. Among these features, faces are the most easily available and easily recognizable feature. The valuable part of any face biometrics is that the recognition

© Springer-Verlag GmbH Germany, part of Springer Nature 2018
M. L. Gavrilova et al. (Eds.): Trans. on Comput. Sci. XXXI, LNCS 10730, pp. 1–19, 2018.
https://doi.org/10.1007/978-3-662-56499-8_1

or authenticate can be done without any expertise. However, by the naked eye without an expert, it is quite impossible to authenticate depending on finger-prints, DNA samples, retinas and ears. Another advantage of face biometric is that a single face consists of a bundle of unique biometric features like eyes, nose, etc. Therefore, in recent years, a lot of work has been done on face biometric authentication based on real life applications. Depending on the broad range of applications, different face recognition algorithms have already been proposed by many researchers [43–45]. The performances of these algorithms are primarily tested on face images collected under well-controlled studio conditions. In effect, most of them have found difficulty in the case of handling natural images, which are captured under different illumination variations. With the variations of illu-mination, the result degrades drastically. On the other hand, different real life applications need faces captured in different situations. Near-infrared cameras are used to capture faces at night, and for illumination-invariant face recognition [1]. To detect liveness by capturing body heat, thermal-infrared (TIR) cameras are used. Often, it may happen that there are no available fingerprints, no avail-able DNA samples and devices, which are present, have captured poor quality images. In those situations, the only solution is the use of face sketches generated by interviewing the eye witness. Hence we can say that various scenarios and necessities create different modalities of faces. In situations like this, it becomes difficult to use conventional face recognition systems. Therefore, an interesting and challenging field of face biometric recognition has emerged for forensics, called heterogeneous face recognition (HFR) [2].

The problem of heterogeneous face recognition has received increasing atten-tion in recent years. Up to now, many different techniques has been proposed in the literature to solve the problem. We can easily classify these solutions into three broad categories: image synthesis based methods, common subspace learn-ing based methods and modality-invariant feature representation based methods.

- **Image synthesis:** In this category, a pseudo-face or pseudo-sketch is gener-ated using synthesis techniques to transform one modality image into another modality and then some classification technique is used. The pioneering work of Tang and Wang [3], where they introduced an eigen transformation based sketch-photo synthesis method. The same mechanism was also used by Chen *et al.* [4] for NIR-VIS synthesis. Gao *et al.* [5] proposed an embedded hidden markov model and a selective ensemble strategy to synthesise sketches from photos. Wang and Tang [6] again proposed a patch based Markov Random Field (MRF) model for the sketch-photo synthesis. Li *et al.* [7] used the same MRF model for TIR-VIS synthesis. Gao *et al.* [8] proposed a sparse represen-tation based pseudo-sketch or pseudo-photo synthesis. Another sparse feature selection (SFS) and support vector regression for synthesis was proposed by Wang *et al.* [9]. Wang *et al.* [10] proposed a transductive learning based face sketch-photo synthesis (TFSPS) framework. Recently, Peng *et al.* [11] pro-posed a multiple representation based face sketch-photo synthesis.
- **Common Subspace learning:** In this category, different modality face images are projected into a subspace for learning. Lin and Tang [12]

introduced a common discriminant feature extraction (CDFE) for face sketch-photo recognition. Yi *et al.* [13] proposed a canonical correlation analysis based regression method for NIR-VIS face images. A coupled spectral regression (CSR) based learning for NIR-VIS face images was proposed by Lei and Li [14]. A partial least square (PLS) based subspace learning method was proposed by Sharma and Jacobs [15]. Mignon and Jurie [16] proposed a cross modal metric learning (CMML) for heterogeneous face matching. Lei *et al.* [17], proposed a coupled discriminant analysis for HFR. A multi-view discriminant analysis (MvDA) technique for single discriminant common space generation was proposed by Kan *et al.* [18].

- **Modality-invariant feature representation:** In this category, images of different modalities are represented using some modality-invariant feature representation. Liao *et al.* [19] used difference of Gaussian (DoG) filter and multi-block local binary pattern (MB-LBP) features for both NIR and VIS face images. Klare *et al.* [20] employed the scale invariant feature transform (SIFT) and multi-scale local binary pattern (MLBP) features for forensic sketch recognition. A coupled information-theoretic encoding (CITE) feature was proposed by Zhang *et al.* [21]. Bhatt *et al.* [22] used a multi-scale circular Weber's local descriptor (MCWLD) for semi-forensic sketch matching. Klare and Jain [23] proposed a kernel prototype random subspace (KP-RS) on MLBP features. Zhu *et al.* [24] used a Log-DoG filter based LBP and a histogram of oriented gradient (HOG) features with transductive learning (THFM) for NIR-VIS face images. Gong *et al.* [25] combined histogram of gradients (HOG) and multi-scale local binary pattern (MLBP) with canonical correlation analysis (MCCA). Roy and Bhattacharjee [26] proposed a geometric edge-texture (GETF) based feature with hybrid multiple fuzzy classifier for HFR. Roy and Bhattacharjee [27] again proposed an illumination invariant local gravity face (LG-face) for HFR. A local gradient checksum (LGCS) feature for face sketch-photo matching was proposed by Roy and Bhattacharjee [28]. Another local gradient fuzzy pattern (LGFP) based on restricted equivalent function for face sketch-photo recognition was again proposed by Roy and Bhattacharjee [29]. A graphical representation based HFR (G-HFR) was proposed by Peng *et al.* [31]. Recently, Roy and Bhattacharjee [30] proposed another edge texture based feature called quaternary pattern of local maximum quotient (QPLMQ) for HFR.

In the synthesis based category, more concentration is applied in the synthesis. The synthesis method itself is a time-consuming technique, where synthesis technique is repeated several times to get a better pseudo sketch or photo. Again, the synthesis mechanism is depending on image quality, and modality i.e. "task-specific". In the common subspace learning category, both modality images are projected into another domain. The projection technique requires huge training data and also generates some loss of information. Due to the loss of information, the accuracy of recognition is also reduced. In the modality-invariant feature representation, local hand-crafted features are directly used, which means no loss of local information and algorithms are more time saving than the other two categories. One and the only problem in this category is to recognize or search features, which are either common to different modalities or invariant in different modalities.

Modality-invariant feature representation methods are neither time-consuming and task-specific synthesis, nor common subspace based learning, but able to consider the local spatial features. Motivated by the advantages of modality-invariant feature representation, in this paper, we propose a modality-invariant feature representation for different modality images. The existing modality-invariant methods [19–25] tried to generate modality-invariant features using the existing popular hand-crafted features. More emphasis is given on classifier. No one tried to develop new modality-invariant features, except [31]. In [26–29], we developed some new hand-crafted features which are actually modality-invariant. From our visual inspection, we conclude that edges are the most important modality-invariant feature. Psychological studies also says that we can recognize a face from its edges only [32]. It is easy to understand that facial components in a face have maximum edges and they belong to high-frequency components of an image. Another feature i.e. texture information is also important for face matching. Since edges and textures in a face image are sensitive to illumination variations, an illumination-invariant domain with the capability of capturing high-frequency information is necessary. LGCS [28] was only applied on sketch-photo recognition CHUCK database. LGFP [29] was developed only for sketch-photo recognition. In GETF [26] and LG-face [27], we tested the features for both sketch-photo and NIR-VIS recognition. Although the results were impressive, the NIR-VIS existing database (CASIA-HFB) has a very small size and still the result was not 100%. Therefore, we need new methods to handle huge databases, where faces not only have variation in modality, but also in pose, illumination, expression and the obstacle. The goal of the proposed method is to recognize the facial features, which are invariant in different modalities, and illumination.

The artist gives more attention towards edges and texture information at the time of drawing a sketch. In the case of NIR images, the high-frequency information is captured. Therefore, selection of edge and texture features for modality-invariant representation is correct in the sense. We propose an illumination-invariant image representation called local extremum logarithm difference ($LELD$), which is a modification of the work explained in [33]. $LELD$ gives only high-frequency image representation at a coarse level. A local micro level feature representation is also important to capture local texture information. Motivated by the superior output results of the local binary pattern (LBP) [34] and LBP-like features in face and texture recognition, we propose one novel local zig zag binary pattern ($LZZBP$). $LZZBP$ measure the binary relation between pixels, which are in a zigzag position in a local square window. $LZZBP$ captures more edge and texture patterns than LBP. Finally, the combination of $LELD$ and $LZZBP$ gives the proposed modality-invariant feature representation for HFR and we call it a zigzag pattern of local extremum logarithm difference ($ZZPLELD$).

Experimental results on different HFR databases show the excellent performance of the proposed methodology. The major contributions are:

1. *LELD* is proposed for capturing illumination-invariant image representation.
2. *LZZBP* is developed to capture the relation between pixels in a zigzag position of a square window.
3. *ZZPLELD* is developed to capture the local texture and edge patterns of the modality-invariant key facial features.
4. Weights learning model is developed to enhance the discrimination power of the proposed *ZZPLELD*.

This paper is organized as follows: in Sect. 2, the proposed *ZZPLELD* is described in detail. Experimental results and comparisons are presented in Sect. 3, and finally, the paper concludes with Sect. 4.

## 2   Proposed Work

In this section, we introduce the way we extract the modality-invariant features for HFR. We start with a detailed idea about illumination-invariant *LELD* based image representation. Finally, we conclude with a detail description of the proposed *ZZPLELD* feature.

### 2.1   Local Extremum Logarithm Difference Based Image Representation

In any face recognition system, one of the main problems is the presence of illumination variations. Due to the presence of illumination variations, the intra-class variation between faces also increase heavily. At the same time, we consider edges as our modality-invariant feature and edges are also sensitive towards illumination. Therefore, we need an illumination-invariant image representation for extracting better edge information. According to the Illumination-Reflectance Model (IRM) [35,36], a gray face image $I(x, y)$ at each point $(x, y)$ is expressed as the product of the reflectance component $R(x, y)$ and the illumination component $L(x, y)$, as shown in Eq. 1

$$I(x, y) = R(x, y) \times L(x, y) \tag{1}$$

Here, the $R$ component consists of information about key facial points, and edges, whereas the $L$ component represents only the amount of light falling on the face. Now, after the elimination of the $L$ component from a face image, the $R$ component is still able to represent the key facial features and edges, which are the most important information for our modality-invariant feature representation. Moreover, the $L$ component corresponds to the low-frequency part of an image, whereas the $R$ component corresponds to the high-frequency part. One widely accepted assumption in the literature [27,37] is that $L$ remains approximately constant over a local $3 \times 3$ neighborhood.

In literature, a wide range of approaches has been proposed to reduce the illumination effect. In those methods, mainly two different mathematical operations are used: division and subtraction. Methods like [37,38] used division operation and methods like [33,42] used subtraction operation. In the case of subtraction operation, at first, the image is converted to the logarithmic domain to convert the multiplicative IRM into an additive one, as shown in Eq. 3. Since, the division operation is "ill-posed and not robust in numerical calculations" [33] due to the problem of divided by zero, it is better to apply subtraction operation to eliminate the $L$ component.

Lai *et al.* [33] proposed a multiscale logarithm difference edgemaps (MSLDE), which used logarithmic domain and subtraction operation to compensate the illumination effect. They calculated a local logarithm difference using the following equation:

$$MSLDE = \sum_{(\hat{x},\hat{y}) \in \aleph_{(x,y)}} (I_{log}(x,y) - I_{log}(\hat{x},\hat{y})), \forall x, \forall y \qquad (2)$$

where $\aleph_{(x,y)}$ is a square neighborhood surrounding a center pixel at $(x,y)$. In MSLDE, only the $R$ component is present. Therefore, MSLDE is an illumination-invariant method. In this method authors considered a long range of square neighborhood from $3 \times 3$ to $13 \times 13$ and all the logarithm difference values are added together. Now, the question is does the $L$ component be constant for such a long neighborhood i.e. $13 \times 13$. We know that $R$ component belongs to high-frequency. Similarly edge and noise also belong to high-frequency. There is no doubt that MSLDE increases the edge information, which is very important in face recognition, by adding all logarithm differences. However, it is also increasing the noise, which causes degradation in true edge detection. The effect of noise is clearly visible in Fig. 2(d), where the proposed MSLDE provides too much false edge information and which are nothing but noise. To solve both the problems i.e. large neighborhood size and presence of noise, we consider the maximum and minimum logarithm difference in a $3 \times 3$ neighborhood (as shown in Fig. 1) and we call it local extremum logarithm difference ($LELD$).

**Theorem 1.** *Given an arbitrary image $I(x,y)$ with illumination effect. The local extremum logarithm difference (LELD) between central pixel and its $3 \times 3$ neighborhood is an illumination invariant feature.*

*Proof.* Let us consider a local $3 \times 3$ window and the center pixel is 'c', as shown in Fig. 1. Applying logarithmic domain, the IRM (1) multiplicative model is converted to additive model as follows

$$I_{log}(x,y) = log\left(R\left(x,y\right) \times L\left(x,y\right)\right)$$
$$\Rightarrow I_{log}(x,y) = log\left(R\left(x,y\right)\right) + log\left(L\left(x,y\right)\right) \qquad (3)$$

where, $I_{log}(x,y)$ is the logarithm representation of the image pixel $I(x,y)$. Now, let us measure the difference between central pixel against all its $3 \times 3$ neighbors and the logarithm differences ($LD$) are represented as follows

$$LD = \{I_{log}(x_i, y_i) - I_{log}(x_c, y_c)\}, (x_i, y_i) \in \aleph_{(x_c, y_c)} \qquad (4)$$

| I (x₄, y₄) | I (x₃, y₃) | I (x₂, y₂) |
|:---:|:---:|:---:|
| I (x₅, y₅) | I (x_c, y_c) | I (x₁, y₁) |
| I (x₆, y₆) | I (x₇, y₇) | I (x₈, y₈) |

**Fig. 1.** Central pixel and its $3 \times 3$ neighborhood.

where $\aleph_{(x,y)}$ is a $3 \times 3$ square neighborhood surrounding a center pixel at $(x_c, y_c)$. Putting the representation of $I_{log}(x, y)$ Eq. (3) into Eq. 4, we have:

$$LD = \{(log\,(R\,(x_i, y_i)) + log\,(L\,(x_i, y_i))) - (log\,(R\,(x_c, y_c)) + log\,(L\,(x_c, y_c))))\}$$
$$\Rightarrow LD = \{(log\,(R\,(x_i, y_i)) - log\,(R\,(x_c, y_c))) + (log\,(L\,(x_i, y_i)) - log\,(L\,(x_c, y_c)))\} \quad (5)$$

Based on the widely accepted assumption that $L$ varies slowly, we can say $L$ is almost equal to a local $3 \times 3$ window. Therefore, we can write:

$$L(x_i, y_i) = L(x_c, y_c)$$
$$\Rightarrow log\,(L\,(x_i, y_i)) = log\,(L\,(x_c, y_c))$$
$$\Rightarrow log\,(L\,(x_i, y_i)) - log\,(L\,(x_c, y_c)) = 0 \quad (6)$$

Now, the Eq. 5 is modified using Eq. 6 as follows:

$$LD = \{log\,(R\,(x_i, y_i)) - log\,(R\,(x_c, y_c))\} \quad (7)$$

The maximum and minimum logarithm differences are calculated as follows:

$$LD_{max} = max\,\{log\,(R\,(x_i, y_i)) - log\,(R\,(x_c, y_c))\}, \forall x_c, \forall y_c \quad (8)$$
$$LD_{min} = min\,\{log\,(R\,(x_i, y_i)) - log\,(R\,(x_c, y_c))\}, \forall x_c, \forall y_c \quad (9)$$

Therefore, the local extremum logarithm difference ($LELD$) is as follows:

$$LELD = \{LD_{max}, LD_{min}\}, \forall x_c, \forall y_c \quad (10)$$

Now, in Eq. 10, we can see that '$LELD$' consists of $R$-part of the IRM. According to this model, $R$ is the illumination invariant feature. Thus, it is proved that the local extremum logarithm difference between central pixel and its $3 \times 3$ neighborhood is an illumination invariant feature.

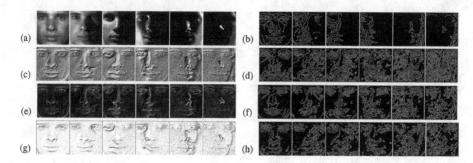

**Fig. 2.** (a) The original images with illumination variations, (b) The canny edge images for (a) images, (c) The corresponding MSLDE images of (a) images as proposed in [33], (d) The canny edge images of MSLDE images, (e) The proposed *LELD* images of (a) images with maximum difference, (f) The canny edge images of (e) images, (g) The proposed *LELD* images of (a) images with minimum difference, (h) The canny edge images of (g) images.

Since we are considering the smallest square neighborhood i.e. $3 \times 3$, the assumption that $L$ is constant in the neighborhood is theoretically true. Again, we are avoiding total sum of differences, therefore, presence of noise is reduced. The results of proposed *LELD* are shown in Fig. 2(e)–(h) and it gives better edge detection result than MSLDE. Finally, we have two different *LELD* methods to convert the different modality face images into an illumination-invariant domain, where important facial key values and edges are almost intact.

## 2.2   Local ZigZag Binary Pattern for *ZZPLELD* Generation

Local binary pattern (LBP) [34] has been used successfully in many fields of image processing and pattern classification problems. It is capable to represent local features in micro structures. LBP implements the binary relation of each and every neighboring pixels with respect to center pixel i.e. if neighboring pixel is greater than or equal to center pixel, then binary value '1' otherwise '0'. Although LBP captures the binary relations between surrounding neighboring pixels with the center pixel, it is not able to capture edge information properly, mainly in diagonal direction. Since our modality-invariant feature is edge related, a local pattern having good edge capturing capability is important. Inspired from the zigzag scanning pattern used for MPEG data compression in discrete cosine transform (DCT) domain, we developed a zigzag binary pattern for the pixels in a zigzag position of a square mask. Figure 3 shows the positions of $3 \times 3$ and $5 \times 5$ zigzag scanning used in our experiment. We use a left to right zigzag scanning (considering top left pixel as the starting point) and right to left zigzag scanning (considering top right pixel as the starting point) in each square mask. Figure 3(a) shows the $3 \times 3$ left zigzag scanning, Fig. 3(b) shows the $3 \times 3$ right zigzag scanning and Fig. 3(c) shows the $5 \times 5$ left zigzag scanning. Again, we consider only 8 bits binary patterns to make the histogram feature vector length up to 256 bins. In case of $5 \times 5$ image pixels we can have a total of 24 bits binary string. To make it with in a small range, we divide it into three 8 bits binary string. Different arrows in Fig. 3(c) shows different sequences of binary string.

Let, the image pixels in a square window are collected in a zigzag pattern, as shown in Fig. 3(a). Then, the pixels are stored in a linear array $Z_P = \{g_1, g_2, g_3, \ldots, g_P\}$, where $P$ is the number of pixels in a square window. For $3 \times 3$ window $P$ is 9 and for $5 \times 5$ window it is 25. Then, we calculate the binary relation between those consecutive pixels according to the following equation (for $P = 8$):

$$LZZBP = \sum_{i=1}^{P-1} 2^{(i-1)} \times f(g_{i+1} - g_i)$$

$$f(a) = \begin{cases} 1, & if \quad a \geq 0 \\ 0, & otherwise \end{cases} \tag{11}$$

In case of $5 \times 5$ window the 24 bits binary string is first broken into 3 parts of 8 bits string and then converted to three separate patterns.

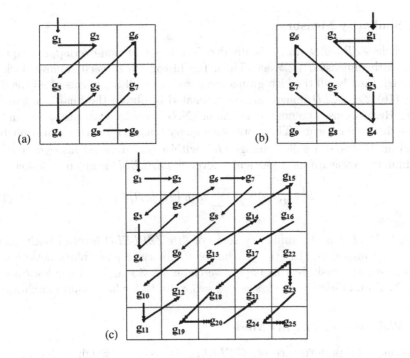

**Fig. 3.** (a) Zigzag scanning in a $3 \times 3$ window starting at top left corner, (b) Zigzag scanning in a $3 \times 3$ window starting at top right corner, (c) Zigzag scanning in a $5 \times 5$ window starting at top left corner. Here 3 different arrows are used to represent 3 different sequences of 8 bits binary strings.

(a)                                             (b)

**Fig. 4.** (a) Sample image and its corresponding LBP and *LZZBP* images. The 2nd image is the $3 \times 3$ LBP image and rest 3rd–4th are $3 \times 3$ *LZZBP* images. (b) The 2nd image is the $5 \times 5$ LBP image and rest 3rd–8th are $5 \times 5$ *LZZBP* images.

The proposed zigzag binary pattern gives better edge preserving texture information. The different LBP images and *LZZBP* images in Fig. 4 shows the edge preserving properties of *LZZBP*. The key facial features are preserved far better than normal LBP in *LZZBP*.

Finally, the proposed *LZZBP* is applied on *LELD* image representation to measure the local patterns of *LELD* image and which give our proposed *ZZPLELD*. For two different extremum *LELD* i.e. maximum and minimum differences, we get 4 different *ZZPLELD* results after applying $3 \times 3$ *LZZBP* and 12 different *ZZPLELD* results after applying $5 \times 5$ *LZZBP*. Therefore, altogether 16 different *ZZPLELD* images. The image features are represented in the form of histogram bins.

### 2.3   Similarity Measure

The whole *ZZPLELD* image is divided into a set of non-overlapping square blocks with dimension $w_b \times w_b$. Then, the histogram of each square block is measured. Finally, all the histograms measured from all the blocks of all the different (16) *ZZPLELD* images are concatenated to obtain the final face feature vector. Here, we use the nearest neighbor (NN) classifier with histogram intersection distance measure. Therefore, for a query image $(I_q)$ with a concatenated histogram $H_q^{i,j}$ and a gallery image $(I_G)$ with a concatenated histogram $H_G^{i,j}$, the similarity measure for a particular level of *ZZPLELD* is given as follows:

$$S^k(I_q, I_G) = - \sum_{i,j} min \left( H_q^{i,j}, H_G^{i,j} \right) \qquad (12)$$

where, $S^k(I_q, I_G)$ is the similarity score of $k$th *ZZPLELD* level of both query and gallery image; $(i,j)$ is the $j$th bin of $i$th block. Square block selection is another essential task. In this paper, we chose $3 \times 3$ and $5 \times 5$ windows pixels for *LZZBP* and different block sizes $w_b = 6, 8, 10, 12$ for histogram matching.

### 2.4   Weighted ZZPLELD Model

To enhance the performance of *ZZPLELD*, we assign a weight value to each *ZZPLELD* patterns. A set of weight values is measured depending on the discriminating ratio proposed in the linear discriminating analysis (LDA). This weight calculation needs a training set consisting of few people and their corresponding different modality images. After calculating the weights from the training set, the values are applied to rest of the database images. A detail idea is given below.

Let, there are '$C$' numbers of different persons i.e. '$C$' number of different classes in the training set. We have 1 to $N$ numbers of different $ZZPLELD$ for one face image (where $N$ is the number of different $ZZPLELD$ patterns). Since there are two different $LELD$ images, for each $LELD$ two different $3 \times 3$ $LZZBP$ and two different $5 \times 5$ $LZZBP$. Again, each $5 \times 5$ $LZZBP$ is partitioned into three different 8-bits patterns. Therefore, altogether $10(2 + 2 + 3 + 3 = 10)$ different 8-bits patterns. Thus the value of $N$ is 10. Now, we calculate the class-wise mean ($\mu_i^C$) and overall mean ($\mu_i$) for the $i$th $ZZPLELD$.

$$\mu_i^C = \frac{1}{n} \sum_{j=1}^{n} ZZPLELD_i^{C,j} \tag{13}$$

where, '$j$' denotes the $j$th number of different modality images (total number of images $n$, which is either 2 for sketch-photo and 4 for NIR-VIS) of a particular person '$C$' and $i \in (1, 2, \ldots, N)$.

$$\mu_i = \frac{1}{C \times n} \sum_{k=1}^{C} \sum_{j=1}^{n} ZZPLELD_i^{C,j} \tag{14}$$

Then, we calculate within-class error ($e_w$) and between-class error ($e_b$):

$$e_w = \sum_{k=1}^{C} \sum_{j=1}^{n} |ZZPLELD_i^{C,j} - \mu_i^C| \tag{15}$$

$$e_b = n \times \sum_{k=1}^{C} |\mu_i^C - \mu_i| \tag{16}$$

If the $ZZPLELD$ has a high discriminating ability, then $e_b$ should be relatively large compared with $e_w$. Hence, we set the ratio between this two as our weights ($\alpha_i$). The normalized weights ($\alpha_i^{norm}$) are

$$\alpha_i = \frac{e_b}{e_w} \tag{17}$$

$$\alpha_i^{norm} = \frac{\alpha_i}{\sum_{i=1}^{P} \alpha_i} \tag{18}$$

Therefore, for each different $ZZPLELD$ pattern we have different $\alpha_i^{norm}$. Now, the similarity between two images, as given in Eq. 12, is modified into the following equation:

$$Sim(I_q, I_G) = \sum_{k=1}^{P} \alpha_k \times S^k(I_q, I_G) \tag{19}$$

The value of $\alpha$ also varies from database to database. Different $\alpha$ values measured during training in different databases are shown in Table 1. The results of weighted $ZZPLELD$ are superior than normal $ZZPLELD$. The recognition accuracy results on different databases are given in a form of tables in the next section and weight learning $ZZPLELD$ is represented as $ZZPLELD$ (weighted).

**Table 1.** Different level weight values for ZZPLELD, measured from training data of CMU-PIE, Extended Yale B, CUFSF, and CASIA NIR-VIS databases

| Levels of weight values | CMU-PIE | Extended Yale B | CUFSF | CASIA NIR-VIS |
|---|---|---|---|---|
| $\alpha_1$ | 0.1021 | 0.0734 | 0.0471 | 0.0841 |
| $\alpha_2$ | 0.0371 | 0.0576 | 0.0501 | 0.0819 |
| $\alpha_3$ | 0.1156 | 0.1008 | 0.0718 | 0.0812 |
| $\alpha_4$ | 0.1097 | 0.0995 | 0.0695 | 0.0964 |
| $\alpha_5$ | 0.1015 | 0.1134 | 0.1094 | 0.1101 |
| $\alpha_6$ | 0.1807 | 0.1693 | 0.1103 | 0.1103 |
| $\alpha_7$ | 0.1503 | 0.1412 | 0.1378 | 0.1145 |
| $\alpha_8$ | 0.0962 | 0.1139 | 0.1230 | 0.1039 |
| $\alpha_9$ | 0.1013 | 0.1200 | 0.1301 | 0.1151 |
| $\alpha_{10}$ | 0.0055 | 0.0109 | 0.1509 | 0.1025 |

## 3 Experimental Results

In this section, *ZZPLELD* is evaluated on one illumination variation scenario and two different HFR scenarios, i.e. face sketch vs. photo recognition and NIR image vs. VIS image recognition respectively on the existing benchmark databases. For illumination variation scenario, we tested our proposed method on CMU-PIE [46], and Extended Yale B Face Database [39,40]. For face sketch vs. photo recognition, we tested the proposed method on the CUHK Face Sketch FERET Database (CUFSF) [21]. CASIA-HFB Face Database [41] is used for NIR face image vs VIS face recognition testing.

At first, proposed *ZZPLELD* is tested on illumination-invariant face recognition. We compared *ZZPLELD* with several other methods, namely LBP, Gradient-face [37], TVQI [38], HF+HQ [42], MSLDE [33] on CMU-PIE and Extended Yale B Face Databases. All the methods mentioned above are well tuned according to their respective published papers.

We compared *ZZPLELD* with several state-of-the-art methods, namely, PLS [15], CITE [21], MCCA [25], TFSPS [10], KP-RS [23], MvDA [18], G-HFR [31], and LGFP [28] on viewed sketch database. We also compared *ZZPLELD* with several state-of-the-art methods, namely, KP-RS, LCKS-CSR [17], and THFM [24] on NIR face image vs VIS face image database. Experimental setups (training and testing samples) and accuracies of the methods mentioned above, except LGFP, are taken from the published papers.

### 3.1 Rank-1 Recognition Results on CMU-PIE

This database contains 41368 images of 68 different subjects. We have tested our proposed method on the illumination subset "C27" with 1428 images of 68 subjects. All the images are in frontal face with pose 27 and 21 different lighting

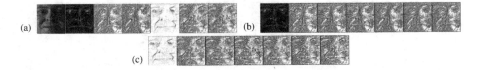

**Fig. 5.** (a) Sample *ZZPLELD* images after applying $3 \times 3$ *LZZBP* on both extremum *LELD* from CMU-PIE Face database. (b) Sample *ZZPLELD* images after applying $5 \times 5$ *LZZBP* on maximum *LELD* from CMU-PIE Face database. (c) Sample *ZZPLELD* images after applying $5 \times 5$ *LZZBP* on minimum *LELD* from CMU-PIE Face database.

**Table 2.** Average rank-1 recognition rates for different methods on CMU-PIE database of 68 subjects

| State-of-the-art methods | Average rank-1 accuracy (%) |
| --- | --- |
| LBP | 69.15 |
| Gradient-face | 93.66 |
| TVQI | 92.94 |
| HF+HQ | 93.86 |
| MSLDE | 94.85 |
| *ZZPLELD* | **95.23** |
| *ZZPLELD (weighted)* | **96.93** |

conditions. In each turn, one image per subject is chosen as the gallery, and the others are tested as query images. All total 21 rank-1 recognition rates for 21 turns. Figure 5 shows few sample face images and their corresponding *ZZPLELD* from CMU-PIE database at different illuminations.

Average rank-1 recognition is shown in Table 2 on CMU-PIE database of 68 subjects. Proposed method is better than other methods in average recognition.

## 3.2 Rank-1 Recognition Results on Extended Yale B Database

This database contains total 2432 images of 38 subjects under 64 different illumination conditions and in a cropped form with a size of $192 \times 168$ pixels. Again, the database is divided into five different subsets according to the illumination angle: Subset 1 ($0°$ to $12°$, 7 images per subject), Subset 2 ($13°$ to $25°$, 12 images per subject), Subset 3 ($26°$ to $50°$, 12 images per subject), Subset 4 ($51°$ to $77°$, 14 images per subject), and Subset 5 ($78°$ and above, 19 images per subject). Figure 6 shows one sample face images under different illumination conditions from the Extended Yale B database and their corresponding *ZZPLELD* images. For the experiment, the image with the most neutral light condition without illumination for each subject from Subset 1 were defined as the gallery, and the remaining images from Subset 1 to Subset 5 were used as query images. A comparison on of the rank 1 accuracy achieved on this database of 38 subjects

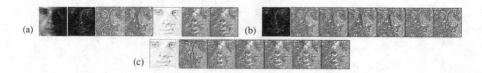

(a)   (b)   (c)

**Fig. 6.** (a) Sample *ZZPLELD* images after applying $3 \times 3$ *LZZBP* on both extremum *LELD* from Extended Yale B Face database. (b) Sample *ZZPLELD* images after applying $5 \times 5$ *LZZBP* on maximum *LELD* from Extended Yale B Face database. (c) Sample *ZZPLELD* images after applying $5 \times 5$ *LZZBP* on minimum *LELD* from Extended Yale B Face database.

**Table 3.** Rank-1 recognition rates for different methods on different subsets of Extended Yale B database of 38 subjects.

| State-of-the-art methods | Rank-1 accuracy (%) | | | | | |
|---|---|---|---|---|---|---|
| | S1 | S2 | S3 | S4 | S5 | Avg |
| LBP | 84.81 | 89.91 | 80.04 | 72.18 | 74.99 | 80.39 |
| Gradient-face | 94.74 | **100** | 83.33 | 75.94 | 84.65 | 87.73 |
| TVQI | 92.28 | 95.20 | 90.27 | 81.39 | 84.32 | 88.69 |
| HF+HQ | 94.81 | 98.76 | 93.18 | 82.90 | 84.43 | 90.82 |
| MSLDE | 96.61 | **100** | 93.20 | 86.66 | 89.33 | 93.16 |
| *ZZPLELD* | **97.01** | **100** | **94.56** | **90.62** | **90.37** | **94.51** |
| *ZZPLELD (weighted)* | **99.01** | **100** | **96.06** | **91.93** | **92.07** | **95.81** |

on the individual subset and after averaged over all subsets is shown in Table 3.

### 3.3  Rank-1 Recognition Results on Viewed Sketch Databases

A CUHK Face Sketch FERET (CUFSF) database has been used for the experimental study, which includes 1194 different subjects from the FERET database. For each person, there is a sketch with shape exaggeration drew by an artist when viewing this photo and a face photo with lighting variations. All the frontal faces in the database are cropped manually by setting approximately the same eye levels and resized to $120 \times 120$ pixels. The proposed method is tested with the existing state-of-the-art methods (PLS, CITE, MCCA, TFSPS, KP-RS, MvDA, G-HFR, and LGFP). Experimental setups and results of other state-of-the-art methods are collected from the published papers. The rank-1 recognition result of proposed *ZZPLELD* on CUFSF database is 96.35% at rank-1, and it is shown in the Table 4. Proposed method outperforms other state-of-the-art methods. Figure 7 shows one sample face photo and sketch image from the CUFSF database and their corresponding *ZZPLELD* images.

**Table 4.** Rank-1 recognition rates for different methods on CUFSF database.

| State-of-the-art methods | Number of training samples (subjects) | Number of testing samples (subjects) | Rank-1 accuracy (%) |
|---|---|---|---|
| PLS | 300 | 894 | 51.00 |
| CITE | 500 | 694 | 89.54 |
| MCCA | 300 | 894 | 92.17 |
| TFSPS | 300 | 894 | 72.62 |
| KP-RS | 500 | 694 | 83.95 |
| MvDA | 500 | 694 | 55.50 |
| G-HFR | 500 | 694 | 96.04 |
| LGFP | 0 | 1194 | 94.47 |
| *ZZPLELD* | 0 | 1194 | **96.35** |
| *ZZPLELD (weighted)* | 500 | 694 | **98.05** |

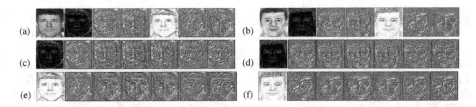

**Fig. 7.** Sample Sketch and photo images and their corresponding *ZZPLELD* images from CUFSF database. (a) Photo-*ZZPLELD* images after applying $3 \times 3$ *LZZBP* on both extremum *LELD*, (b) Sketch-*ZZPLELD* images after applying $3 \times 3$ *LZZBP* on both extremum *LELD*, (c) Photo-*ZZPLELD* images after applying $5 \times 5$ *LZZBP* on maximum *LELD*, (d) Sketch-*ZZPLELD* images after applying $5 \times 5$ *LZZBP* on maximum *LELD*, (e) Photo-*ZZPLELD* images after applying $5 \times 5$ *LZZBP* on minimum *LELD*, (f) Sketch-*ZZPLELD* images after applying $5 \times 5$ *LZZBP* on minimum *LELD*.

## 3.4    Rank-1 Recognition Results on NIR-VIS CASIA-HFB Database

This database has 200 subjects with probe images captured in the near-infrared and gallery images captured in the visible light. Each and every subject has 4 NIR images and 4 VIS images with pose and expression variations. All the frontal faces in the database are cropped manually by setting approximately the same eye levels and resized to $120 \times 120$ pixels. This database follows standard evaluation protocols.

The output result is also tested against other state-of-the-art methods (KP-RS, LCKS-CSR, THFM). Table 5 shows the rank-1 accuracy of the proposed method and other state-of-the-art methods. The rank-1 recognition of all those methods, mentioned above, is found from different published papers. The rank-1 recognition accuracy of the proposed method is 99.39%, and it is

**Table 5.** Rank-1 recognition rates for different methods on CASIA-HFB database of 200 subjects.

| State-of-the-art methods | Number of training samples (subjects) | Number of testing samples (subjects) | Rank-1 accuracy (%) |
|---|---|---|---|
| KP-RS | 133 | 67 | 87.80 |
| LCKS-CSR | 150 | 150 | 81.43 |
| THFM | 100 | 100 | 99.28 |
| *ZZPLELD* | 0 | 200 | **96.01** |
| *ZZPLELD (weighted)* | 100 | 100 | **99.69** |

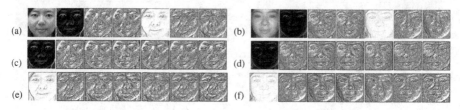

**Fig. 8.** Sample VIS and NIR images and their corresponding *ZZPLELD* images from CASIA-HFB database, (a) VIS-*ZZPLELD* images after applying $3 \times 3$ *LZZBP* on both extremum *LELD*, (b) NIR-*ZZPLELD* images after applying $3 \times 3$ *LZZBP* on both extremum *LELD*, (c) VIS-*ZZPLELD* images after applying $5 \times 5$ *LZZBP* on maximum *LELD*, (d) NIR-*ZZPLELD* images after applying $5 \times 5$ *LZZBP* on maximum *LELD*, (e) VIS-*ZZPLELD* images after applying $5 \times 5$ *LZZBP* on minimum *LELD*, (f) NIR-*ZZPLELD* images after applying $5 \times 5$ *LZZBP* on minimum *LELD*.

better than other methods. One sample NIR-VIS pair image from CASIA-HFB database and its different levels of *ZZPLELD* is shown in Fig. 8.

## 4    Conclusion

We have presented a novel modality-invariant feature representation *ZZPLELD* for HFR. It is a combination of *LELD* and *LZZBP* to boost the performance of HFR. The proposed *LELD* is an illumination-invariant image representation. To capture the local patterns of *LELD* a novel zigzag binary pattern (*LZZBP*) is proposed. Since the entire database images used in the experiment are in a frontal mode without rotation, we have not thought about whether *LZZBP* will work good in huge rotation variations or not.

Experimental results on illumination variations, sketch-photo and NIR-VIS databases, it shows the supremacy in rank-1 recognition than other compared methods. The result shows *ZZPLELD* has a good verification and discriminating ability in heterogeneous face recognition.

*LELD* can easily be used as a preprocessing stage to remove illumination variations, and to enhance edge features. Therefore, it has a long range of applications for illumination variations to heterogeneous face recognition. Since the entire database images used in the experiment are in a frontal mode without rotation, we have not thought about whether *LZZBP* will work well on huge rotation variations or not. In future a rotation-invariant *LZZBP* can be thought of texture analysis. Again, how *ZZPLELD* will work on other facial variations like pose, expression, etc. that also need a further investigation. At the same time, a further investigation is also required to search other application domains for *ZZPLELD*.

# References

1. Li, S., Chu, R., Liao, S., Zhang, L.: Illumination invariant face recognition using NIR images. IEEE Trans. Pattern Anal. Mach. Intell. **29**(4), 627–639 (2007)
2. Li, S.: Encyclopaedia of Biometrics. Springer, Boston (2009)
3. Tang, X., Wang, X.: Face sketch recognition. IEEE Trans. Circ. Syst. Video Technol. **14**(1), 50–57 (2004)
4. Chen, J., Yi, D., Yang, J., Zhao, G., Li, S., Pietikainen, M.: Learning mappings for face synthesis from near infrared to visual light images. In: Proceedings of IEEE International Conference on Computer Vision and Pattern Recognition, pp. 156–163 (2009)
5. Gao, X., Zhong, J., Li, J., Tian, C.: Face sketch synthesis algorithm on e-hmm and selective ensemble. IEEE Trans. Circ. Syst. Video Technol. **18**(4), 487–496 (2008)
6. Wang, X., Tang, X.: Face photo-sketch synthesis and recognition. IEEE Trans. Pattern Anal. Mach. Intell. **31**(1), 1955–1967 (2009)
7. Li, J., Hao, P., Zhang, C., Dou, M.: Hallucinating faces from thermal infrared images. In: Proceedings of the IEEE International Conference on Image Processing, pp. 465–468 (2008)
8. Gao, X., Wang, N., Tao, D., Li, X.: Face sketchphoto synthesis and retrieval using sparse representation. IEEE Trans. Circ. Syst. Video Technol. **22**(8), 1213–1226 (2012)
9. Wang, N., Li, J., Tao, D., Li, X., Gao, X.: Heterogeneous image transformation. Elsevier J. Pattern Recogn. Lett. **34**, 77–84 (2013)
10. Wang, N., Tao, D., Gao, X., Li, X., Li, J.: Transductive face sketch-photo synthesis. IEEE Trans. Neural Netw. **24**(9), 1364–1376 (2013)
11. Peng, C., Gao, X., Wang, N., Tao, D., Li, X., Li, J.: Multiple representation-based face sketch-photo synthesis. IEEE Trans. Neural Netw. **27**(11), 1–13 (2016)
12. Lin, D., Tang, X.: Inter-modality face recognition. In: Leonardis, A., Bischof, H., Pinz, A. (eds.) ECCV 2006. LNCS, vol. 3954, pp. 13–26. Springer, Heidelberg (2006). https://doi.org/10.1007/11744085_2
13. Yi, D., Liu, R., Chu, R., Lei, Z., Li, S.: Face matching between near infrared and visible light images. In: Proceedings of International Conference on Biometrics, pp. 523–530 (2007)
14. Lei, Z., Li, S.: Coupled spectral regression for matching heterogeneous faces. In: Proceedings of IEEE International Conference on Computer Vision and Pattern Recognition, pp. 1123–1128 (2009)
15. Sharma, A., Jacobs, D.: Bypassing synthesis: PLS for face recognition with pose, low-resolution and sketch. In: Proceedings of IEEE International Conference on Computer Vision and Pattern Recognition, pp. 593–600 (2011)

16. Mignon, A., Jurie, F.: CMML: a new metric learning approach for cross modal matching. In: Proceedings of Asian Conference on Computer Vision, pp. 1–14 (2012)
17. Lei, Z., Liao, S., Jain, A.K., Li, S.Z.: Coupled discriminant analysis for heterogeneous face recognition. IEEE Trans. Inf. Forensics Secur. **7**(6), 1707–1716 (2012)
18. Kan, M., Shan, S., Zhang, H., Lao, S., Chen, X.: Multi-view discriminant analysis. IEEE Trans. Pattern Anal. Mach. Intell. **38**(1), 188–194 (2016)
19. Liao, S., Yi, D., Lei, Z., Qin, R., Li, S.: Heterogeneous face recognition from local structure of normalized appeaaranceshared representation learning for heterogeneous face recognition. In: Proceedings of IAPR International Conference on Biometrics (2009)
20. Klare, B.F., Li, Z., Jain, A.K.: Matching forensic sketches to mug shot photos. IEEE Trans. Pattern Anal. Mach. Intell. **33**(3), 639–646 (2011)
21. Zhang, W., Wang, X., Tang, X.: Coupled information-theoretic encoding for face photo-sketch recognition. In: Proceedings of IEEE International Conference on Computer Vision and Pattern Recognition, pp. 513–520 (2011)
22. Bhatt, H.S., Bharadwaj, S., Singh, R., Vatsa, M.: Memetically optimized MCWLD for matching sketches with digital face images. IEEE Trans. Inf. Forensics Secur. **7**(5), 1522–1535 (2012)
23. Klare, B.F., Jain, A.K.: Heterogeneous face recognition using kernel prototype similarities. IEEE Trans. Pattern Anal. Mach. Intell. **35**(6), 1410–1422 (2013)
24. Zhu, J., Zheng, W., Lai, J., Li, S.: Matching NIR face to VIS face using transduction. IEEE Trans. Inf. Forensics Secur. **9**(3), 501–514 (2014)
25. Gong, D., Li, Z., Liu, J., Qiao, Y.: Multi-feature canonical correlation analysis for face photo-sketch image retrieval. In: Proceedings of ACM International Conference on Multimedia, pp. 617–620 (2013)
26. Roy, H., Bhattacharjee, D.: Heterogeneous face matching using geometric edge-texture feature (getf) and multiple fuzzy-classifier system. Elsevier J. Appl. Soft Comput. **46**, 967–979 (2016)
27. Roy, H., Bhattacharjee, D.: Local-gravity-face (LG-face) for illumination-invariant and heterogeneous face recognition. IEEE Trans. Inf. Forensics Secur. **11**(7), 1412–1424 (2016)
28. Roy, H., Bhattacharjee, D.: Face sketch-photo matching using the local gradient fuzzy pattern. IEEE J. Intell. Syst. **31**(3), 30–39 (2016)
29. Roy, H., Bhattacharjee, D.: Face sketch-photo recognition using local gradient checksum: LGCS. Springer Int. J. Mach. Learn. Cybern. **8**(5), 1457–1469 (2017)
30. Roy, H., Bhattacharjee, D.: A novel quaternary pattern of local maximum quotient for heterogeneous face recognition. Elsevier Pattern Recogn. Lett. (2017). https://doi.org/10.1016/j.patrec.2017.09.029
31. Peng, C., Gao, X., Wang, N., Li, J.: Graphical representation for heterogeneous face recognition. IEEE Trans. Pattern Anal. Mach. Intell. **39**(2), 1–13 (2016)
32. Sinha, P., Balas, B., Ostrovsky, Y., Russell, R.: Face recognition by humans: Nineteen results all computer vision researchers should know about. Proc. IEEE **94**, 1948–1962 (2006)
33. Lai, Z., Dai, D., Ren, C., Huang, K.: Multiscale logarithm difference edgemaps for face recognition against varying lighting conditions. IEEE Trans. Image Process. **24**(6), 1735–1747 (2015)
34. Ojala, T., Pietikinen, M., Menp, T.: Multiresolution gray-scale and rotation invariant texture classification with local binary patterns. IEEE Trans. Pattern Anal. Mach. Intell. **24**(7), 971–987 (2002)

35. Land, E.H., McCann, J.J.: Lightness and retinex theory. J. Opt. Soc. Am. **61**(1), 1–11 (1971)

36. Horn, B.K.P.: Robot Vision. MIT Press, Cambridge (2011)

37. Zhang, T., Tang, Y.Y., Fang, B., Shang, Z., Liu, X.: Face recognition under varying illumination using gradientfaces. IEEE Trans. Image Process. **18**(11), 2599–2606 (2009)

38. An, G., Wu, J., Ruan, Q.: An illumination normalization model for face recognition under varied lighting conditions. Elsevier J. Pattern Recogn. Lett. **31**, 1056–1067 (2010)

39. Belhumeur, P., Georghiades, A., Kriegman, D.: From few to many: Illumination cone models for face recognition under variable lighting and pose. IEEE Trans. Pattern Anal. Mach. Learn. **23**(6), 643–660 (2001)

40. Lee, K.C., Ho, J., Kriegman, D.: Acquiring linear subspaces for face recognition under variable lighting. IEEE Trans. Pattern Anal. Mach. Learn. **27**(5), 684–698 (2005)

41. Li, S.Z., Lei, Z., Ao, M.: The HFB face database for heterogeneous face biometrics research. In: Proceedings of IEEE International Workshop on Object Tracking and Classification Beyond and in the Visible Spectrum, Miami (2009)

42. Fan, C.N., Zhang, F.Y.: Homomorphic filtering based illumination normalization method for face recognition. Elsevier J. Pattern Recogn. Lett. **32**, 1468–1479 (2011)

43. Turk, M., Pentland, A.: Eigenfaces for recognition. J. Cogn. Neurosci. **3**(1), 71–86 (1991)

44. Lawrence, S., Giles, C.L., Tsoi, A., Back, A.: Face recognition: a convolution neural-network approach. IEEE Trans. Neural Netw. **8**(1), 98–113 (1997)

45. Wiskott, L., Fellous, J.M., Kruger, N., Malsburg, C.V.: Face recognition by elastic bunch graph matching. IEEE Trans. Pattern Anal. Mach. Intell. **19**(7), 775–779 (1997)

46. Sim, T., Baker, S., Bsat, M.: The CMU pose, illumination, and expression database. IEEE Trans. Pattern Anal. Mach. Intell. **25**(12), 1615–1618 (2003)

# Automatic Identification of *Tala* from *Tabla* Signal

Rajib Sarkar$^{(\boxtimes)}$ ⓘ, Anjishnu Mondal, Ankita Singh, and Sanjoy Kumar Saha

CSE Department, Jadavpur University, Kolkata 700032, West Bengal, India
rjbskar@gmail.com, anjishnu@outlook.com, singh.ankita91@outlook.com,
sks_ju@yahoo.co.in

**Abstract.** *Tabla* is the most common rhythmic instrument in Indian Classical music. A *bol* the fundamental unit of *tabla* play and it is produced by striking either or both of the two drums of *tabla*. *Tala* (rhythm) is formed with a basic sequence of *bols* that appears in a cyclic pattern. In this work, *bols* are automatically segmented from *tabla* signal following Attack-Decay-Sustain-Release (ADSR) model. Subsequently segmented *bols* are recognized using low level spectral descriptors and support vector machine (SVM). The identified *bol* sequence generates transcript of *tabla* play. A template based matching approach is used to identify *tala* from the transcript. Proposed system tested successfully with a variety of collection of *tabla* signal of different *talas* and it can be utilized in rhythm analysis of music. Moreover, for the learners also the system can help in analyzing their performance.

**Keywords:** Tabla signal · Bol segmentation · ADSR model
Bol identification · Tala transcript · Tala identification

## 1 Introduction

In Indian music, *Tabla* is the most widely used rhythmic instrument. It is used to maintain the rhythm of the music. The percussion instrument has two drums namely, *bayan* and *dayan*. *Bayan* is the bass drum and *dayan* is the treble drum. Drums are played using the palm and fingers. The heel of the hand can also be used on *bayan* to control the pitch of the sound. Moreover, different regions of the drums give rise to various notes. Various *bols* are generated as the outcome of playing style with palm, fingers and the drum region being struck. The *bols* form the basic unit of *tabla* signal. Each *tala* is characterized by a sequence of *bols*. This sequence gets repeated. Thus, *tala* of *tabla* signal has a cyclic pattern.

A stroke on any drum gives rise to a *bol* (note). Such a *bol* is categorized as single stroke. Often two strokes are made simultaneously on two drums and that gives rise to another category of *bol* termed as combined stroke. The sound generated by such strokes is a mixture of bass and treble. For example, *Na* is a single stroke played on the *dayan*. It is played by tapping with the index finger and by imposing relatively high pressure. *Khe* is a single stroke played on the *bayan*. Playing configuration is light slap with a completely flat palm and all the

M. L. Gavrilova et al. (Eds.): Trans. on Comput. Sci. XXXI, LNCS 10730, pp. 20–30, 2018.
https://doi.org/10.1007/978-3-662-56499-8_2

five fingers make contact with the drum. *Dha* is a combined stroke obtained by playing *Na* on *dayan* and *Ghe* on *bayan* simultaneously. Similarly, *Teen* on *dayan* and *Ghe* on *bayan* together generates *Dhin*.

In order to analyze the rhythmic properties of a music, it is important to look into the accompanying percussion signal. *Tabla* being the most important rhythmic instrument, it is essential to analyze the corresponding signal. Locating the *bols* can help in measuring the tempo, identification of the *bols* leads to automatic generation of the transcript. Finally, *tala* can be identified by analyzing the transcripts. A collection of *tabla* signals can also be organized according to their *tala*. It enables structured storage and retrieval. Furthermore, a robust and automated system can be of great assist in analyzing and evaluating the performance of a learner. It has motivated us to develop a methodology to extract and identify the *bols* and extend it further to identify the *talas*.

The paper is organized as follows. Section 2 presents the survey on past work. Proposed methodology is elaborated in Sect. 3. Experimental result and concluding remarks are put in Sects. 4 and 5 respectively.

## 2 Past Work

In order to identify the *tala* of a *tabla* signal, one will have to extract the basic sequence of *bols* that characterizes the *tala*. The process involves extraction and recognition of the individual *bols* at first level. Thereafter, the *bol* pattern that repeats in a cycle has to be identified for understanding the *tala*. The situation is rather simple in Western music. In instruments like drum, beats are generated in linear fashion to maintain the rhythm. But, *tabla* offers more variety in terms of different *bols* and their sequencing. Still it is worth to study the work on different aspects of rhythm analysis in Western music. Although most of the works are on onset detection, it provides an insight to get into the complex domain of notes/*bols* in *tabla* signal.

A significant work has been done on onset detection in Western music. Bello et al. [1] combined energy difference based function and phase based approach to detect the onsets. Energy based approach captures percussive onsets and the phase based approach captures soft onsets. Further improvement has been achieved by adding a pre-processing step to decompose the signal into multiple bands. Thereafter different reduction methods are applied on the bands to determine the onsets [2]. Dixon [3] extended the work of Bello et al. [1,2]. An onset detection function was proposed that combines the weighted phase deviation, normalized weighted phase deviation and half wave rectified complex domain information. Grosche et al. [4] also adopted similar method to detect onsets. The amplitude and phase information are combined to identify the onsets. Strokes are then extracted based on the steady state assumptions. Scheirer in his work [5] divided the audio signal into multiple bands and sub-band envelopes, for accurate rhythm detection. Klapuri [6] implemented the psycho-acoustic knowledge described by Scheirer [5]. The concept of novelty curve presented by Foote [7]. He proposed a methodology for onset detection [8] using novelty curve.

This approach is well in use in various applications like beat tracking, tempo detection.

Gillet and Richard [9] worked on *bol* identification from *tabla* signal. They applied a low threshold on low frequency envelope for segmentation. Spectral based features are extracted from the segmented *bol*s. Hidden Markov Model (HMM) classifier is used to identify the *bol*s. Chordia [10] presented a methodology for *bol* segmentation and identification. Gillet et al. [9] used spectral features such as centroid, skewness, kurtosis and rolloff as feature for representing the *bol*s. They also included Mel-frequency cepstrum co-efficient (MFCC), temporal centroid, attack-time and zero crossing rate (ZCR). Four different classifiers, Multivariate Gaussian model, Feed-forward Neural Network, Probabilistic Neural Network and Tree classifier were used for classification of the *bol*s. A similar system is utilized to develop a real time recognition system [11]. Marius-Miron [12] extended the work of [11] and proposed a method for automatic recognition of *bol*s. Each *bol* is modeled using Gaussian Mixture Model (GMM) and the models are used in classifying the segmented units. Gupta et al. [13] worked on *bol* pattern generation. They used MFCCs as descriptors of segmented *bol*s. The *bol*s are then classified using HMM classifier. The identified *bol* sequence is used for *bol* pattern extraction. They have used Rough Longest Common Sub-sequence (RLCS) algorithm to search a query pattern in output *bol* sequence. But only *teental* is considered in their work.

In case of *tabla*, *tala* is the higher level semantic and it is played according to a *tala* to maintain the rhythm. Thus, it is more meaningful to identify the *tala* from the signal. It is observed that reported works are mostly focused on *bol* segmentation and identification. It provides the foundation to go further towards the identification of *tala*. In this work, we present a composite methodology for extracting and identifying the *bol*s from the signal. Finally, from extracted *bol* sequence, *tala* is identified.

## 3    Proposed Methodology

In order to detect the *tala* from a *tabla* signal, the first step is to segment the individual *bol*s present in the signal. Once the *bol*s are extracted, these are to be identified. It enables the generation of transcript from the signal. Finally, the characterizing sequence of the *tala*s are matched with the sub-sequence of the transcript to identify the *tala*. The major modules of the proposed methodology are as follows:

– Automatic segmentation of *bol* from *tabla* signal based on ADSR model
– *Bol* identification
– *Tala* identification

The proposed methodology is the extension of our early work presented in [14] where segmentation methodology has been elaborated. For the sake of understanding we shall present the same in brief and describe the other modules in the following subsections.

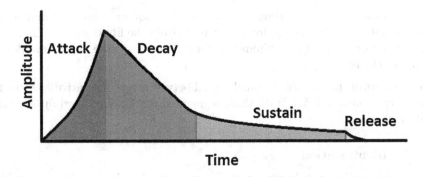

**Fig. 1.** Attack Decay Sustain Release (ADSR)

### 3.1 Segmentation of *Bol* from *Tabla* Signal

The segmentation methodology exploits Attack Decay Sustain Release (ADSR) model as shown in Fig. 1 adhered by a *bol* played on *tabla*. The attack phase is the start of *bol*. The attack period extends from the start of the *bol* to the instance of reaching maximum energy (peak). After reaching the peak, energy decays for certain duration. In decay, the energy losing rate is very high. After losing the energy at sharp rate, the *bol* has considerably steady energy level. Then the energy is gradually dropped denoting the release period. The ADSR model is the best approach to segment a *bol*. Due to the oscillatory behavior of audio signal, segmenting the *bol* directly from the time domain *tabla* signal is not suitable. Hence, the change in energy pattern is the key to segment a *bol* more accurately. The segmentation steps are as follows.

- **Novelty curve generation:** The *tabla* signal is divided into small frames (frame size 256 samples). Short-time Fourier transform (STFT) [15] is computed for each frame. For each spectral band, spectral difference over consecutive frames are computed which reflects the variation of spectral energy over time in the individual band. Corresponding elements of all the bands are averaged to obtain the novelty curve.
- **Selection of Peaks:** The local maximas of the novelty curve are selected as the peaks. This selection may include some spurious peaks. To remove spurious peaks, we first normalized the novelty curve by its maximum value. From the normalized novelty curve, the peaks above the threshold $Th_{peak}$ are considered. Here,

$$Th_{peak} = \mu - 0.5 \times \sigma$$

  where $\mu$ and $\sigma$ are the average and standard deviation of local maxima values respectively.
- The time instance of the detected peaks are mapped to the original signal. This indicates the estimated peak position of a *bol* in the original *tabla* signal.
- To recognize actual attack position, we used backtracking algorithm. From the peak position, we backtrack towards actual attack position. A straight

line is fitted trough the time samples by least square regression and it is extrapolated till the energy drops to zero. Within the fitted straight line, the position corresponding to minimum energy is taken as the actual attack or start of the *bol.*

Once the start of the *bols* are obtained, signal between two consecutive such start points corresponds to a *bol.* With these segmented units, we proceed further for its identification.

## 3.2   *Bol* Identification

In order to identify the *bols*, we need to consider the descriptors which are to be computed from the segmented unit. Based on those descriptors classification is to be achieved. The details of computation of features and classification process are as follows.

**Computation of Features:** Spectral features estimate the spectral density of a signal. The spectral density characterizes the frequency content in a signal. The Fourier transformation of a audio signal produces a frequency spectrum which contains all of the information about the signal in frequency domain. Short term Fourier transform (STFT) [15] is used to compute the frequency spectrum from the segmented unit. Based on the co-efficients of STFT, the following spectral features are computed.

- **Spectral Centroid:** It indicates the center of mass of the spectrum and provides the impression of brightness of the signal. It is computed as follows [16].

$$centroid = \frac{\sum_{n=0}^{N-1} n \times f(n)}{\sum_{n=0}^{N-1} f(n)}$$

  where $f(n)$ represents the magnitude of frequency bin number $n$ obtained after STFT. The segmented signal is divided into window of $N$ samples.
- **Spectral Flatness:** High spectral flatness indicates that the spectrum has a similar amount of power in all spectral bands. Low spectral flatness indicates that the spectral power is concentrated in relatively small number of bands. It is computed as [16]

$$flatness = \frac{\sqrt[N]{\Pi_{n=0}^{N-1} f(n)}}{\frac{\sum_{n=0}^{N-1} f(n)}{N}}$$

  where $f(n)$ represents the magnitude of frequency bin number $n$ obtained after STFT.
- **Spectral Skewness:** Skewness [16] of the components of STFT are used as a descriptor. The duration and energy distribution of a *bol* are likely to influence the measure.
- **Spectral Kurtosis:** Spectral kurtosis [16] is a ratio that accounts the deviation of the spectral components form Gaussianity. It provides a means of determining which frequency bands contains a signal of maximum impulsivity. It is computed as

- **Spectral Roll Off:** Spectral rolloff [16] point is defined as the $k^{th}$ percentile of the power spectral distribution. In our case $k$ is taken as 85.
- **Mel Frequency Cepstral Coefficients (MFCC):** MFCCs are the results of a cosine transform of the real logarithm of the spectrum expressed on a mel-frequency scale [16,17]. It resembles human perception of hearing. First 13 co-efficients are used as part of descriptor.

The extracted *bol* segment is divided into frames of equal size (256 samples per frame, in our case). Spectral features are computed for each frame. Average and standard deviation of the feature values over the frames constitute the final 34 dimensional descriptor. It is worth to mention that in our early [14] the features were computed separately for attack, decay, sustain and release regions. It is quite difficult to identify the individual regions for every type of *bols*. As a result approximation creeps into the descriptor. Hence, in this work, features are computed for the complete *bol*. It also reduces the feature dimension.

*Bol* **Classification:** Each segmented *bol* is represented by the feature descriptor. Then Support Vector Machine (SVM) [18] is used to classify the *bols*. The algorithm incorporated in Weka [19] has been used for this purpose. An iterative optimization algorithm called Sequential Minimal Optimization (SMO) [20] is used to solve the quadratic programming problem that arises during the training of support vector machines for solving such optimization problem. It makes SVM training process faster.

### 3.3  *Tala* Identification

Each *tala* has a unique *bol* sequence which is repeated when the *tala* is played. We refer to this characterizing *bol* sequence as template. Table 2 shows the template for different *talas*. *Dadra tala* is a sequence of six *bols*. Corresponding template is *dha, dhin, na, na, teen, na*. Sometimes two or more *bols* sit together and forms a composite *bol*. In Table 2, *ektal* has two composite *bols DhaGhe* and *TiRaKiTa*. *Bol DhaGhe* consists of *dha* and *ghe*. Similarly *bol TiRaKiTa* is the composition of *ti, ra, ki* and *ta*. To produce a composite *bol*, a *tabla* player plays all individual *bols* in quick succession on same and/or different drums of *tabla*. Thus, the template of *ektal* has twelve *bols* but, in signal level it has twenty *bols*. Similarly, *teental* has sixteen *bols* in its template but seventeen *bols* in signal level for the composite *bol TehTe*.

In order to detect the *tala* of a *tabla* signal, *bols* are first segmented and identified. Putting the name of the identified *bols* in a sequence the transcript for the signal is generated. Templates of the *talas* are matched with the transcript of the signal. *Tala* corresponding to the best matched template is considered as the *tala* of the signal. Thus, it comes down to substring matching as the template string is to be matched in the larger string corresponding to the transcript of the signal. While matching, the concept of composite *bol* is ignored. For such cases, each individual *bols* are considered separately. Due to the variety in playing style of the artists, variety of the *bols*, their composite nature it is difficult to achieve precise segmentation and identification of the *bols*. Thus, it is likely that transcript generated for the signal may not be completely correct. Moreover, the template shows one cycle of the basic *bol* sequence. Thus, finding the offset in transcript *i.e.* from which position the *bols* are to be matched with corresponding one in the template will be compared is an issue. Keeping all these in mind and relying on the robustness of our *bol* segmentation and identification methodology, we consider a simple matching process as follows.

– Each *tala* has unique *bol* pattern as shown in Table 2, is considered as the template ($Tem$) for the *tala*.
– A *tala* transcript ($Trans$) generated from a excerpt of *tabla* signal is used as search space for *tala* identification.
– Let $L_{tr}$ be the length of $Trans$
– For each template $Tem_i$,
  • Let $L_{tm}$ be the length of $Tem_i$
  • The template $Tem_i$ is matched with the *bols* in $Trans$, starting from $j$-th position in $Trans$.
  • Corresponding match-score, $S_j^i$ is computed as

$$S_j^i = \frac{1}{L_{tm}} \Sigma_{k=1}^{L_{tm}} f_{match}(Trans, Tem_i, j, k)$$

and

$$f_{match}(Trans, Tem_i, j, k) = \left\{ \begin{array}{ll} 1 & if, \ Trans(j+k-1) = Tem_i(k) \\ 0 & if, \ Trans(j+k-1) \neq Tem_i(k) \end{array} \right\}$$

  • Final Match score between $Trans$ and $Tem_i$, $S^i = max\{S_j^i\}$ where j varies from 1 to $L_{tr} - L_{tm} + 1$.
– Let $S_k = max\{S_i\}$
– *Tala* corresponding to $Tem_k$ is taken as the *tala* for the signal corresponding to $Trans$.

## 4   Experimental Results

In order to carry out the experiment we have prepared a dataset which reflects wide variety. It contains recordings of the *tabla* recitals of number of artists with different skill-set. Solo recordings of four different *talas* namely *Teental*, *Dadra*, *Kaharba* and *Ektal* are there. Again the playing style varies depending on *gharana* (school of practice). Each *tala* is played in three different *gharanas*. Seven artists have played the *talas*. *Tabla* was also tuned at different frequencies. Tempo varied from 80 BPM to 180 BPM. All these have made the dataset more realistic in nature. Sampling rate is 44.1 kHz. Different *tablas* are used for recordings and those are tuned at different frequencies. The duration of the dataset is 75 min.

The performance of the *bol* identification is very important. Sarkar et al. [14] extracted the feature descriptor from four basic part of a *bol*- attack, decay, sustain and release portion. But when *tabla* played at high tempo, next *bols* of the *tala* played before the current *bol*'s energy releases. Sometime, two consecutive

**Table 1.** Identification of Bols

| Bol name | # of extracted segment | Detection accuracy (%) |
|---|---|---|
| Dha | 648 | 85.96 |
| Dhin | 1034 | 86.27 |
| Na | 1117 | 87.02 |
| Teen | 310 | 85.16 |
| Ti | 110 | 100.00 |
| Ra | 110 | 90.00 |
| Ki | 110 | 90.00 |
| Tu | 154 | 93.30 |
| Ka | 154 | 81.82 |
| Ghe | 99 | 90.91 |
| Te | 196 | 80.61 |
| Khe | 98 | 75.51 |
| Ta | 154 | 98.00 |
| Overall | 4294 | 87.33 |

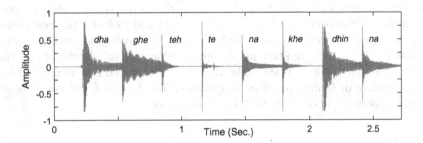

**Fig. 2.** Kaharba tala (signal level).

*bol*s are played so frequently that before completion of decay region of current *bol*, next *bol* appears. In this work, we have generated *bol* descriptors from the whole segmented *bol*. The spectral features are calculated from the complete *bol*. Ten fold cross validation is applied to measure the classification accuracy and it has been shown in Table 1. The performance of *bol* detection is improved by 3% compared to early work reported in [14]. The detailed performance of *bol* identification methodology is presented in Table 1. A signal of *dadra tala* and corresponding identified *bol*s shown in Fig. 2.

The grammar of *tala*s (as shown in Table 2) reflects its characterizing *bol* sequence. Such sequence is taken as the template for the *tala*. The tabla signal clips are of around 45 s duration. So, in each clip, the *bol* sequence are expected to repeat. In order to obtain the meaningful match score with a template the start of the cycle is to be synchronized. Inaccuracy in segmentation and *bol*

**Table 2.** Grammar of Talas

| Tala | Grammar of Tala |
|---|---|
| Teental | Dha, Dhin, Dhin, Dha, Dha, Dhin, Dhin, Dha, Na, Teen, Teen, Na, TehTe, Dhin, Dhin, Dha |
| Kaharba | Dha, Ghe, Teh, Te, Na, Khe, Dhin, Na |
| Dadra | Dha, Dhin, Na, Na, Teen, Na |
| Ektal | Dhin, Dhin, DhaGhe, TiRaKiTa, Tu, Na, Ka, Ta, DhaGhe, TiRaKiTa, Dhin, Na |

**Table 3.** Identification of *Tala*

| Tala | Correctly identified (in %) |
|---|---|
| Teentala | 92.00 |
| Ektala | 93.33 |
| Dadra | 100.00 |
| Kaharba | 100.00 |

identification may make this task difficult. In the proposed matching process, the template slides over the whole signal transcript and looks for the best match score. As a result it well addresses the issue of cycle mapping or synchronization and also surmounts the limitations of segmentation and *bol* identification. *Tala* identification performance is shown in Table 3. It is observed that number of *bols* in the template of *Dadra* appear in templates of *Teental* and *Ektal* and it results into mis-classification of those *talas* in certain cases.

## 5   Conclusion

*Tabla* is the mostly used percussion instrument in Indian classical music. In this work, we have presented a novel scheme for automated system for identifying the *tala* from *tabla* signal. *Tabla* is played according to a *tala*. Each *tala* is characterized by a sequence of *bols* which repeats itself. Such sequence is taken as the template for the *tala*. *Bol* is the basic building block of *tabla signal*. In our work, *bols* are automatically segmented based on Attack-Decay-Sustain-Release (ADSR) model. Segmented *bols* are represented using spectral descriptors and SVM is used for their identification. Thus, a transcript showing the *bol* sequence for a given signal is automatically generated. Finally, a simple matching scheme is proposed to match the *tala* templates and transcript of the given signal. *Tala* corresponding to the best matched template is identified as the *tala* for signal under test. Experiment is carried out with a wide variety of dataset and the performance of the proposed methodology is satisfactory. A robust system may be of immense help for organized archival of the music according to *tala* and also for evaluating the performance of self learner. In future, deep learning approaches may be deployed for identifying the *tala*.

# References

1. Bello, J.P., Duxbury, C., Davies, M., Sandler, M.: On the use of phase and energy for musical onset detection in the complex domain. IEEE Signal Process. Lett. **11**(6), 553–556 (2004)
2. Bello, J.P., Daudet, L., Abdallah, S., Duxbury, C., Davies, M., Sandler, M.B.: A tutorial on onset detection in music signals. IEEE Trans. Speech Audio Process. **13**(5), 1035–1047 (2005)
3. Dixon, S.: Onset detection revisited. In: Proceedings of the 9th International Conference on Digital Audio Effects, vol. 120, pp. 133–137 (2006)
4. Grosche, P., Müller, M.: Extracting predominant local pulse information from music recordings. IEEE Trans. Audio, Speech Lang. Process. **19**(6), 1688–1701 (2011)
5. Scheirer, E.D.: Tempo and beat analysis of acoustic musical signals. J. Acoust. Soc. Am. **103**(1), 588–601 (1998)
6. Klapuri, A.: Sound onset detection by applying psychoacoustic knowledge. In: IEEE International Conference of Acoustics, Speech and Signal Processing, Washington, DC, USA, vol. 6, pp. 115–118 (1999)
7. Foote, J.: Visualizing music and audio using self-similarity. In: ACM International Conference on Multimedia (Part 1), MULTIMEDIA 1999, pp. 77–80. ACM, New York (1999)
8. Foote, J.: Automatic audio segmentation using a measure of audio novelty. In: IEEE International Conference on Multimedia and Expo (I), pp. 452–455. IEEE Computer Society (2000)
9. Gillet, O., Richard, G.: Automatic labelling of tabla signals. In: Proceedings of the 4th International Society for Music Information Retrieval Conference (2003)
10. Chordia, P.: Segmentation and recognition of tabla strokes. In: ISMIR, pp. 107–114 (2005)
11. Chordia, P., Rae, A.: Tabla gyan: a system for realtime tabla recognition and resynthesis. In: ICMC (2008)
12. Miron, M.: Automatic detection of hindustani talas. Master's thesis, Universitat Pompeu Fabra, Barcelona, Spain (2011)
13. Gupta, S., Srinivasamurthy, A., Kumar, M., Murthy, H.A., Serra, X.: Discovery of syllabic percussion patterns in tabla solo recordings. In: International Society for Music Information Retrieval Conference, pp. 385–391 (2015)
14. Sarkar, R., Singh, A., Mondal, A., Saha, S.K.: Automatic extraction and identification of bol from tabla signal. In: ACSS (2017)
15. Fulop, S.A., Fitz, K.: Algorithms for computing the time-corrected instantaneous frequency (reassigned) spectrogram, with applications. J. Acoust. Soc. Am. **119**(1), 360–371 (2006)
16. Zhang, T., Kuo, C.C.J.: Audio content analysis for online audiovisual data segmentation and classification. IEEE Trans. Speech Audio Process. **9**(4), 441–457 (2001)
17. Logan, B., et al.: Mel frequency cepstral coefficients for music modeling. In: ISMIR (2000)
18. Suykens, J.A., Vandewalle, J.: Least squares support vector machine classifiers. Neural Process. Lett. **9**(3), 293–300 (1999)

19. Witten, I.H., Frank, E., Hall, M.A., Pal, C.J.: Data Mining: Practical Machine Learning Tools and Techniques. Morgan Kaufmann, Burlington (2016)
20. Zeng, Z.Q., Yu, H.B., Xu, H.R., Xie, Y.Q., Gao, J.: Fast training support vector machines using parallel sequential minimal optimization. In: 3rd International Conference on Intelligent System and Knowledge Engineering, vol. 1, pp. 997–1001. IEEE (2008)

# A Novel Approach of Retinal Disorder Diagnosing Using Optical Coherence Tomography Scanners

Maciej Szymkowski[1(✉)] and Emil Saeed[2]

[1] Faculty of Computer Science, Bialystok University of Technology, Bialystok, Poland
szymkowskimack@gmail.com
[2] Department of Ophthalmology, Faculty of Medicine, Medical University of Bialystok,
Bialystok, Poland
emilsaeed1986@gmail.com

**Abstract.** OCT is a promising technology that allows getting a lot of data in each sample. Authors hope that it is possible to create a system that would automatically diagnose various retinal diseases basing on OCT images with the accuracy of 95% which may revolutionize and shorten diagnostic pathway. At the beginning authors focus on automatic distinguishing the healthy images from pathological retinas. In this paper a novel approach has been presented. The algorithm has been described and results have been revealed and discussed. OCT is a way for detecting many various diseases. However, the amount of information to be processed is much more numerous so the task seems to be more difficult than it is in fundus imaging. In this paper some advanced diseases with the macular oedema detection algorithm basing on OCT images are presented.

**Keywords:** Optical coherence tomography · OCT · Diabetes mellitus
Age-related macular degeneration · Exudates · Retina disorders · Image processing
Classification · Computer detection algorithm · Automated diagnosis

## 1 Introduction

Optical Coherence Tomography (OCT) is a medical non-invasive imaging method of optical signal reception and processing. It is based on the interferometry which is typically performed using near-infrared light. Three-dimensional images from within biological tissues, as an optical scattering media, can be captured. OCT provides high-resolution images of the retina. Each of the retina distinctive layers can be seen in vivo. The thickness of the tissue can be measured and the retinal map can be created [1]. Optical coherence tomography recently has revolutionized ophthalmology. Some eye diseases such as age-related macular degeneration and diabetic retinopathy, retinal vein occlusion or glaucoma can be diagnosed and their progression could be monitored using OCT.

Diabetes mellitus is one of the most common and dangerous diseases. More than 400 million people in the world have diabetes nowadays and this number is expected to rise to nearly 600 million by 2035. The longer patients have diabetes, the higher the prevalence of diabetes retinopathy. Age-related macular degeneration, in turn, is the

© Springer-Verlag GmbH Germany, part of Springer Nature 2018
M.L. Gavrilova et al. (Eds.): Trans. on Comput. Sci. XXXI, LNCS 10730, pp. 31–40, 2018.
https://doi.org/10.1007/978-3-662-56499-8_3

main cause of treatable blindness in the developed world. Quickly diagnosed may be treated using anti-VEGF injections [2].

However, there are some other diseases, for example cataract or vitreous hemorrhage that may change the transparency of the eye. In such cases, the view to the eye fundus and OCT imaging become impaired.

The purpose of this study is to work out and implement an OCT graph based algorithm that can diagnose eye diseases. Moreover, the OCT application itself would find out other useful diagnosis. All these and other algorithm applications will be given in the next chapters of this work.

Recently, a considerable attention has been paid to prevent rather than treat diseases. Little research has been done in this particular field in the world so far. In this paper the authors will consider the OCT - Optical Coherence Tomography in detail. Figure 1 shows healthy retina in OCT.

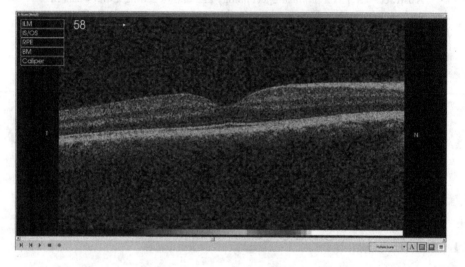

**Fig. 1.** Normal macula in OCT

## 2   Optical Coherence Tomography in Retinal Lesions Diagnostics

Authors are considering retina diseases where the macular region is affected and treatment is needed whilst visual acuity is reduced - such as macular oedema in diabetic retinopathy (Fig. 2). Macular oedema impairs visual acuity significantly [3] and can be noticed even in early stages of diabetic retinopathy [4]. There are some differences detected in literature in this field between female and male - a central subfield thickness was significantly greater in males relative to females [5]. Macular oedema may also occur in patients who undergo cataract surgery [6].

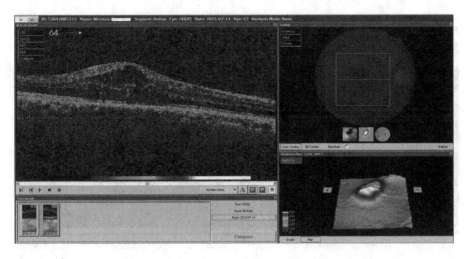

**Fig. 2.** OCT graph of macular oedema in diabetic retinopathy

Retinal vein occlusion may also go with the oedema in macular region showing another odd case for OCT. It is presented in Fig. 3.

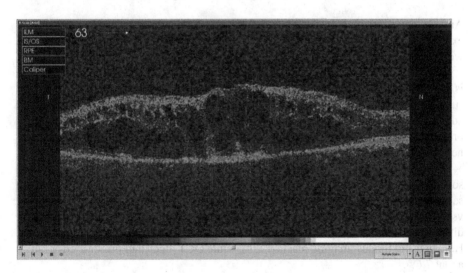

**Fig. 3.** Macular oedema in retinal vein occlusion

Blood and protein leakage may appear below the macula in wet type of age-related macular degeneration [7]. Figure 4 shows the OCT illustration of this case.

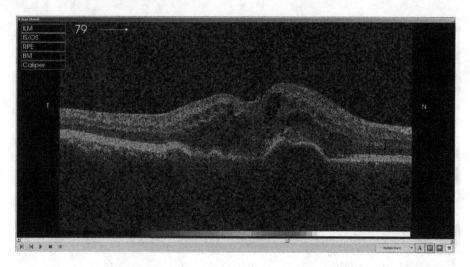

**Fig. 4.** Age-related macular degeneration – wet type

## 3   How Others See It

Authors could not find in the literature a method for automated retinal oedema or exudates detection basing on OCT images. Most of the works available today are the works basing on fundus photography.

The works presenting OCT processing methods are less because the imaging method is quite new itself. What is more the OCT scanners are quite expensive. Here in the field such approaches as [8] can be mentioned, where a preliminary algorithm of locating edemas on OCT images is presented. In this work classification algorithm was not presented. A number of research works introduced automatic methods of retinal thickness measurement in wet AMD or diabetic macular edema [9, 10].

In [11] authors prepared an algorithm for analyzing hard exudates and their precursors in patients with diabetic macular edema using polarization-sensitive OCT. One can see in the results the comparison between manual grading basing on fundus photography vs automated classification basing on OCT images. Authors present the result as a difference in diagnose between two manual graders and the result automatic algorithm. Human using fundus imaging reached 2,7% while OCT algorithm presents error rate at about 7,6%.

Another interesting approach to OCT image processing was presented in [12]. Authors prepared a comparison between different noise reduction algorithms that could be used in OCT images. Tested algorithms included different filtering methods, anisotropic diffusion, soft wavelet thresholding and multiframe wavelet thresholding. Precision of the denoising process was evaluated on the basis of automated retina layers segmentation results. Experiments were conducted with a set of 10 healthy scans and 10 samples with vitreoretinal pathologies. Authors claimed that anisotropic diffusion and wavelet thresholding give the best results and allow for better retina segmentation for both of sets. Interesting results were obtained with multiframe wavelet thresholding but this approach provided significant improvement only for retinas with pathological changes.

When it comes to fundus photography there are few works in the field of automated disorder detection. For example in [13] authors present an algorithm to detect exudates and optic disks in retinal images using curvelet transform. Their algorithm allows to detect the diseases with the average success rate at about 95% depending on the database used. In [14] authors present computer aided hard exudates detection method on fundus images using morphology and multi-resolution analysis. A $k$-NN based algorithm has been used with 35 training samples and has been run on four databases. Another interesting approach has been introduced in [15]. Authors present a novel method for glaucoma detection using digital fundus image and OCT image. The combined features from fundus and OCT images were analyzed. The system proposed turned to be able to classify glaucoma automatically with the accuracy of Back Propagation Neural Networks of 90.76% and Support Vector Machine Classifiers of 96.92%.

## 4 Authors' Approach

This method carries lots of information and allows to diagnose various diseases. This is why it is quite a big challenge facing the authors to design and implement the algorithm that will allow to support the doctors and even OCT technicians to present the patient a preliminary diagnosis with the highest possible accuracy. In this early stage of the research, authors propose the method to distinguish healthy retinas from deformed due to some apparent exudates. Images representing fluid under retina layers that authors have been working on comes mainly from patients suffering from wet AMD and diabetes mellitus.

As every image processing algorithm, authors' solution starts with input image preprocessing. At the beginning image is being narrowed by cutting 24% of the original width from the left and from the right. This way parts of the image that may introduce unnecessary information noise are being removed. This was in align with the suggestion of our team OCT expert member.

In the following step the image is being rescaled with bicubic interpolation and antialiasing. This way the noise is being reduced before the next segmentation step. Another step leaves only green pixels that are selected according to a rule that the green channel subpixel value is at least a 0.45 part of the sum of all pixel channels values as presented on (1) where $x$ and $y$ are the position on the X and Y axis respectively and $R$ is red channel pixel value at the given location. Accordingly $G$ is for green channel value and $B$ is for blue.

$$\frac{G_{x,y}}{R_{x,y} + G_{x,y} + B_{x,y}} > 0.45 \tag{1}$$

After getting only green pixels, median filter with a mask of $5 \times 5$ is used in order to remove all the remaining noise. The last operation applied to the image in the preprocessing section is morphological closing of green pixels. Closing means morphological dilation applied on previously eroded image. This stage leaves us with the most important part of the image - the tissue distribution. In Fig. 5 one can observe the algorithm diagram presenting how preprocessing phase was organized.

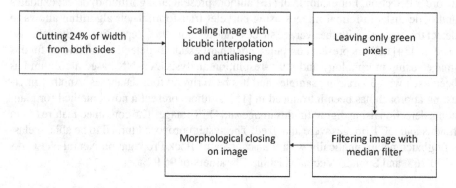

**Fig. 5.** A diagram presenting preprocessing methods used in the authors' algorithm

In Figs. 6 and 7 one can observe results of preprocessing stage of the algorithm on both distorted and healthy retina. All watery tissue has been removed from the image leaving only solid tissue. What is more interesting the most of the artifacts has been removed allowing us to easily process the image and the changes in retina thickness.

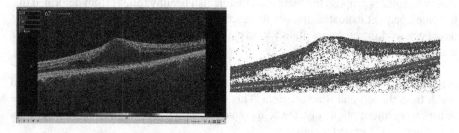

**Fig. 6.** Using an example of distorted retina the comparison of original OCT image on the left with the preprocessed image on the right is presented.

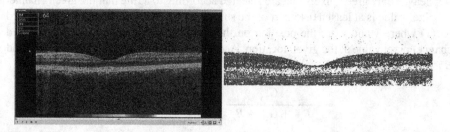

**Fig. 7.** Using an example of healthy retina the comparison of original OCT image on the left with the preprocessed image on the right is presented.

Another step is a feature vector building. Authors build a histogram representing a "thickness of a tissue". This is done by measuring the distance between the first and the last green pixel in each column. As the histogram is ready, it is being divided to several sections. For each section the average tissue thickness is being calculated. This method allows to get more general information. After that rather than storing the floating point values, the variability of the graph is being calculated. This mean if the next section has lower average height it is called a reduction and the opposite is the increase. If changes fit into a given margin the section is called insignificant. Margin value allows us to handle slight image rotations and slight or dry disorders. Computer representation of authors' algorithm was implemented with Java Programming Language. The flow chart of worked out computer program is given in Fig. 8.

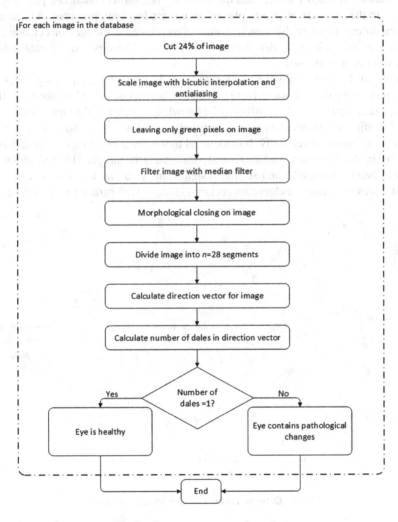

**Fig. 8.** Computer program flow chart

In the first approach authors focus only on significant exudations. More subtle differences will be a matter of further examination as a continuation of this work. However before starting more insight analyze, authors would like to dissolve really noticeable changes. So in this step it is assumed that the eye is sick when there is more than one increase after the reduction what represents one expected retina dale. All other anomalies in the vector course will indicate a lesion.

## 5    Results of the Experiment

In order to get precise results, sample database has been divided into two groups one of which consists of healthy retinas and the other one is a subset containing pathological changes. In the experiment 20 samples of each class has been provided. All samples represent different eyes of different patients. As mentioned in the previous chapter, our main goal at this point is to detect the most observable lesions and separate healthy retinas from unhealthy ones.

To obtain the best results we've changed the classification setup many times. As there is no training dataset in use, there will be no classifier described. Authors use their own approach implemented according to the knowledge shared by the Ophthalmologist. One of the adjustable parameters is sections count which describes on how many sections the image has been cut vertically. It is identical to the count of average macula heights calculated by the algorithm. And the second parameter is the margin which decides when to ignore height variability and set the insignificant value on the feature vector. In Fig. 9 it is presented how the algorithm accuracy changes with parameters modifications.

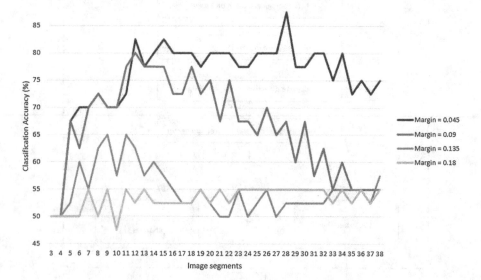

**Fig. 9.**  Detection accuracy of macular disorders

As one can see in the Fig. 9 using following setup results of correct classification range up to 87.5% when detecting macular degenerations. As the accuracy measure the Equal Error Rate (EER) [16] has been chosen which means that correct decision was made. No matter whether if it was a false negative or a false positive classification. The best EER score has been obtained when the value margin is equal to 0.045 and the number of sections is 28. In short the feature vector in this setup consists of 27 values each of them carries the information either there was a height value reduction, an increase or the change is insignificant.

Authors see the potential in this method and possibility to obtain even much better results, however some other mathematical model should be used in rejecting the insignificant changes. When the database grows even more common classifiers could be tested, especially good idea seems to be the use of Artificial Neural Networks on such feature vector.

## 6  Conclusions and Future Work

In the presented work only evident lesions were taken into consideration. Tenuous impairment, however, has been left to future work. The main reason is that the authors' work subject is dealt with for the first time, or at least up to their knowledge no such subject has been a topic of other medical or computer science researchers' work. Therefore, it has been decided to divide their work observations, results and achievements into current and future works. In the first part, namely this paper, authors have shown a detailed study to the subject of OCT presenting the basic concepts, related diseases and the necessary computer engineering contribution. This has ended with an algorithm and its computer implementation to automatically pick up the sick eye cases such as diabetes retinopathy and exudative type of age-related macular degeneration. According to the prepared algorithm, the decision about the disease stage can be taken as an output from the computer program. This is essential for the physician to know how critical the patient state is. The role of the physician will be limited to give his final decision about the necessary therapy. The results have shown that it is possible to automatically detect anomalies in retina structure.

In the nearest future authors plan to improve the accuracy of proposed algorithm and expand the variousity of retinal diseases to be detected. The final algorithm should diagnose subtle lesions such as small exudates. The satisfying level of final solution overall classification accuracy should be no lower than 95%.

**Acknowledgements.**  We would like express our sincere thanks to Medical University of Bialystok, Department of Ophthalmology. No work could be done without the generous help in sharing the data to process as well as the expertise.

This work was supported by grant S/WI/1/2013 from Bialystok University of Technology and funded with resources for research by the Ministry of Science and Higher Education in Poland.

# References

1. Kelty, P.J., Payne, J.F., Trivedi, R.H., et al.: Macular thickness assessment in healthy eyes based on ethnicity using stratus OCT Optical Coherence Tomography. Invest. Ophthalmol. Vis. Sci. **49**(6), 2668–2672 (2008)
2. Shah, A.R., Williams, S., Baumal, C.R., et al.: Predictors of response to intravitreal anti-vascular endothelial growth factor treatment of age-related macular degeneration. Am. J. Ophthalmol. **163**, 154–166 (2016)
3. Chen, Y., Li, J., Yan, Y., et al.: Diabetic macular morphology changes may occur in the early stage of diabetes. BMC Ophthalmol. **16**(12) (2016)
4. Gooding, K.M., Shore, A.C., Ling, R., et al.: Regional differences in macular thickness in the early stages of diabetic retinopathy in type 2 diabetes. Diabetologia **58**(1), S526 (2015)
5. Bressler, N.M., Edwards, A.R., Antoszyk, A.N., et al.: Retinal thickness on stratus Optical Coherence Tomography in people with diabetes and minimal or no diabetic retinopathy. Am. J. Ophthalmol. **145**(5), 894–901 (2008)
6. Chen, X., Song, W., Cai, H., et al.: Macular edema after cataract surgery in diabetic eyes evaluated by optical coherence tomography. Int. J. Ophthalmol. **9**(1), 81–85 (2016)
7. Mokwa, N.F., Ristau, T., Keane, P.A., et al.: Grading of age-related macular degeneration: comparison between color fundus photography, fluorescein angiography, and spectral domain optical coherence tomography. J. Ophthalmol. (2013). Article ID 385915
8. Swiebocka-Wiek, J.: The detection of the retina's lesions in Optical Coherence Tomography (OCT). In: Kulczycki, P., Kóczy, László T., Mesiar, R., Kacprzyk, J. (eds.) CITCEP 2016. AISC, vol. 462, pp. 179–195. Springer, Cham (2017). https://doi.org/10.1007/978-3-319-44260-0_11
9. Lee, J.Y., Stephanie, J.C., Pratul, P.S., et al.: Fully automatic software for retinal thickness in eyes with diabetic macular edema from images acquired by cirrus and spectralis systems. Invest. Ophthalmol. Vis. Sci. **54**(12), 7595–7602 (2013)
10. Chen, X., Niemeijer, M., Zhang, L., et al.: 3D segmentation of fluid-associated abnormalities in retinal OCT: probability constrained graph-search-graph-cut. IEEE Trans. Med. Imaging **31**(8), 1521–1531 (2012)
11. Lammer, J., Bolz, M., Baumann, B., Pircher, M., Gerendas, B., Schlanitz, F., Hitzenberger, C.K., Schmidt-Erfurth, U.: Detection and analysis of hard exudates by polarization-sensitive optical coherence tomography in patients with diabetic maculopathy. Invest. Ophthalmol. Vis. Sci. **55**(3), 1564–1571 (2014)
12. Stankiewicz, A., Marciniak, T., Dąbrowski, A., Stopa, M., Rakowicz, P., Marciniak, E.: Denoising methods for improving automatic segmentation in OCT images of human eye. Bull. Pol. Academic. Sci. Tech. Sci. **1** (2017)
13. Esmaeili, M., Rabbani, H., Dehnavi, A.M., Dehghani, A.: Automatic detection of exudates and optic disk in retinal images using curvelet transform. IET Image Process. **6**(7), 1005–1013 (2012)
14. Rokade, P.M., Manza, R., Jonathan, P.: Computer aided hard exudates detection on digital fundus images using morphology and multi-resolution analysis. Int. J. Adv. Comput. Technol. (IJACT) **4**(5), 20–27 (2015)
15. Ganesh Babua, T.R., Shenbaga Devi, S., Venkateshc, R.: Optic nerve head segmentation using fundus images and optical coherence tomography images for glaucoma detection. Biomed. Pap. Med. Fac. Univ. Palacky Olomouc Czech Repub. **159**(4), 607–615 (2015)
16. Saeed, K., Nagashima, T.: Biometrics and Kansei Engineering. Springer, New York (2012). https://doi.org/10.1007/978-1-4614-5608-7

# Algebraic and Logical Emulations
# of Quantum Circuits

Kenneth Regan[1](✉) ⓘ, Amlan Chakrabarti[2], and Chaowen Guan[1]

[1] University at Buffalo (SUNY), Buffalo, USA
regan@buffalo.edu
[2] University of Calcutta, Kolkata, India

**Abstract.** Quantum circuits exhibit several features of large-scale distributed systems. They have a concise design formalism but behavior that is challenging to represent let alone predict. Issues of scalability—both in the yet-to-be-engineered quantum hardware and in classical simulators—are paramount. They require sparse representations for efficient modeling. Whereas *simulators* represent both the system's current state and its operations directly, *emulators* manipulate the images of system states under a mapping to a different formalism. We describe three such formalisms for quantum circuits. The first two extend the polynomial construction of Dawson et al. [1] to (i) work for any set of quantum gates obeying a certain "balance" condition and (ii) produce a single polynomial over any sufficiently structured field or ring. The third appears novel and employs only simple Boolean formulas, optionally limited to a form we call "parity-of-AND" equations. Especially the third can combine with off-the-shelf state-of-the-art third-party software, namely *model counters* and *#SAT solvers*, that we show capable of vast improvements in the emulation time in natural instances. We have programmed all three constructions to proof-of-concept level and report some preliminary tests and applications. These include algebraic analysis of special quantum circuits and the possibility of a new classical attack on the factoring problem. Preliminary comparisons are made with the libquantum simulator [2–4].

## 1 A Brief but Full QC Introduction

A *quantum circuit* is a compact representation of a computational system. It consists of some number $m$ of *qubits* represented by *lines* resembling a musical staff, and some number $s$ of *gates* arrayed like musical notes and chords. Here is an example created using the popular visual simulator [5]:

The circuit $C$ operates on $m = 5$ qubits. The input is the binary string $x = 10010$. The first $n = 4$ qubits see most of the action and hold the nominal input $x_0 = 1001$ of length $n = 4$, while the fifth qubit is an *ancilla* initialized to 0 whose purpose here is to hold the nominal output bit. The circuit has thirteen *gates*. Six of them have a single *control* represented by a black dot; they activate if and only if the control receives a 1 signal. The last gate has two controls and

© Springer-Verlag GmbH Germany, part of Springer Nature 2018
M. L. Gavrilova et al. (Eds.): Trans. on Comput. Sci. XXXI, LNCS 10730, pp. 41–76, 2018.
https://doi.org/10.1007/978-3-662-56499-8_4

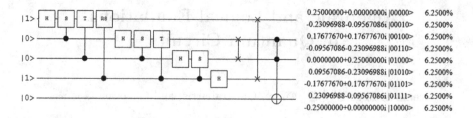

| | |
|---|---|
| 0.25000000+0.00000000i  \|00000> | 6.2500% |
| -0.23096988-0.09567086i  \|00010> | 6.2500% |
| 0.17677670+0.17677670i  \|00100> | 6.2500% |
| -0.09567086-0.23096988i  \|00110> | 6.2500% |
| 0.00000000+0.25000000i  \|01000> | 6.2500% |
| 0.09567086-0.23096988i  \|01010> | 6.2500% |
| -0.17677670+0.17677670i  \|01101> | 6.2500% |
| 0.23096988-0.09567086i  \|01111> | 6.2500% |
| -0.25000000+0.00000000i  \|10000> | 6.2500% |

**Fig. 1.** A five-qubit quantum circuit that computes a Fourier transform on the first four qubits.

a *target* represented by the parity symbol $\oplus$ rather than a labeled box. Called a *Toffoli gate*, it will set the output bit if and only if *both* controls receive a 1 signal. The two gates before it merely *swap* the qubits 2 and 3 and 1 and 4, respectively. They have no effect on the output and are included here only to say that the first twelve gates combine to compute the *quantum Fourier transform* $\mathrm{QFT}_4$. This is just the ordinary discrete Fourier transform $F_{16}$ on $2^4 = 16$ coordinates.

The actual output $C(x)$ of the circuit is a *quantum state* $\mathcal{Z}$ that belongs to the complex vector space $\mathbf{C}^{32}$. Nine of its entries in the *standard basis* are shown in Fig. 1; seven more were cropped from the screenshot. Sixteen of the components are absent, meaning $\mathcal{Z}$ has 0 in the corresponding coordinates. Despite the diversity of the nine complex entries $\mathcal{Z}_L$ shown, each has magnitude $|\mathcal{Z}_L|^2 = 0.0625$. In general, $|\mathcal{Z}_L|^2$ represents the probability that a *measurement*—of all qubits— will yield the binary string $z \in \{0,1\}^5$ corresponding to the coordinate $L$ under the standard ordered enumeration of $\{0,1\}^5$. Here we are interested in those $z$ whose final entry $z_5$ is a 1. Two of them are shown; two others (11101 and 11111) are possible and also have probability $\frac{1}{16}$ each, making a total of $\frac{1}{4}$ probability for getting $z_5 = 1$. Owing to the "cylindrical" nature of the set $B$ of strings ending in 1, a measurement of just the fifth qubit yields 1 with probability $\frac{1}{4}$.

Where does the probability come from? The physical answer is that it is an indelible aspect of nature as expressed by quantum mechanics. For our purposes the computational answer is that it comes from the four gates labeled H, for *Hadamard gate*. Each supplies one bit of nondeterminism, giving four bits in all, which govern the sixteen possible outcomes of this particular example. It is a mistake to think that the probabilities must be equally spread out and must be multiples of $1/2^h$ where $h$ is the number of Hadamard gates. Appending just one more Hadamard gate at the right end of the third qubit line creates nonzero probabilities as low as $0.0183058\ldots$ and as high as $0.106694\ldots$, each appearing for four outcomes of 24 nonzero possibilities. This happens because the component values follow wave equations that can *amplify* some values while reducing or zeroing the amplitude of others via *interference*. Indeed, the goal of quantum computing is to marshal most of the amplitude onto a small set of desired outcomes, so that measurements—that is to say, quantum *sampling*—will reveal one of them with high probability.

All of this indicates the burgeoning complexity of quantum systems. Our original circuit has 5 qubits, 4 nondeterministic gates, and 9 other gates, yet there are $2^5 = 32$ components of the vectors representing states, 32 basic inputs and outputs, and $2^4 = 16$ branchings to consider. Adding the fifth Hadamard gate creates a new fork in every *path* through the system, giving 32 branchings. The whole circuit $C$ defines a $32 \times 32$ matrix $U_C$ in which the $I$-th row encodes the quantum state $\Phi_I$ resulting from computation on the standard basis vector $x = e_I$. The matrix is *unitary*, meaning that $U_C$ multiplied by its conjugate transpose $U_C^*$ gives the $32 \times 32$ identity matrix. Indeed, $U_C$ is the product of thirteen simpler matrices $U_\ell$ representing the respective gates ($\ell = 1, \ldots, s$ with $s = 13$). Here each gate engages only a subset of the qubits of arity $r < m$, so that $U_\ell$ decomposes into its $2^r \times 2^r$ unitary *gate matrix* and the identity action (represented by the $2 \times 2$ identity matrix I) on the other $m - r$ lines. Here are some single-qubit gate matrices:

$$H = \frac{1}{\sqrt{2}}\begin{bmatrix} 1 & 1 \\ 1 & -1 \end{bmatrix}, \quad X = \begin{bmatrix} 0 & 1 \\ 1 & 0 \end{bmatrix}, \quad Y = \begin{bmatrix} 0 & -i \\ i & 0 \end{bmatrix}, \quad Z = \begin{bmatrix} 1 & 0 \\ 0 & -1 \end{bmatrix}, \quad S = \begin{bmatrix} 1 & 0 \\ 0 & i \end{bmatrix}, \quad T = \begin{bmatrix} 1 & 0 \\ 0 & e^{i\pi/4} \end{bmatrix}, \quad R_8 = \begin{bmatrix} 1 & 0 \\ 0 & e^{i\pi/8} \end{bmatrix}.$$

The *phase gate* S is also called $R_2$ and the *twist gate* T is also called $R_4$. Multiplying a quantum state by a unit scalar changes none of the magnitudes so the unconditional global *phase shift* by the scalar has no effect on outcomes. The conditional phase shift on a 1 signal embodied by the lower-right entry of all these matrices does matter, and unconditionally effects a rotation of the qubit line through its own $2 \times 2$ space.

Adding *controls* is one way to extend effects to other qubits. The gate X, which is also called the NOT gate for the negation it effects on the classical bit corresponding to the qubit line, yields the controlled forms CX (aka. CNOT) and CCX (aka. Tof for the Toffoli gate) at left and right:

$$\text{CNOT} = \begin{bmatrix} 1 & 0 & 0 & 0 \\ 0 & 1 & 0 & 0 \\ 0 & 0 & 0 & 1 \\ 0 & 0 & 1 & 0 \end{bmatrix}, \quad \text{CS} = \begin{bmatrix} 1 & 0 & 0 & 0 \\ 0 & 1 & 0 & 0 \\ 0 & 0 & 1 & 0 \\ 0 & 0 & 0 & i \end{bmatrix}, \quad \text{Tof} = \begin{bmatrix} 1 & 0 & 0 & 0 & 0 & 0 & 0 & 0 \\ 0 & 1 & 0 & 0 & 0 & 0 & 0 & 0 \\ 0 & 0 & 1 & 0 & 0 & 0 & 0 & 0 \\ 0 & 0 & 0 & 1 & 0 & 0 & 0 & 0 \\ 0 & 0 & 0 & 0 & 1 & 0 & 0 & 0 \\ 0 & 0 & 0 & 0 & 0 & 1 & 0 & 0 \\ 0 & 0 & 0 & 0 & 0 & 0 & 0 & 1 \\ 0 & 0 & 0 & 0 & 0 & 0 & 1 & 0 \end{bmatrix}.$$

Note that the NAND of $u, v$ equals $\text{Tof}(u, v, 1)$ so the Toffoli gate alone can efficiently code any classical computation. The controlled versions of the Z, T, and $R_8$ gates, as also employed in our example circuit, are defined similarly. Here is a simple circuit using one Hadamard gate and the standard symbol for CNOT:

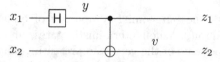

Here $x_1, x_2$ and $z_1, z_2$ are variables that stand for the input and output viewed as binary strings, while $y$ and $v$ are internal variables following the scheme laid out in Sect. 3 below. On input $a = 00$, which is represented by the vector $(1, 0, 0, 0)$ in $\mathbf{C}_4$, the final quantum state $\mathcal{Z}$ is $\frac{1}{\sqrt{2}}(1, 0, 0, 1)$. The outcomes $b = 00$ and $b = 11$ are possible with probability $\frac{1}{2}$ each, but the outcomes 01 and 10 are impossible. So the two qubits are constrained to give the same binary value. When a quantum state $\mathcal{Z}$ cannot be written as a tensor product of two other vectors—as implied here by the lack of probabilistic independence of the output bits $b_1$ and $b_2$—it is *entangled*.

The matrix of the Swap gate is the special $4 \times 4$ permutation matrix that fixes coordinates 1 and 4 corresponding to the strings 00 and 11 but sends 2 to 3 and 3 to 2 so that 01 switches with 10. We have now completed the description of the circuit $C$ in Fig. 1. Two quirks of the notation must be noted:

- If the qubits engaged by $U_j$ are not contiguous, then we may not get $U_j$ as a literal tensor product of its gate matrix and identity matrices, but we can write $U_j = P^{-1} U_j' P$ where $U_j'$ is such a product and $P$ induces a permutation of the qubit lines in the manner of the swap matrix above.
- We read the circuits left-to-right but matrices are composed and applied to column vectors right-to-left.

Above we have ignored the swapping in the former point by writing the matrices with *control lines* first. The second point looks ignorable because all our matrices happen to be symmetric, but when the gate Y is included this is no longer so. The single-qubit gates X, Y, Z (plus I for completeness) are called *Pauli gates*, while adding H, S, and CZ creates a basis for the set of *Clifford gates*, which also include CNOT but not Tof, CS, T, or $R_8$. Adding any one of the latter four gates creates a gate set that is *universal* in that any quantum circuit $C$ can have its states $\Phi = C(a)$ approximated to arbitrary precision with comparable efficiency by a circuit $C'$ using only gates from the set. Indeed, the set consisting of just H and Tof is universal in a weaker sense that encodes the real and complex parts of $\Phi$ separately and approximates the probabilities of the basic outcomes. Two minimal universal sets that keep $r \leq 2$ are $\{H, CS\}$ and $\{H, T, CNOT\}$.

To complete our description of quantum computation, we note that to compute a mapping $f$ from inputs $x \in \{0, 1\}^n$ to outcomes $z_0 \in \{0, 1\}^q$ it is conventional to use $m = n + m_0 + q$ qubits with the latter $m_0 + q$ initialized to 0 and produce outcomes of the form $x \cdot 0^{m_0} \cdot y$. This can be effected by using only the initial $n$ qubits plus $m_0$ more qubits for "scratch space" for the main computation, then using $q$ CNOT gates to copy out desired results into the last $q$ qubits—in like manner to how the fifth qubit was employed in our example. Finally one can restore the first $n + m_0$ qubits to their initial state by repeating the conjugate transposes of the gates of the main computation in reverse order. The extra cost of the "copy" and "uncompute" steps after the main computation stays within a linear factor in terms of the visible hardware—that is, the count $m + s$ of qubits and gates (presuming bounded arity $r$ of any one gate). The convention works even if $f$ is not one-to-one.

We can implement traditional definitions of computing functions $f :$ $\{0, 1\}^n \rightarrow \{0, 1\}^q$ and deciding membership in languages $L$ with high probability of success or correctness. Say $f$ is (*quantum*) *efficiently computable* if there is a polynomial $p(n)$ such that for all $\epsilon > 0$ and all $n$ we can build a circuit $C_{n,\epsilon}$ of size $m + s \leq p(n + \log(1/\epsilon))$ such that for all inputs $x$, the measurement gives $x0^{m_0} f(x)$ with probability at least $1 - \epsilon$. Applying this criterion to the 0–1 valued characteristic functions of $L$ defines the quantum complexity class BQP standing for "Bounded-error Quantum Polynomial time." Functions and even multi-valued mappings $f$ are also said to belong to BQP with the understanding that computing $f(x) \mapsto z$ is equivalent to deciding $L_f = \{(x, y) : \text{some legal}$ value $z$ has $y$ as an initial substring$\}$. But the primary utility may come from the quantum ability to *sample* the joint distribution of $(x, z)$ where $z$ is a legal value of $f$ and see what the induced distribution on $x$ may highlight.

## 2    A System View: Simulation and Emulation

What is the "true" complexity of the system we have described? We can first ask about its effective size:

(a) Is it the simple count $m + s$ of qubits and gates, perhaps multiplied by some function of $r$?

(b) Or is it the dimension $2^m$ of the ambient space, and/or the size $2^h$ of the branching paths?

(c) Or is the "real size" something in-between?

Two ideas of "in-between" are whether the layout size $m \times s$ of the grid should be counted and whether entanglements render its effective cross-section as more than the number $m$ of qubits. The former still leaves the size polynomial in $n$ while it seems hard to argue the latter higher than the number of possible binary entanglements, which is $O(m^2)$. Moreover, there is a dearth of natural mathematical functions between polynomial (or quasi-polynomial: $n^{(\log n)^{O(1)}}$) and exponential ($2^{n^{\Omega(1)}}$).

The polynomial versus exponential divide is burnished by Shor's algorithm [6] for factoring $n$-bit integers $M$. Its quantum circuits $C_n$ sit inside a non-quantum program loop that samples integers $a < M$, runs $C(a, M)$, measures all qubits of the resulting state $\mathcal{Z}$, and tries to infer a factor of $M$ from the outcome $b$. The circuits $C_n$ are relatively simple; they use the gates in Fig. 1 plus one call to the quantum Fourier transform on $n$ qubits, and are known to have size no worse than slightly above $O(n^2)$. Classical algorithms, however, are conjectured to require time $2^{n^c}$ with $c$ not much smaller than $1/3$ (see [7]) on *many* instances

$M$. The security of RSA and many other cryptographic protocols depends on this hardness assumption or a similar one for the discrete logarithm problem, which is also solved by Shor's algorithm. If one subscribes both to the classical hardness of factoring and to our circuit modeling correctly metering quantum mechanics as a true theory of nature, the upshot is:

> Nature can compute efficiently in ways that symbolic operations are far from emulating.

This is stronger than concluding that classical physical systems cannot approximate the quantum sampling $C(a, M) \mapsto b$ as above. It says that no human system of notation for describing quantum circuits can execute their calculations with comparable efficiency—nor any reasonable efficiency. Somewhere we must face an exponential blowup. To riff on the enigmatic final words in Latin of Umberto Eco's novel *The Name of the Rose*, all the QC notations we can hold are "bare names" that miss the pristine mechanism through which the quantum "rose" abides unsullied by notation.

Of course, this is a *challenge* for the description of computational systems. Formal analysis tools for computing systems are legion but this system—after we needed only a few pages to specify its components fully and indicate how signals are processed—spits fire saying it can't be done. There are two levels of demands we can make on the description, one stronger and the other weaker:

(a) At any time $t$, it should describe with high fidelity the state of the system at time $t$.

(b) On any input, it should reproduce with high fidelity the *final* state of the system.

We identify these capabilities with the distinction made by Häner et al. [8] between (a) a *simulator* and (b) an *emulator* of quantum circuits. As described in Sect. 2 of their papers, simulators to date have directly manipulated the gate matrices under sparse representations and using hardware systems dedicated to such matrix operations. We read the essence as being that the simulators can on request deliver a "census" of active system elements and their microstates as they stand after multiplying $j$ of the matrices, for any $j$ from 0 to $s$. As such, they need to grapple with the exponential blowup at the first stages where it is in force. *Emulators* are freed from having to comply with such requests, and in particular are entitled to ignore the synchrony imposed by $j$ and the $m \times s$ grid view of the circuit. Their prime goal is to postpone the blowup as long as possible and perhaps—in enough important cases—to avoid it.

In this paper we present three formalisms for describing quantum circuits that begin with the capability of simulation but promote non-quantum, non-physical manipulations that may yield faster emulation. The first two represent circuits $C$ by single polynomials $P_C$ and $Q_C$ over various finite fields or rings, the third by simple quantifier-free Boolean formulas $\phi_C$. In their brute-force rendition they can perform simulation, and we show that the Boolean one is competent on simple hardware. The former two may connect to existing software packages that perform algebraic manipulations such as equation solving and reduction using Gröbner bases, such as *Singular* [9,10]. The latter immediately connects to existing *model counters* and #SAT *solvers* such as *sharpSAT* [11] and *Cachet* [12–14]. Both $P_C$ and $\phi_C$ have size $O(m + s)$. The blowup is entirely handed off to the algebraic system or solution counter.

The first express conversion to (sets of) polynomials was by Dawson et al. [1] and programmed by Gerdt and Severyanov [15]. It applied only to the universal set {H, CNOT, Tof} of gates with ±1 entries, except for remarks in [1] about "mixed mode (mod-2/mod-8) arithmetic." Bacon et al. [16] tailored a construction to (singly and doubly) controlled phase-changing gates modulo various values of $K$, like those for $K = 4, 8, 16$ in the last section's example, plus the Fourier transform $F_K$. All of these constructions constitute proofs that BQP polynomial-time reduces to the complexity class #P of functions and its decision analogue PP [17]. Fortnow and Rogers [18] improved this to place BQP inside a "low" subclass of PP called AWPP and characterized by one evaluation of the difference $f(x) - g(x)$ of two functions $f, g \in$ #P that obey a further restriction. We claim to give the first "global" presentation of polynomial constructions $P_C$, including a trick to produce polynomials $Q_C$ of bounded degree at the cost of using more variables. Our translation into Boolean formulas $\phi_C$ appears to be entirely new as we discuss later. But to be sure, the constructions are elementary enough that they could have been done soon after these papers or even the seminal gate papers [19,20]. Perhaps motives are stronger now amid greater development of algebraic system-analysis tools, the increasing success of heuristic SAT and #SAT solvers, and ramped-up efforts at high-performance emulation of quantum systems represented recently by [8,21,22].

Our formalisms employ the *path* concept promoted by Richard Feynman, whose papers [23,24] are often jointly credited with Deutsch [25,26] as originating quantum computing. Each path contributes a unit amount to a term in the matrix product $U_s U_{s-1} \cdots U_2 U_1$ applied to an input vector $x$ when everything is multiplied out. It begins in some row $I$, $0 \le I \le 2^m - 1$, of the column vector $x$ and enters column $I$ of $U_1$. It may exit $U_1$ at any row $J$ for which $U_1[J, I] \ne 0$ and then enters column $J$ of $U_2$. Finally, it exits $U_s$ at some row $L$, which we call the final *location* of the path. The matrices of most elementary gates satisfy the following condition:

**Definition 1.** *A quantum gate matrix is* balanced *if all nonzero entries have the same magnitude.*

If $r_\ell$ is the magnitude for each gate $\ell$, then the final path value is a unit complex scalar $e^{i\theta}$ divided by $R = r_1 \cdot r_2 \cdots r_s$ which is independent of the path. The $\theta$ is the *phase* of the path. We can identify a path's *current phase and location* at any stage $j$ upon exiting $U_j$. Tracking this explicitly for all $j$ and all paths would constitute what we have called a simulation. The freedom of emulation we desire will come from (i) treating paths individually without the idea of "stage $j$," (ii) combining and transforming their representations into the small objects $P_C$ and $\phi_C$, and hopefully (iii) further algebraic and formal manipulations that may break the association with gates and matrices but gather the final locations and phases into outcomes more efficiently than by census.

The contributions of the present paper are:

- Main theorems showing how to convert quantum circuits $C$—using all common gate sets—into polynomials $P_C, Q_C$ and Boolean formulas $\phi_C$ that produce amplitudes $\langle b| C |a \rangle$ for every basic input $a$ and output $b$.
- Further theorems building polynomials $\mathcal{P}_C, \mathcal{Q}_C$ and formulas $\Phi_C$ that compute probabilities, foster partial measurements, and enable an exact emulation of quantum sampling.
- Examples of algebraic and logical calculations, including a new proof of the *Gottesman-Knill theorem* that draws an especially fine line between BQP and P.
- Very preliminary experiments showing that on reasonable cases up to several dozen qubits and nondeterministic gates, #SAT solvers not only soundly beat intelligent brute force but *scale* much better as the problem size increases.

## 3   The Common Architecture

The two main structural parameters are the number $m$ of qubits and the *minimum phase denominator* $K$, which is the minimum $K$ such that all matrix entries $re^{i\theta}$ have $\theta$ an integer multiple of $2\pi/K$. We assume $K$ is a power of 2, $K = 2^k$. The architecture maintains the phase $J \in \{0, \ldots, K-1\}$ and location in $\{0,1\}^m$ of any one path. The following elements are common to the descriptions by polynomials and by formulas:

- All variables range over 0 and 1 only. (Theorem 4 will allow values in $\mathbf{Z}_4$.)
- The input $a_1 \cdots a_m \in \{0,1\}^m$ designates the one initial location for all paths.
- Variables $X = x_1, \ldots, x_m$ are placeholder variables assigned $a_1, \ldots, a_m$ when an input $a \in \{0,1\}^m$ is given.
- Variables $Z = z_1, \ldots, z_m$ can be fully or partially substituted by *targets* $b_i$ for $i \in I \subseteq \{1, \ldots, m\}$, in order to define desired and undesired final locations.
- The *value(s)* of the polynomial or formula represent only a path's phase, not its location.
- The current location of a path is embodies by *line designators* $u_1, \ldots, u_m$ which are not variables but rather references to already-existing variables. Initially they refer to $x_1, \ldots, x_m$, respectively.
- Upon finishing the circuit, algebraic terms or logical equations are added to force $z_1, \ldots, z_m$ to be equal to the variables designated by $u_1, \ldots, u_m$ upon finishing the circuit. They may also be substituted by some or all target values $b_1, \ldots, b_m$ prefatory to executing measurements.
- *Free variables* $Y = y_1, \ldots, y_h$ represent nondeterministic bits (from Hadamard and some other gates) and are the main variables over which solutions are counted. When a designator $u_i$ refers to a free variable $y_j$ it denotes a fork in the path tied to line $i$ but affecting every location.

- *Forced variables* $V = v_1, \ldots, v_s, \ldots$ are placed on qubit lines $i$ and become the new $u_i$ when placed. Their values are forced—else the path being built is zeroed out or cancels itself out or fails a satisfaction filter.
- Extra variables $\Upsilon$ in terms $\Upsilon_\ell$ may be used to enforce constraints by making failure fork the path into the whole range of phases—equally weighted—so that its net contribution is zero.
- The polynomial's *value* may—or may not—be maintained in *phase variables* $W_\ell = \{(w_j)_\ell\}$ at any juncture $\ell$, with $1 \le j \le k$ in binary. These variables are also forced, and the designations "$V$" and "$W$" will be flexible in context.

We will also consider liberalizing $u_1, \ldots, u_m$ to refer to arbitrary subterms, not just variables (or their negations). In the simple Hadamard plus CNOT example in Sect. 1 we could replace the forced variable $v$ by its algebraic value $2x_2 y - x_2 - y$ or its Boolean value $x_2 \oplus y$ instead of creating a polynomial term or Boolean clause to constrain $v$ to have that value. Our general theorem, however, uses only fresh single variables $y$ as the internal *annotations* on qubit lines. Absorbing this architecture may be enough to treat Sect. 5 as self-justifying and skip over the full proof of the general theorem in the next section.

## 4    General Simulation

To state the main theorem, we call a ring $\mathcal{R}$ *adequate* for a quantum circuit $C$ of min-phase denominator $K$ if there is a 1-to-1 mapping $h$ from the $K$-th roots of unity into $\mathcal{R}$ such that, letting $\omega = e^{2\pi i/K}$, we have $h(\omega^{I+J}) = h(\omega^I)h(\omega^J)$ for all $I, J \le K$. Since the range of $h$ cannot include zero, $\mathcal{R}$ must have at least $K+1$ elements. In this multiplicative case, zero will annihilate terms that would denote impossible paths. Our theorem will also include a 1-to-1 function $h'$ such that $h'(\omega^{I+J}) = h'(\omega^I) + h'(\omega^J)$ in a different ring $\mathcal{R}'$ while translating $C$ into a polynomial $Q_C$ over $\mathcal{R}'$. For simplicity we will fix $\mathcal{R}' = \mathbf{Z}_K$, the integers modulo $K$, and fix $h'(\omega^I) = I$ as the mapping. Now zero is in the range: $0 = h'(1)$. We will use the additivity to make impossible paths yield a net-zero effect by having them cause a corresponding constraint expression $\gamma$ to have value 1 rather than 0. In the Boolean case we will have $k$ variables $W_\ell = (w_0, \ldots, w_{k-1})$ that represent the values $0, \ldots, K-1$ in binary notation, while an impossible path will correspond to a truth assignment that is immediately unsatisfying—that will satisfy none of the formulas $\phi_J = \phi_C[W_\ell = J]$ expressing that the final value is $J$. The "indicators" $u_1, \ldots, u_m$ are not actual variables but rather references to variables in $X \cup Y \cup V$.

Finally, given a polynomial $p$ in $h$ variables, let $\#binsols(p)$ denote the number of zeros of the polynomial in $\{0,1\}^h$. If some variables in $p$ are substituted by constants, we note that in square brackets and may subscript the non-substituted variables for emphasis. We similarly use $\#sat(\phi)$ for the number of satisfying assignments to a formula $\phi$. The counting runs over $\{0,1\}^q$ where $q$ is the number of non-substituted variables. If $q = 0$, then $\{0,1\}^q$ still has one member, so the count of solutions will be 1 or 0 according to whether the resulting constant

$p$ is zero or $\phi$ is reduced to the constant $\top$ (true) function. Although "$V$" will be unused in the proof for $P_C$ and $Q_C$, we keep it in the theorem statement to cover usage in the next section.

**Theorem 1.** *There is an efficient uniform procedure that transforms any balanced $m$-qubit quantum circuit $C$ of min-phase $K = 2^k$ with $s$ gates of maximum arity $r$ into constants $R, R'$, polynomials $P_C$ over an adequate ring and $Q_C$ over $\mathbf{Z}_K$, and a Boolean formula $\phi_C$—all with variables from $V, W, X, Y, \Upsilon, Z$ as in Sect. 3—such that for all $a, b \in \{0, 1\}^m$:*

$$\langle b| C |a\rangle = \frac{1}{R} \sum_{J=0}^{K-1} \omega^J \#binsols_{V,Y}(P_C[X = a, Z = b] - h(\omega^J)) \tag{1}$$

$$= \frac{1}{R'} \sum_{J=0}^{K-1} \omega^J \#binsols_{V,Y,\Upsilon}(Q_C[X = a, Z = b] - J) \tag{2}$$

$$= \frac{1}{R} \sum_{J=0}^{K-1} \omega^J \#sat_{V,Y}(\phi_C[X = a, Z = b, W = J]). \tag{3}$$

*The objects $P_C, Q_C, \phi_C$ all have formulas of size $O(2^{2r}msk)$ and can be written down in time $\tilde{O}(m + 2^{2r}sk)$, where the $\tilde{O}$ means to ignore logarithmic factors coming from the variable labels.*

*Proof.* We first describe the construction of $P_C$, then indicate the adjustments needed to produce $Q_C$ and $\phi_C$. On input $a$, let $U_s U_{s-1} \cdots U_2 U_1 a$ be the matrix computation. We will first treat each $U_\ell$ as a general $2^m \times 2^m$ matrix engaging all $m$ qubits, then show how things simplify for arity $r$. We maintain a running polynomial $P_\ell$ in stages $\ell = 0, 1, 2, \ldots, s$. This will give $P_C = P_s E_C$ where

$$E_C = \prod_{i=1}^m (1 + 2u_i z_i - u_i - z_i),$$

using whatever variables (or alternatively subterms) are designated by $u_1, \ldots, u_m$ at the end. On 0–1 arguments, $E_C$ gives 1 if $u_i = z_i$ for all $i$ and 0 otherwise. We can also put $P_{C,\ell} = P_\ell E_C$ for any $\ell$ using the variables the $u_i$ refer to on completing stage $\ell$.

Initially, $P_0 = 1$, $R = 1$, and the indicators $u_1, \ldots, u_m$ refer to the variables $x_1, \ldots, x_m$, which themselves will be substituted by the binary arguments $a_1, \ldots, a_m$. If $s = 0$, i.e., if $C$ has no gates, then we will have $u_i = x_i = a_i$ and $z_i = b_i$ for all $i$, yielding 1 if $b = a$ and 0 otherwise. Since we have $\langle b| I |a\rangle = 1$ when $b = a$ and 0 otherwise, (1)–(3) hold by the convention on counting over empty domains before the theorem statement.

As we add gates in stages $\ell = 1$ to $s$, we will maintain the invariant that paths from $a$ to some current location $L$ giving current phase $J$ are in 1-to-1 correspondence with solutions to $P_C[X = a, Z = L] - h(\omega^J) = 0$. Suppose this is true for stage $\ell - 1$ (as initially when $\ell = 1$) and consider the matrix $U_\ell$. Each path enters in some column $L$ and exits in some row $I$. Using the $m$-bit binary code for each $L$, define the *indicator term*

$$t_L = \prod_{j:L_j=0} (1 - u_j) \prod_{j:L_j=1} u_j.$$

Then $t_L = 1$ if the current entering location given by $(u_1, \ldots, u_m)$ equals $L$ and $t_L = 0$ otherwise. Let $g$ stand for the current number of $Y$-variables allocated so far $(g = m(\ell - 1)$ before we simplify), allocate new variables $y_{g+1}, \ldots, y_{g+m}$, and for each possible $I$ define

$$t_I = \prod_{j:I_j=0} (1 - y_{g+j}) \prod_{j:I_j=1} y_{g+j}.$$

For each $I, L$ we either have $U_\ell[I, L] = 0$ or we have $U_\ell[I, L] = r\omega^d$ for some $d$, where $r$ is independent of $I, L$ by the balance condition. Multiply $R$ by $r$ and define $P_\ell$ to be $P_{\ell-1}$ multiplied by the term

$$p_\ell = \sum_{I,L:U_\ell[I,L]=r\omega^d \neq 0} t_I t_L h(\omega^d).$$

Finally, re-assign $u_1, \ldots, u_m$ to refer to the newly-created variables $y_{g+1}, \ldots, y_{g+m}$. This completes stage $\ell$.

We claim that this preserves the invariant. The main point is that each 0–1 assignment to the variables previously designated by $u_1, \ldots, u_m$ and thew new variables $y_{g+1}, \ldots, y_{g+m}$ makes exactly one product $t_I t_L$ nonzero. So it corresponds to the path segment that enters at $L$ and exits at $I$. If $U_\ell[I, L] = 0$ then any extension of that assignment will make $P_C$ have value 0, so it cannot be a solution to any equation $P_C - h(\omega^J) = 0$. Else, the segment advances the phase of any path it extends by $d$. Hence for paths that are in location $I$ and have current phase $J$ after $U_\ell$ we know:

- There is some $L$ and $d$ such that the path came into $U_\ell$ by column $L$ and $p_\ell = t_I t_L h(\omega^d)$. On entry it had phase $\omega^{J-d}$ with the exponent wrapped mod $K$.
- By the inductive invariant, there is a unique assignment to the variables appearing in $P_{C,\ell-1}[X = a, Z = L]$ that gives value $h(\omega^{J-d})$. Those are all variables in $P_{C,\ell}$ except $y_{g+1}, \ldots, y_{g+m}$.
- Setting $y_{g+1}, \ldots, y_{g+m} = I$ generates a solution to $P_{C,\ell}[X = a, Z = I] - h(\omega^J) = 0$.

Now we need to show that every solution uniquely defines a path:

- Given a solution to $P_{C,\ell}[X = a, Z = I] - h(\omega^J) = 0$, that solution must give some value $L$ to the variables that were designated by $u_1, \ldots, u_m$ entering stage $\ell$.
- We have $p_\ell \neq 0$ since the assignment is a solution.

- No assignment can give the sum in $p_\ell$ more than one nonzero summand, so $p_\ell$ evaluates to $h(\omega^d)$ where $U_\ell[I, L] = r\omega^d$, taking $d$ and $r$ from above.
- Hence the assignment induces a solution to $P_{C,\ell-1}[X = a, Z = L] - h(\omega^{J-d}) = 0$.
- By the induction invariant, the assignment induces a unique path from $a$ to location $L$ entering $U_\ell$ and with phase $\omega^{J-d}$. (There may be other paths that converge in that location with the same phase, but they are induced by other assignments.)
- Forming $P_{C,\ell}$ from $P_\ell$ involved equating $y_{g+1}, \ldots, y_{g+m}$ to the respective variables $z_1, \ldots, z_m$, which were substituted by $I$ in the equation, so the solution correctly induces the unique extension of the path into column $L$ of $U_\ell$ and out row $I$.

This establishes the needed invariant after stage $\ell$ and completes the induction. So (1) holds. Before optimizing the polynomials $P_\ell$ obtained, we adapt this construction and proof to $Q_C, \phi_C$ and the analogous inductively defined $Q_\ell, \phi_\ell$, which are this time based on $Q_0 = 0$ and $\phi_0 = \top$.

In forming and evaluating $Q_C$ we are taking logarithms base $\omega$ so that products become sums. We can use the same indicator subterms $t_L, t_I$ as above, except that the matrix gives an additive $d$ not a multiplicative $h(\omega^d)$. Note that if $U[I, L] = 1$ we will get an additive 0. The issue is what to do with the cases $U[I, L] = 0$—what to use in place of the logarithm of 0? The answer is to allocate $k$ variables $v_0, \ldots, v_{k-1}$, put $\Upsilon = v_0 + 2v_1 + \cdots 2^{k-1}v_{k-1}$, and define

$$q_\ell = \sum_{d,I,L:U_\ell[I,L]=r_\ell\omega^d \neq 0} t_I t_L \cdot d \quad + \sum_{I,L:U_\ell[I,L]=0} t_I t_L \cdot \Upsilon.$$

And now instead of multiplying $R$ by $1/r_\ell$ we multiply it by something also involving $k$. The reason is that a path entering $U_\ell$ in column $L$ and exiting in row $I$ now induces $2^k$ assignments rather than just one, counting all those to $v_0, \ldots, v_{k-1}$. If $U_\ell[I, L] \neq 0$ the latter assignments are irrelevant because $\Upsilon$ is multiplied by 0 but the variables $v_0, \ldots, v_{k-1}$ are still present in the formula. (Unless, that is, $U_\ell$ is a matrix like $\mathsf{QFT}_m$ which has no zero entries—in which case we do nothing more.) If $U_\ell[I, L] = 0$ then the corresponding assignment $c$ to the other variables multiplies $\Upsilon$ by 1. Now we can associate to $c$ the $K$ assignments to $v_0, \ldots, v_{k-1}$, producing $K$ assignments $c_J$ in all, $0 \leq J < K$. Each of these assignments gives a different final phase value $J'$. When we sum over those assignments, they augment each of the solution counts multiplying $\omega^{J'}$ in (2), giving a net-zero contribution to the whole sum equated to $\langle b| C |a \rangle$.

When using this trick multiple times one needs to use distinct suites $\Upsilon_\ell$ of variables. The reason is that if the number $n_c$ of violated constraints, each contributing $+1$, becomes a positive multiple of $K$, the contribution from $\sum_{J'=0}^{K-1} \omega^{n_c J'}$ in (2) is no longer zero but $K$. The number $N_c$ of constraints will be at most $s + m$ and so the bump in formula size will be $O(sk + mk)$. We also need to multiply $R$ by $\sqrt{K^{N_c}}$, but otherwise we can ignore all assignments inducing illegal paths while repeating the above correctness analysis.

We need to use the same trick to handle the final equations with the output variables $z_j$. Define

$$E'_C = \sum_{i=1}^{m}(u_i + z_i - 2u_i z_i)\Upsilon,$$

and finally,

$$Q_C = E'_C + \sum_{\ell=1}^{s} q_\ell.$$

Note that whereas the degree of $P_C$ is linear in $s$, the degree of $Q_C$ depends only on the maximum arity $r$—not even on $k$.

To define a Boolean formula $\phi_C$ we do not need this "$\Upsilon$ trick" but instead introduce suites $W_\ell = (w_{0,\ell}, \ldots, w_{k-1,\ell})$ to track the phase at each stage $\ell$. In place of the "indicator terms" $t_I, t_L$ we use sub-formulas defined as follows: For any column value $L \in \{0,1\}^m$, $u_L$ denotes the unique conjunction of signed literals $\pm u_i$ (over $i = 1$ to $m$) whose value is 1 on $L$ and 0 for all $L' \neq L$. For instance, if $L = 01101$ then $u_L = (\bar{u}_1 \wedge u_2 \wedge u_3 \wedge \bar{u}_4 \wedge u_5)$. We denote row conjuncts $y_I$ similarly using the newly allocated variables $y_{g+1}, \ldots, y_{g+m}$ defined as before. Entering stage $\ell$ of the circuit, we consider all possible phases $J_{\ell-1}$ coded by the variables $W_{\ell-1} = (w_{0,\ell-1}, \ldots, w_{k-1,\ell-1})$. For all pairs $I, L$ we add clauses as follows:

- If $U_\ell[I, L] = 0$ then we add $\neg(u_L \wedge y_I)$, which becomes a clause of $2m$ disjoined literals.
- If $U_\ell[I, L] = r_\ell \omega^d$ then we add for $j = 0$ to $k - 1$ the clauses

$$(u_L \wedge y_I) \rightarrow (w_{j,\ell} = w_{j,\ell-1} \oplus F_d(W_{\ell-1})),$$

where $F_d$ is the fixed finite function true on all $c$ such that $c + d$ causes a flip in bit $j$.

Note that $F_d$ can be a function of the variables $w_{0,\ell-1}, \ldots, w_{j,\ell-1}$ alone. We can alternately consider that over $j = 0$ to $k - 1$ alone we have added the single clauses

$$w_{j,\ell} = w_{j,\ell-1} \oplus F'(u_1, \ldots, u_m, y_1, \ldots, y_m, w_0, \ldots, w_j),$$

where $F'$ takes into account all the phases $d$ that arise in the matrix entries $U_\ell[I, J]$ as specified by the values $L$ for $u_1, \ldots, u_m$ and $I$ for $y_{g+1}, \ldots, y_{g+m}$. Economizing $F'$ will occupy much attention later, but for this proof we reason about $F_d$ for all the $u_L$ and $v_I$.

Finally we note that $y_{g+1}, \ldots, y_{g+m}$ become "$u_1, \ldots, u_m$" for the next stage if there is one, else we conjoin the clauses $\wedge_{i=1}^{m}(y_{g+i} = z_i)$ (or just substitute $z_1, \ldots, z_m$ directly). The last act is to add the clauses $\wedge_j \bar{w}_{j,0}$ and declare "$W$" in the theorem statement to refer to the terminal $w_{j,s}$ phase variables. Then $V$

in the theorem statement ranges over $w_{j,\ell}$ for $1 \le \ell \le s - 1$ and $Y$ ranges over variables $y_{g+i,\ell}$ introduced as "$y_{g+i}$" in the corresponding stages $\ell$. (We will say more below.) This finishes the construction of $\phi_C$.

To see that it is correct, first consider any path $P$ from $a$ to $b$ whose phase changes by $J$. First we substitute $\boldsymbol{x} = a$ and $\boldsymbol{z} = b$ and $W_s = J$. In the base case $s = 0$ with empty circuit, $P$ can only be a path from $a$ to $b = a$ with $J = 0$. Then we have $W_s = W_0$ and substituting $J$ gives $\top$ if $b = a$ and $J = 0$, $\bot$ otherwise. For $s \ge 1$, to $P$ there is a unique assignment of row and column values

$$a = L_1, \quad I_1 = L_2, \quad \ldots, \quad I_{s-1} = L_s, \quad I_s = b$$

to literals designated "$u_i$" and "$y_{g+i}$" at each stage $\ell$. For all $(I, L) \ne (I_\ell, L_\ell)$, all clauses $(u_I \wedge v_L) \to (\ldots)$ are vacuously satisfied. This leaves the clause

$$(u_{L_\ell} \wedge y_{I_\ell}) \to (w_{j,\ell} = w_{j,\ell-1} \oplus F_d(W_{\ell-1})),$$

where $d$ is the phase of the nonzero entry $U_\ell[I, L]$. By induction, the values of $W_{\ell-1}$ in the assignment either have the phase $J_{\ell-1}$ of the path entering that stage or the assignment is already determined to be unsatisfying. These determine the value $F_d(W_{\ell-1})$ and hence collectively over $j$ these clauses determine that $W_\ell$ must have the correct value $J_{\ell-1} + d$ modulo $K$, else they are not satisfied. Since the values of the variables in $W_\ell$ are forced, we have a unique continuation of a satisfying assignment. In the last stage, the current phase value must become $J$. Hence we have mapped $P$ to one satisfying assignment of $\phi_C[X = a, Z = b, W = J]$ (with $W_0$ already zeroed).

Going the other way, suppose $c$ is any satisfying assignment to $\phi_C$ (again with $W_0 = 0$). We argue that $c$ maps uniquely to a path $P_c$. We get $a = L_1$ from the values assigned to $X$, then the values $L_2, \ldots, L_s$ of the other column entries, and finally the exit row $I_s$ which gives a $b$. The values of phases along the path are likewise determined by the assignment and must be correct. Hence the assignment yields a unique path. The path must be legal: at any stage the left-hand side of one clause of the form $(u_J \wedge y_I) \to (\cdots)$ holds so its consequent must be made true. Thus the correspondence of counting paths and counting satisfying assignments is parsimonious for each phase value $L$, so the Eq. (3) follows.

It remains to reduce the objects $P_C$, $Q_C$, and $\phi_C$ down to the stated size, without changing the numbers of solutions or of satisfying assignments. For $P_C$, consider any qubit line $i$ that is not involved in gate $\ell$, so that $U_\ell$ acts as the identity on $i$. The product terms in $p_\ell$ involving line $i$ divide into four groups with $u_i y_{g+i}$, $(1 - u_i)(1 - y_{g+1})$, $z u_i (1 - y_{g+1})$, and $(1 - u_i) y_{g+i}$, respectively. Because $U_\ell$ acts as the identity on line $i$, the latter two groups occur only for entries $U_\ell[I, L]$ that are 0, so they vanish. Since having $u_i = 0$ while $y_{g+1} = 1$ or vice-versa zeroes out the former two groups as well, any 0–1 solution to $P_C[X = a, Z = b] - h(\omega^J) = 0$ must have $y_{g+i} = u_i$. Hence without changing the number of binary solutions, we may for each such $i$ substitute $y_{g+i} = u_i$, delete the terms for the vanishing groups, and make the factors on the surviving groups just $u_i$ and $(1 - y_{g+i})$, respectively. Doing so cuts the size of $p_\ell$ down by a factor of $2^{m-r}$. But since $p_\ell$ is a sum of $2^{2r}$ terms, each a product of $2r$-many factors, this is not yet good enough.

Again focusing on qubit line $i$, the remaining terms have the forms $y_{g+i}H_1$ and $(1 - u_i)H_2$. Because $U_\ell$ acts as the identity on qubit $i$, every entry $U[I, L]$ where $I_i = L_i = 1$ equals the entry $U[I', L']$ where $I'_i = L'_i = 0$ with the other bits the same as in $I$ and $L$. Hence terms in $H_1$ pair off with equal terms in $H_2$. We claim that we can replace the remaining terms in $p_\ell$ by just $H_1$ ($= H_2$). Doing this does not add any new solutions, because if a solution makes $u_i = 1$ then the original $p_\ell$ got the same contribution from $H_1$ as it gets now (with $H_2$ being zeroed), and similarly for $u_i = 0$. Nor does doing this remove any solutions—nor does it remove all dependence on $u_i$ because line $i$ may be involved in $U_{\ell+1}$. It does allow us to avoid introducing the new variable $y_{g+i}$, so entering stage $\ell + 1$, $u_i$ refers to the same variable as previously (and $g$ counts only the new variables added). Applying this second process cuts the number of terms in $p_\ell$ down by another factor of (at least) $2^{m-r}$, and also cuts the degrees of terms down from $m$ to $r$. The polynomial $P$ obtained by doing this for all stages thus has size $O(m + sk2^{2r})$ as claimed.

Similar remarks apply to $Q_C$ with possible occurrences of $\Upsilon_\ell$ absorbed into the overall size factor $k$ for coefficients in $0 \ldots K - 1$. For $\phi_C$, the size reduction boils down to saying that whenever $I$ and $I'$ vis-à-vis $L$ and $L'$ agree on the $r$ qubit lines touched by the gate, their clauses can be identified, leaving at most $2^{2r}$ distinct clauses of size $O(k)$ added at stage $\ell$. The rest of the size estimation is similar. Also in each case, the objects can be computed in time linear in their size in one "pass" that introduces the terms or clauses for each gate one-by-one.    □

We will re-prove this theorem for all the gates covered in Sect. 1. This will show more cases in which it is unnecessary to put a new variable $y_{g+i}$ even for lines $i$ involved in the gate. It will also increase the role of "V" via further cases in which a new variable is forced to have a certain argument value in any solution or satisfying assignment. Then it will be named $v_{f+i}$ instead where $f$ counts the forced line variables. The dedicated constructions will reveal structural properties of these gates and some particular points of elegance.

## 5    Simulation of Common Gates

Most of the gates have min-phase $K = 2$, 4, or 8. Indeed, $K = 2$ suffices for a universal set able to approximate probabilities and $K = 4$ for a set (namely H and CS) able to approximate all complex amplitudes. Adequacy of the target ring for $P_C$ entails $-1 \neq 1$, so $1 + 1 \neq 0$, so 2 exists, though $2 = -1$ is possible. Accordingly we write $-1$ in place of $h(-1)$ but write $h(i)$ in place of $i$ and so on. For $Q_C$, however, we prefer to write $K/2$ rather than specify 1 when $K = 2$ or 2 when $K = 4$, etc. In defining $\phi_C$ we avoid the double-subscripting in the phase variables $W_\ell = \{w_{j,\ell}\}$ by letting $p_\ell$ distinguish the top of the circle from the bottom, $q_\ell$ the first and third quadrants, and $r_\ell$ the odd eighths from the even eighths. For instance, when $K = 8$ and $J$ is the phase after stage $\ell$, $p_\ell = 0$ means $J \in \{0, 1, 2, 3\}$, $q_\ell = 0$ means $J \in \{0, 1, 4, 5\}$, and $r_\ell = 0$ means $J \in \{0, 2, 4, 6\}$.

Initializing $P = 1$, $Q = 0$, and $\phi = \top$, we describe running changes as gates are appended one-by-one in stages $\ell = 1, 2, 3, \ldots$ When we use $\ell$ as a subscript on a variable or term $T_\ell = t_0 + 2t_1 + \cdots 2^{k-1}t_{k-1}$ multiplying a constraint for $Q$, it means "the next available index in that category"—thought we could make it literally agree with the stage number by inserting dummies.

- Hadamard gate $\mathsf{H} = \frac{1}{\sqrt{2}} \begin{bmatrix} 1 & 1 \\ 1 & -1 \end{bmatrix}$ on line $i$: Allocate a new top-phase variable $p_\ell$, allocate a new free variable $y_g$ on line $i$, and change the objects as follows:

$$P \ * = (1 - 2u_i y_g)$$
$$Q \ + = (u_i y_g K/2)$$
$$\phi \ \wedge = (p_\ell = p_{\ell-1} \oplus (u_i \wedge y_g)).$$

Finally, multiply $R$ by $\sqrt{2}$ and set $u_i = y_g$.

The remaining elementary gates are either deterministic or are expressible using Hadamard and deterministic gates. We now regard $g$ as keeping a running count of all free variables up to $h$ total. A deterministic change of location in qubit $i$ (as opposed to phase) is reflected by a variable we denote by $v_f$ rather than $y_g$ being placed "on" line $i$ so that $u_i$ denotes it after the stage. This comes with a *constraint* of the form $v_f = E$ where $E$ is 0–1 valued. Multiplying $P$ by $(1 + 2Ev_f - v_f - E)$ kills paths that violate the constraint and preserves ones that obey it (with no phase change). Adding $T_\ell(v_f + E - 2Ev_f)$ has a similar effect for $Q$. Two alternatives are worth noting:

- We can add $(v_f = E)$ as a separate equation. Indeed, we can also keep the final $(z_i = u_i)$ equations separate. Then instead of one large $P_C$ we have a system of small equations and a smaller $P'_C$, with only $P'_C - h(\omega^J)$ changing for different phases $J$.
- We can avoid introducing $v_f$ and make $u_i$ subsequently refer to $E$ rather than a variable. It is OK for $u_i$ to refer to arbitrary 0–1 valued subterms. The complexity of subsequent terms, including later expressions $E'$, can be compounded, however.

For $\phi$ we can conjoin $(v_f = E)$ as a Boolean term, or alternatively introduce nothing and revise $u_i$ to refer to $E$. Again this is OK above for $\mathsf{H}$ and below for all the other gates but can cause terms "on" the qubit lines to mushroom.

It is of course possible that the phase may change as well. Then we multiply $P_C$ by other functions of $v_f$ and $E$ that either kill the path or implement the phase change. Gates with diagonal matrices can change the phase but do not change the location and so do not allocate a $v_f$ or change $u_i$ in any case. Now we see the details for particular gates:

- Pauli gate $\mathsf{X} = \begin{bmatrix} 0 & 1 \\ 1 & 0 \end{bmatrix}$ on qubit line $i$: Allocate a new line variable $v_f$ on line $i$ and implement the equation $v_f = 1 - u_i$ by:

$$P * = (u_i + v_f - 2u_i v_f)$$
$$Q + = \Upsilon_\ell (1 - u_i - v_f + 2u_i v_f)$$
$$\phi \wedge = (v_f = \neg u_i).$$

There is no change to other variables or to $R$. Finally, update $u_i = v_f$. The alternative is to substitute whatever subterm $u_i$ referred to into $1 - u_i$ and let the "new $u_i$" refer to that.

- CNOT $= \begin{bmatrix} \mathsf{I} & 0 \\ 0 & \mathsf{X} \end{bmatrix}$ with *control* on line $i$ and *target* on line $j$: Allocate new $v_f$ on line $j$ and implement the equation $v_f = u_i \oplus u_j$, numerically $v_f = u_i + u_j - 2u_i u_j$, by:

$$P * = (1 - u_i - u_j - v_f + 2u_i u_j + 2u_i v_f + 2u_j v_f - 4u_i u_j v_f)$$
$$Q + = \Upsilon_\ell \cdot (2u_i u_j v_f - 2u_i u_j - 2u_i v_f - 2u_j v_f + u_i + u_j + v_f)$$
$$\phi \wedge = (v_f = u_j \oplus u_i).$$

Finally, update $u_j$ to refer to $v_f$. Alternatives: revise $u_j$ to refer to $u_i + u_j - 2u_i u_j$ with no change to $P$ or to $Q$, and in the case of $\phi$, call $u_i \oplus u_j$ the new $u_j$.

- Toffoli gate Tof $= \begin{bmatrix} \mathsf{I} & 0 \\ 0 & \mathsf{CNOT} \end{bmatrix}$ with controls on $i, j$ and target on $k$: Allocate new $v_f$ on line $k$ and implement the equation $v_f = u_k \oplus (u_i \wedge u_j)$, numerically $v_f = u_i u_j + u_k - 2u_i u_j u_k$, by:

$$P * = (1 - u_i u_j - u_k - v_f + 2u_i u_j u_k + 2u_i u_j v_f + 2u_k v_f - 4u_i u_j u_k v_f)$$
$$Q + = \Upsilon_\ell \cdot (2u_i u_j u_k v_f - 2u_i u_j u_k - 2u_i u_j v_f - 2u_k v_f + u_i u_j + u_k + v_f)$$
$$\phi \wedge = (v_f = u_k \oplus (u_i \wedge u_j)).$$

Finally, update $u_k$ to refer to $v_f$. Alternatives: revise $u_k$ to refer to $u_i u_j + u_k - 2u_i u_j u_k$ with no change to $P$ or to $Q$, and in the case of $\phi$, call $u_i u_j \oplus u_k$ the new $u_k$.

The Swap gate on qubits $i, j$ can be implemented simply by interchanging $u_i$ and $u_j$ woth no growth in formulas. The *Fredkin* gate on $i, j, k$ is the $i$-controlled swap of $j, k$ and needs new forced variables $v_j, v_k$ on the latter two lines with terms expressing $v_j = (u_i \vee u_j) \wedge (\bar{u}_i \vee u_k)$ and similarly for $v_k$.

Although Hadamard and Toffoli are radically different gates—with radically different changes to $P$ and to $Q$—the updates to $\phi$ have the same form. In general we call a Boolean formula of the form

$$p' = p \oplus (\wedge_{i=1}^{j} u_i) \tag{4}$$

a *parity of AND equation*, or *pae* for short, of *order* $j$. It is elegant that H and Tof are both entirely coded by one *pae* of order 2, with the most overt difference being that the one for H introduces a free variable $y_g$ whereas the one for Tof does not. The *pae* form is natural for carry propagation and adding controls as shown in what follows.

- Pauli gate $\mathsf{Z} = \begin{bmatrix} 1 & 0 \\ 0 & -1 \end{bmatrix}$ on qubit line $i$: Allocate new top-phase variable $p_\ell$ and do the following with no other change:

$$P \;*\; = (1 - 2u_i)$$
$$Q \;+\; = (K/2)u_i$$
$$\phi \;\wedge\; = (p_\ell = p_{\ell-1} \oplus u_i).$$

- Pauli gate $\mathsf{Y} = \begin{bmatrix} 0 & -i \\ i & 0 \end{bmatrix}$ on qubit line $i$: Allocate $v_f$ on line $i$, and for $\phi$, allocate new top and quarter-phase variables $p_\ell$ and $q_\ell$. Since this matrix is not symmetric, it is important to remember that the columns are $(1 - u_i)$ and $u_i$ whereas the rows are $(1 - v_f)$ and $v_f$. Accordingly:

$$P \;*\; = h(i)(1 - 2u_i)(u_i + v_f - 2u_i v_f)$$
$$Q \;+\; = (K/4) - (K/2)u_i + \Upsilon_\ell(1 + 2u_i v_f - u_i - v_f)$$
$$\phi \;\wedge\; = (v_f = \neg u_i) \wedge (q_\ell = \neg q_{\ell-1}) \wedge (p_\ell = p_{\ell-1} \oplus u_i \oplus q_{\ell-1}).$$

The last conjunct for $\phi$ is not a *pae*, but since $\mathsf{Y} = i\mathsf{XZ}$, we can instead compose the actions for $\mathsf{Z}$ and $\mathsf{X}$ and $i$. The scalar multiplication by $i$ is optional, but it seems helpful to say we are tracking phases of paths exactly especially when we use *conjugation* in the next section. To update $\phi$ for multiplication by $i$, make $q_{\ell+1} = \neg q_\ell$ and $p_{\ell+1} = p_\ell \oplus q_\ell$. For the conjugate multiplication by $-i$ the latter is $p_{\ell+1} = p_\ell \oplus \bar{q}_\ell$ instead. The matrix $\mathsf{Y}$ is self-adjoint, i.e., $\mathsf{Y}^* = \mathsf{Y}$, so we do not need to give conjugate forms. But for the gates that follow, we will indicate the conjugate forms $P^*, Q^*, \phi^*$, which are likewise initialized to 1, 0, and $\top$, respectively.

- Phase gate $\mathsf{S} = \begin{bmatrix} 1 & 0 \\ 0 & i \end{bmatrix}$: Allocate new $p_\ell, q_\ell$ and do:

$$P \;*= (1 - u_i + h(i)u_i) \qquad\qquad P^* \;*= (1 - u_i + h(-i)u_i)$$
$$Q \;+= (K/4)u_i \qquad\qquad\qquad Q^* \;+= (3K/4)u_i$$
$$\phi \;\wedge= (q_\ell = q_{\ell-1} \oplus u_i) \qquad\qquad \phi^* \;\wedge= (q_\ell = q_{\ell-1} \oplus u_i)$$
$$\wedge(p_\ell = p_{\ell-1} \oplus (u_i \wedge q_{\ell-1})) \qquad\qquad \wedge(p_\ell = p_{\ell-1} \oplus (u_i \wedge \bar{q}_{\ell-1})).$$

- $\mathsf{T} = \begin{bmatrix} 1 & 0 \\ 0 & \omega^{K/8} \end{bmatrix}$: Allocate all new $p_\ell, q_\ell, r_\ell$ with equations:

$$P \;*= (1 - u_i + h(\omega^{K/8})u_i) \qquad\qquad P^* \;*= (1 - u_i + h(\omega^{7K/8})u_i)$$
$$Q \;+= (K/8)u_i \qquad\qquad\qquad\qquad Q^* \;+= (7K/8)u_i$$
$$\phi \;\wedge= (r_\ell = r_{\ell-1} \oplus u_i) \qquad\qquad \phi^* \;\wedge= (r_\ell = r_{\ell-1} \oplus u_i)$$
$$\wedge(q_\ell = q_{\ell-1} \oplus (r_{\ell-1} \wedge u_i)) \qquad\qquad \wedge(q_\ell = q_{\ell-1} \oplus (\bar{r}_{\ell-1} \wedge u_i))$$
$$\wedge(p_\ell = p_{\ell-1} \oplus (q_{\ell-1} \wedge r_{\ell-1} \wedge u_i)) \qquad \wedge(p_\ell = p_{\ell-1} \oplus (\bar{q}_{\ell-1} \wedge \bar{r}_{\ell-1} \wedge u_i)).$$

The controlled gate $\mathsf{CS}$ forms a universal set with $\mathsf{H}$ that also approximates complex amplitudes. So does $\mathsf{T}$ when added to $\mathsf{H}$ and either $\mathsf{CNOT}$ or $\mathsf{CZ}$. Now we show the progression of controlled phase gates, which leave $R$ unchanged and allocate no variables except phase variables for $\phi$:

$$- \; \mathsf{CZ} = \begin{bmatrix} \mathsf{I} & 0 \\ 0 & \mathsf{Z} \end{bmatrix} = \begin{bmatrix} 1 & 0 & 0 & 0 \\ 0 & 1 & 0 & 0 \\ 0 & 0 & 1 & 0 \\ 0 & 0 & 0 & -1 \end{bmatrix} \quad \text{with source } i \text{ and target } j:$$

$$P \; *= (1 - 2u_i u_j)$$
$$Q \; += (K/2)u_i u_j$$
$$\phi \; \wedge = (p_\ell = p_{\ell-1} \oplus (u_i \wedge u_j)).$$

Note that all three forms are symmetrical in $u_i$ and $u_j$, expressing the fact that with $\mathsf{CZ}$ it does not matter which line is considered the control. As with the gates before $\mathsf{S}$, the conjugate forms change the same way so they are not shown.

$$- \; \mathsf{CS} = \begin{bmatrix} \mathsf{I} & 0 \\ 0 & \mathsf{S} \end{bmatrix} = \begin{bmatrix} 1 & 0 & 0 & 0 \\ 0 & 1 & 0 & 0 \\ 0 & 0 & 1 & 0 \\ 0 & 0 & 0 & i \end{bmatrix} \quad \text{with source } i \text{ and target } j:$$

$$\begin{aligned}
P \; *= (1 - u_i u_j + h(i)u_i u_j) \qquad & P^* \; *= (1 - u_i u_j + h(-i)u_i u_j) \\
Q \; += (K/4)u_i u_j \qquad & Q^* \; += (3K/4)u_i u_j \\
\phi \; \wedge = (q_\ell = q_{\ell-1} \oplus (u_i \wedge u_j)) \qquad & \phi^* \; \wedge = (q_\ell = q_{\ell-1} \oplus (u_i \wedge u_j)) \\
\wedge (p_\ell = p_{\ell-1} \oplus (q_{\ell-1} \wedge u_i \wedge u_j)) \qquad & \wedge (p_\ell = p_{\ell-1} \oplus (\bar{q}_{\ell-1} \wedge u_i \wedge u_j)).
\end{aligned}$$

$$- \; \mathsf{CT} = \begin{bmatrix} \mathsf{I} & 0 \\ 0 & \mathsf{T} \end{bmatrix} = \begin{bmatrix} 1 & 0 & 0 & 0 \\ 0 & 1 & 0 & 0 \\ 0 & 0 & 1 & 0 \\ 0 & 0 & 0 & \omega^{K/8} \end{bmatrix} \quad \text{with source } i \text{ and target } j:$$

$$\begin{aligned}
P \; *= (1 - u_i u_j + h(\omega^{K/8})u_i u_j) \qquad & P^* \; *= (1 - u_i u_j + h(\omega^{7K/8})u_i u_j) \\
Q \; += (K/8)u_i u_j \qquad & Q^* \; += (7K/8)u_i u_j \\
\phi \; \wedge = (r_\ell = r_{\ell-1} \oplus (u_i \wedge u_j)) \qquad & \phi^* \; \wedge = (r_\ell = r_{\ell-1} \oplus (u_i \wedge u_j)) \\
\wedge (q_\ell = q_{\ell-1} \oplus (r_{\ell-1} \wedge u_i \wedge u_j)) \qquad & \wedge (q_\ell = q_{\ell-1} \oplus (\bar{r}_{\ell-1} \wedge u_i \wedge u_j)) \\
\wedge (p_\ell = p_{\ell-1} \oplus (r_{\ell-1} \wedge q_{\ell-1} \wedge u_i \wedge u_j)) \qquad & \wedge (p_\ell = p_{\ell-1} \oplus (\bar{r}_{\ell-1} \wedge \bar{q}_{\ell-1} \wedge u_i \wedge u_j)).
\end{aligned}$$

The controlled $\mathsf{R_8}$ in the circuit in Sect. 1 has $K/16$ in place of $K/8$ for $P$ and $Q$ and updates another phase variable $s_\ell$ for $\phi$, so that the *pae* for $p_\ell$ has order 5. By using more variables to denote *carries* and sharing intermediate results we can code arbitrary (controlled) rotations $\mathsf{R_K}$ using $O(K)$ rather than quadratically many occurrences of variables in *pae*'s of orders 3 and 4. The next gates break the *pae* form when coded directly but can be written as compositions of gates or otherwise similarly broken down into small *pae*'s.

- $Y^{1/2} = \frac{1+i}{2}\begin{bmatrix}1 & -1\\ 1 & 1\end{bmatrix} = \frac{\omega^{K/8}}{\sqrt{2}}\begin{bmatrix}1 & -1\\ 1 & 1\end{bmatrix}$: Introduce one nondeterministic variable

$y_g$, plus $p_\ell, q_\ell, r_\ell$ to update $\phi$. We keep the scalar multiplication by $\omega^{K/8}$ but must remember to conjugate it:

$$P \mathrel{*}= h(\omega^{K/8})(2u_i y_g - 2u_i + 1) \qquad P^* \mathrel{*}= h(\omega^{7K/8})(2u_i y_g - 2u_i + 1)$$
$$Q \mathrel{+}= (K/8) + (K/2)u_i(1 - y_g) \qquad Q^* \mathrel{+}= (7K/8) + (K/2)u_i(1 - y_g)$$
$$\phi \wedge= (r_\ell = \neg r_{\ell-1}) \qquad\qquad \phi^* \wedge= (r_\ell = \neg r_{\ell-1})$$
$$\wedge(q_\ell = q_{\ell-1} \oplus r_{\ell-1} \oplus (u_i \wedge \bar{y}_g)) \qquad \wedge(q_\ell = q_{\ell-1} \oplus \bar{r}_{\ell-1} \oplus (u_i \wedge \bar{y}_g))$$
$$\wedge(p_\ell = p_{\ell-1} \oplus \rho) \qquad\qquad \wedge(p_\ell = p_{\ell-1} \oplus \rho^*),$$

where $\rho = (r_{\ell-1} = q_{\ell-1}) \wedge (r_{\ell-1} \oplus (u_i \wedge (\bar{y}_g)))$ and $\rho^* = (r_{\ell-1} = q_{\ell-1}) \wedge (\bar{r}_{\ell-1} \oplus (u_i \wedge (\bar{y}_g)))$. Finally, multiply $R$ by $\sqrt{2}$, and note that $y_g$ becomes the new $u_i$.

- $R_x(\pi/2) = \frac{1}{\sqrt{2}}\begin{bmatrix}1 & -i\\ -i & 1\end{bmatrix} = \omega^{-K/8} \cdot V$ on line $i$: Allocate a new nondeterministic

variable $y_g$, and for $\phi$, new phase variables $p_\ell$ and $q_\ell$. Multiply $R$ by $\sqrt{2}$ and do:

$$P \mathrel{*}= (1 + (h(-i) - 1)(u_i + y_g - 2u_i y_g)) \quad P^* \mathrel{*}= (1 + (h(i) - 1)(u_i + y_g - 2u_i y_g))$$
$$Q \mathrel{+}= (3K/4)(u_i + y_g) - (K/2)u_i y_g \qquad Q^* \mathrel{+}= (K/4)(u_i + y_g) - (K/2)u_i y_g$$
$$\phi \wedge= (q_\ell = q_{\ell-1} \oplus u_i \oplus y_g) \qquad\quad \phi^* \wedge= (q_\ell = q_{\ell-1} \oplus u_i \oplus y_g)$$
$$\wedge(p_\ell = p_{\ell-1} \oplus (\bar{q}_{\ell-1} \wedge (u_i \oplus y_g))) \qquad \wedge(p_\ell = p_{\ell-1} \oplus (q_{\ell-1} \wedge (u_i \oplus y_g))).$$

The equation $Y^{1/2} = HZ \cdot \omega^{K/8}$, where again the scalar multiplication can be ignored, gives an efficient alternative. The conjugate is $ZH \cdot \omega^{7K/8}$. The gate $V = \omega^{K/8}R_x(\pi/2)$ satisfies $V^2 = X$ and hence is also called $X^{1/2}$ or $\sqrt{\text{NOT}}$. The identity $V = HSH$ plus (optionally) multiplying by the scalar $\omega^{-K/8} = e^{7\pi i/4}$ thus allows coding $R_x(\pi/2)$ by $pae$'s, on pain of introducing one more nondeterministic variable. The conjugate matrix $R_x(-\pi/2)$, which has positive-signed entries $i$ on the off-diagonals, can be handled similarly. If these identities are used, then all *free* variables are assigned when placing Hadamard gates.

The sequence of equations, as gates are placed in left-to-right order (with matrices composed in right-to-left order), obeys the following invariant:

**Lemma 1.** *For any 0-1 assignment $c = (c_1, c_2, \ldots, c_h)$ to the free variables, input $a = a_1 \cdots a_m$ to the variables $x_i$, and initialization of the phase variables (to zero phase, say), the product of terms in $P_C$, sum of terms in $Q_C$, and conjunction of equational clauses in $\phi_C$, can be evaluated in order with all right-hand side values defined in the initialization or in previous steps.* □

This enables an "intelligent backtrack" routine that, when incrementing $c \in \{0, 1\}^h$ to the next $c'$ in standard order, need only roll back to the first term or $pae$ containing $y_g$, where $c$ and $c'$ agree in the first $g - 1$ bits. Roughly speaking, this saves a factor of one-half the number $h$ of free variables when carrying out the brute-force iteration through $c$ to tabulate the results of each path. For $Q_C$ the variables in $\Upsilon$ count as free, but if there are fewer than $K$ uses of $\Upsilon_\ell$ they can all be identified, so that the extra branching is only $K$ and $R' = R\sqrt{K}$.

The invariant is particularly notable with our Boolean logic emulation. It means that for every gate, the equations typified by $p = q \oplus (u \wedge v)$ for every gate are interpreting the '=' as assignment, not just equality. Only the equations setting the output variables $z_i$ to specified target values $b_i$ (after the $z_i$ have been filled by the equations $z_i = u_i$) have a constraining effect. We have found references using Boolean formulas to specify and SAT-solvers to test equivalence of portions of quantum circuits [27,28] but not for conducting emulation. The significance of the invariant for a SAT solver or #SAT counter involves how resolvents of clauses (or rather their negated terms) are propagated. To give an intuitive example, consider a Boolean formula $\phi(x_1, \ldots, x_n, y_1, \ldots, y_n, z_1, \ldots, z_n)$ expressing the multiplication relation $x \cdot y = z$ for the numbers $x, y, z$ encoded by the variables in binary. If only $z$ is given then we have the factoring problem in the form known to be tough for SAT solvers. In our case, however, the $x$ will be given by the values of incoming line references $u_i$. The $y$ may come from nondeterministic variables. Any setting of those variables will produce $z$ by propagation. In any event, we are not in the situation where only $z$ is given. Thus although the same Boolean relation $\phi$ is being used, the manner in which it is approached makes a big difference for solvers—as we demonstrate partially in Sect. 8. Before that we show how our logic emulation binds this Boolean relation up with the Fourier transform.

# 6    Quantum Fourier Transform, Measurements, and Sampling

The *quantum Fourier transform* QFT$_n$ on $n$ qubits is represented (in the standard basis) by the ordinary $N \times N$ discrete Fourier matrix $F_N$ where $N = 2^n$. It has entries

$$F_N[I, J] = \omega^{I \cdot J},$$

where $\omega = e^{-2\pi i/N}$. If the incoming phase is $c$ then the new phase is $c' = c + I \cdot J$ modulo $N$. Hence the only equations we need to add are

$$W_\ell = W_{\ell-1} + I \cdot J \pmod{N}. \tag{5}$$

We can emulate QFT$_n$ via the general recursion implied by the example in Sect. 1. This uses $\Theta(n^2)$ gates—in particular, $\Theta(n^2)$ cases of CR$_{2^k}$ for $k \geq n/2$, each of which uses $\Theta(n)$ variables once we apply the optimization by representing carries discussed in the last section regarding R$_8$. This gives no better than $O(n^3)$ as a size guarantee. We can further observe in Fig. 1 that partial results from carries can be shared among the formulas for the adjacent CR$_{2^k}$ gates, which promises $O(n^2)$. However, (5) has Boolean circuit complexity $O(n \log n \log \log n)$ by the celebrated result of Schönhage and Strassen [29]. The asymptotically-small circuits include gates for each output bit of $W_\ell$ using the $3n$ input gates for $W_{\ell-1}$, $I$, and $J$. Each Boolean gate can be directly converted into one *pae* of order 3 or 4. Hence the size blowup should be only $\tilde{O}(n)$, i.e., *quasi-linear*. However, the advantage is asymptotic and is only known to take precedence when $n > 10,000$ or so, and the question of how best to emulate $\mathsf{QFT}_n$ for relevant ranges of the number of qubits seems still open (compare [30–33]).

Shor's algorithm [6] applies $\mathsf{QFT}$ in conjunction with *sampling*. To factor a given $n$-bit integer $M$, it starts by choosing $Q = 2^\ell$ where $\ell = 2n + 1$, so that $M^2 < Q < 2M^2$, and a random $a < M$ which we may presume is relatively prime to $M$ (else $\gcd(a, M)$ gives a factor at once). The quantum circuit $C$ used by its inner loop starts with Hadamard gates on the first $\ell$ of $2\ell$ qubit lines. It then places a deterministic circuit $C_0$ that maps any binary-encoded number $x < Q$ to $f_a(x) = a^x \pmod{M}$. More precisely, $C_0$ maps $x \cdot 0^\ell$ to the concatenation $x \cdot y$ where $y = f_a(x)$ as an $\ell$-bit number. The combination with the Hadamard gates creates the *functional superposition*

$$\Phi = \frac{1}{\sqrt{Q}} \sum_x |x f_a(x)\rangle.$$

The quantum circuit then applies $\mathsf{QFT}_\ell$ to the first $\ell$ lines and measures them to get an output $b < Q$. With substantial probability, $b$ reveals a *period* $r$ such that $f_a(x) = f_a(x + r)$ for all $x$ and $r$ in turn reveals a factor.

Thus far we have organized our software system to give the amplitude and probability of specific outcomes $b$ but not to generate $b$ from the set of possible outcomes. In order to emulate algorithms like Shor's, we want to sample according to the distribution

$$\mathcal{D}_{C,a}(b) = \Pr[C(a) = b] = |\langle b|\, C\, |a\rangle|^2.$$

Also let $\mathcal{D}_{C,a}(B)$, for any set $B \subset \{0,1\}^m$, be the sum of $|\langle b|\, C\, |a\rangle|^2$ over all $b \in B$. We will reduce quantum sampling to the *uniform generation* problem on the set $S$ of 0–1 roots of polynomials $P, Q$ or of satisfying assignments to a formula $\phi$. First we review the classical reduction from counting to uniform generation. It starts with one call to #$sat$ to compute the cardinality of $S$.

– Using one call to #$sat$, compute $|S_0| = |\{x \in S : x_1 = 0\}|$, so $|\{x \in S : x_1 = 1\}| = |S| - |S_0|$.
– Set $x_1 = 0$ with probability $|S_0|/|S|$ and $x_1 = 1$ otherwise.
– Substitute the value of $x_1$ into $\phi$ and recurse on $x_2$ and so on.

The $k$-th iteration deals with sets of outcomes sharing a common prefix $x_1 x_2 \ldots x_k$. Given any ordered subset $I = \{i_1, i_2, \ldots, i_k\}$ of the line indices $1, \ldots, m$ and string $\beta \in \{0,1\}^{|I|}$, define the *cylinder* $B_{I,\beta}$ to be the set of strings $b \in \{0,1\}^m$ such that $b_{i_1} b_{i_2} \cdots b_{i_k} = \beta$. If $I$ is omitted then it is the subset $1, \ldots, |w|$.

A naive attempt to emulate the above process beginning with $B_0$ would substitute $z_1 = 0$ but leave the variables $z_2, \ldots, z_m$ open in the first formula $\phi_0$. Applying the counting in (1)–(3) to the phase-shifted formulas derived from $\phi_0$ would fail, however, because it would attempt to cancel counts of solutions with different final locations $b_2, \ldots, b_m$ whose waves do not interfere. The fix is to maintain the probabilities directly rather than the amplitudes in a way that preserves the cylindrical structure. We write $[Z_I = \beta]$ for the act of substituting the variables $z_i$ for $i \in I$ by the respective bits in $\beta$.

**Theorem 2.** *For any $C, a, m$ as in Theorem 1 and $K = 2$ or $4$ we can find constants $R, R'$ and build a polynomial $\mathcal{P}_C$ over any adequate ring, a polynomial $\mathcal{Q}_C$ over $\mathbf{Z}_K$, and a Boolean formula $\Phi$ with the same variables as $\phi_C$ plus an extra variable $w$ such that for any cylinder $B = (I, \beta)$:*

$$\mathcal{D}_{C,a}(B) = \frac{1}{R^2}\left[\#binsols(\mathcal{P}_C[X = a, Z_I = \beta] - 1) - \#binsols(\mathcal{P}_C[X = a, Z_I = \beta] + 1)\right] \quad (6)$$

$$= \frac{1}{R'^2}\left[\#binsols(\mathcal{Q}_C[X = a, Z_I = \beta]) - \#binsols(\mathcal{Q}_C[X = a, Z_I = \beta] - K/2)\right] \quad (7)$$

$$= \frac{1}{R^2}\left[\#sat(\Phi[X = a, Z_I = \beta, w = 0] - \#sat(\Phi[X = a, Z_I = \beta, w = 1]\right]. \quad (8)$$

*The same asymptotic size limits as for $P_C, Q_C, \phi_C$ in Theorem 1 apply to $\mathcal{P}, \mathcal{Q}, \oplus$.*

*Proof.* We use the conjugates $P_C^*, Q_C^*, \phi_C^*$ with the proviso that they share the input and output variables $X, Z$ but have their own copies $V', W', Y'$ (and $\Upsilon'$) of line, phase, and nondeterministic variables. We also make $\phi'_C$ to be a similar non-conjugated copy of $\phi_C$. We prove (7) first. For any $b$, abbreviating $Q_C[X = a, Z = b]$ to $Q_{a,b}$, we have

$$\Pr[C(a) = b] = \langle b| \, C \, |a\rangle \langle b| \, C \, |a\rangle^* = \frac{1}{R'^2} \sum_{J,L=0}^{K-1} \omega^{L+J} \#binsols(Q_{a,b} - J) \#binsols(Q_{a,b}^* - L). \quad (9)$$

For $K = 4$ with $\omega = i$, the terms for odd powers cancel. So as with $K = 2$ we are left only a positive term with $L = K - J$ and a negative term with $L = \frac{K}{2} - J$, both modulo $K$. So $R'^2 \Pr[C(a) = b]$ equals

$$\sum_{J=0}^{K-1} \#binsols(Q_{a,b} - J) \#binsols(Q_{a,b}^* + J) - \sum_{J=0}^{K-1} \#binsols(Q_{a,b} - J) \#binsols(Q_{a,b}^* + J - \frac{K}{2})$$

$$= \#binsols(Q_{a,b} + Q_{a,b}^*) - \#binsols(Q_{a,b} + Q_{a,b}^* - \frac{K}{2}).$$

So put $\mathcal{Q}_C = Q_C + Q_C^*$. Since the right-hand side has no phase dependence anymore,

$$R'^2 \Pr[C(a) \in B] = \sum_{b \in B} R'^2 \Pr[C(a) = b]$$

$$= \sum_{b \in B} \#binsols(\mathcal{Q}_C[X = a, Z = b]) - \sum_{b \in B} \#binsols(\mathcal{Q}_C[X = a, Z = b] - \frac{K}{2})$$

$$= \#binsols(\mathcal{Q}_C[X = a, Z_I = \beta]) - \#binsols(\mathcal{Q}_C[X = a, Z_I = \beta] - \frac{K}{2}).$$

In like manner we obtain $\mathcal{P}_C = P_C \cdot P_C^*$ (with shared $X, Z$), and using $h(1) = 1$, $h(-1) = -1$ per remarks before Theorem 1, we obtain

$$R^2 \Pr[C(a) \in B] = \#binsols(\mathcal{P}[X = a, Z_I = \beta] - 1) - \#binsols(\mathcal{P}[X = a, Z_I = \beta] + 1).$$

It is notable that no absolute value bars are needed here. For $\Phi_C$ there is a final twist. Let $W_s, W_s^*, W_s'$ be the final suites of phase variables in $\phi_C, \phi_C^*, \phi_C'$ and similarly abbreviate $\phi_C[X = a, Z = b]$ to $\phi_{a,b}$. We get that $R^2 \Pr[C(a) = b]$

$$= \sum_{J,L=0}^{K-1} \omega^{J+L} \#sat(\phi_{a,b}[W_s = J]) \#sat(\phi_{a,b}^*[W_s^* = L])$$

$$= \sum_{J=0}^{K-1} \#sat(\phi_{a,b}[W_s = J]) \#sat(\phi_{a,b}^*[W_s^* = K - J]) - \#sat(\phi_{a,b}[W_s = J]) \#sat(\phi_{a,b}^*[W_s^* = \frac{K}{2} - J])$$

$$= \sum_{J=0}^{K-1} \#sat(\phi_{a,b}[W_s = J]) \#sat(\phi_{a,b}'[W_s' = J]) - \#sat(\phi_{a,b}[W_s = J]) \#sat(\phi_{a,b}'[W_s' = \frac{K}{2} + J])$$

Now unpacking $W_s = w_0, \ldots, w_{k-1}$ and similarly for $W_s'$, define

$$\Phi_C = \phi_C \wedge \phi_C' \wedge (w_{k-1} = w_{k-1}') \wedge \cdots \wedge (w_1 = w_1') \wedge (w_0 \oplus w_0' = w).$$

Then $\Phi_C[w = 0]$ equates $W_s' = W_s$ and so by the disjointness of $Y, V, W$ from $Y', V', W'$,

$$\#sat(\Phi_C[X = a, Z = b, w = 0]) = \sum_{J=0}^{K-1} \#sat(\phi_{a,b}[W_s = J]) \#sat(\phi_{a,b}'[W_s' = J]).$$

Because adding $K/2$ is the same as flipping the top phase,

$$\sum_{J=0}^{K-1} \#sat(\phi_{a,b}[W_s = J]) \#sat(\phi_{a,b}'[W_s' = J + \frac{K}{2}]) = \#sat(\Phi_C[X = a, Z = b, w = 1]).$$

The rest involving cylinders $B$ is similar to before.                          □

For $K \geq 8$ the terms for $J$ not a multiple of $\frac{K}{4}$ need not cancel, so simplifying (9) leaves a sum over phases. The simple one-qubit circuit HTH consisting of a twist gate flanked by two Hadamard gates gives probabilities $\frac{1}{2} + \sqrt{\frac{1}{8}} = 0.85355\ldots$ and $\frac{1}{2} - \sqrt{\frac{1}{8}}$, which are not (dyadic) rational numbers. We still get the benefit in Theorem 2 of having a single expression that encompasses all possible final locations $z$, but the sum over phases entails a number of calls to an equation solver or #SAT solver that is proportional to $K$. For universal circuits $C$ with $K \leq 4$, however, we conclude:

**Theorem 3.** *The distribution $\mathcal{D}_C$ projected onto any cylinder $B = (I, \beta)$ can be computed with $m - |I|$ evaluations of $\#sat(\Phi_C[X = a, Z_{I'} = \beta', w = 0]) - \#sat(\Phi_C[X = a, Z_{I'} = \beta', w = 1])$ for successive extensions $I'$ of $I$ and $\beta'$ of $\beta$. Assuming constant arity, this needs only $O(m + sk)$ time* **and space** *apart from the #sat invocations.*

*Proof.* Theorem 2 enables using the classical polynomial-time oracle procedure given before it.                          □

Thus sampling can be emulated via #SAT solvers but at the cost of linearly many invocations (rather than one or two), and most important, of doubling the number $h = |Y|$ of nondeterministic variables. The tradeoff is that the double rail entirely saves the space previously used to build a dictionary of counts for each location. With regard to Eq. (5) and the idea of emulating Shor's algorithm, it can be objected that the logic uses the multiplication relation $K = I \cdot J$ for numbers $I, J, K$ of the same order as the number $M$ we are trying to factor—indeed, on the order of $M^2$. We have attempted to rebut this already with the remarks at the end of Sect. 5 about the flow of processing.

What is the meaning of, say, $\phi_C[z_1 = b]$ where $b \in \{0, 1\}$ without the "double-rail" use of $\phi'_C$? Theorem 2 also justifies the interpretation that $\phi_C[u_1 = b]$ (at any time, not just at the end when $u_1$ is equated to $z_1$) represents *the state of the system after measuring the first qubit and getting the outcome b*. After the measurement, the constant $R$ needs to be re-normalized by multiplying it by the square root of the probability of getting the outcome $b$ as computed via Theorem 2. This enables continuing to represent the system as quantum operations are added to $C$ after the measurement is executed. The use of $\phi_C[u_1 = b]$ is also consonant with the *principle of deferred measurement*, which states that if $b$ on line $i$ is used only in a test "if $b$ then do G else do nothing" on other qubits, then the results are the same as removing the measurement, replacing G by the controlled gate CG with source on $i$, and including $i$ and result $b_i$ in any final measurement.

We finish our systems toolkit with two more observations. First, define $C*$ to be the mirror image of $C$ with the former outputs $b_1, \ldots b_m$ now being designated as inputs and vice-versa for $a_1, \ldots, a_m$, and with each gate $G$ reversed by substituting its adjoint $G^*$. Note that this is not the same as conjugating each gate but keeping the sequence from $a$ to $b$ the same, which is what is modeled by $P_C^*$, $Q_C^*$, and $\phi_C^*$.

**Proposition 1.** *For every quantum circuit $C$, $P_{C*} = P_C$, $Q_{C*} = Q_C$, and $\phi_{C*} = \phi_C$ (up to re-labeling of variables).*

*Proof.* Since the adjoint of a "bra" is a "ket," $\langle b| C^* |a \rangle = \langle a| C |b \rangle$, so we may picture the original $C$ running right-to-left with $a$ and $b$ interchanged. Since the general-case construction in the proof of Theorem 1 is symmetrical for each gate until the $z_i = u_i$ step, and the only substitution is to equate two variables, the resulting $P_{C*}$ is the same polynomial as $P_C$, up to interchanging the substituted variables and $a$ with $b$. The same goes for $Q_C$ and $\phi_C$. □

The *tensor product* $C_1 \otimes C_2$ of two quantum circuits $C_1$ and $C_2$ simply consists of laying them side-by-side, with no gates between their respective qubit lines.

**Proposition 2.** *For any quantum circuits $C_1$ and $C_2$ of min-phase $K$, $P_{C_1 \otimes C_2}$ can be taken as $P_{C_1} \cdot P_{C_2}$, $Q_{C_1 \otimes C_2}$ can be taken as $Q_{C_1} + Q_{C_2}$ (mod K), and $\phi_{C_1 \otimes C_2}$ can be taken as $\phi_{C_1} \wedge \phi_{C_2}$.*

*Proof.* We can regard $C_1 \otimes C_2$ as a single quantum circuits in which the gates are introduced in any left-to-right order. The sequencing does not affect which variables are "$u_i$" on any qubit line when each gate is placed.    □

The *compute-uncompute* structure mentioned in Sect. 1 combines several of these elements. We have our initial circuit $C$ with some set $I$ of $r$ qubit lines intended for output. Then $r$ CNOT gates are placed with controls in $I$ and targets in $r$ fresh ancilla lines initialized to 0. Then $C^*$ is placed on the initial $m$ lines so that $C(x)$ is "uncomputed" and measurements of the $m+r$ lines will always give $xy$ for some output $y$. It is noteworthy that the composition of $C^*$ after $C$ gives almost the same product, sum, and AND forms, respectively, as Theorem 2 for the computation of probabilities. Further processing on $y$ alone is in parallel with $C^*$ and is modeled by multiplying, adding, or AND-ing in more terms. The only distinction from the completely-parallel situation of Proposition 2 comes from the forced variables $v_j$ and terms connecting $v_j$ to $u_i$ and $u_j$ (where $j = m + i$ with $i \in I$) when the CNOT gates are placed.

# 7    Examples and Prospective Applications

First, we take stock. We have defined a three-pronged framework that not only handles some universal set of gates and decision problems in BQP, but directly implements a wide range of quantum operations: exact quantum Fourier transform, sampling, on-the-fly measurement, and some circuit combinations. Our formal objects *remain small* and yet maintain full information about the quantum system. They are conducive to further manipulation by computer algebra and formal logic packages. They not only postpone the ostensible exponential blowup but raise the prospect that heuristic solvers—honed with high effort apart from the quantum context—can avoid it altogether. We give some examples that hint at the manner and plausibility of advances obtained this way.

One problem to attack is, *which restricted forms of quantum circuits can be emulated in classical polynomial time?* A fundamental case is the Gottesman-Knill theorem (see [34, 35]):

**Theorem 4.** *Quantum circuits that use only Hadamard, the Pauli gates, the phase gate* S, CNOT, CZ, *and swaps can be simulated in classical deterministic polynomial time. In particular, languages defined in the manner of Sect. 1 by uniform families of such circuits belong to* P.

Many proofs of this theorem have been given, including one in the related polynomial framework of [16]. Ours uses the even newer high-level result in [36] (also in Sect. 12 of [37]) that computing functions of the form (2) for polynomials of degree 2 belongs to P. It shows an even finer line than one of degree between polynomial-time computability and hardness.

*Proof.* Build the additive representation $Q_C$ of a circuit $C$ using these gates with $K = 4$. Note that $Z = S^2$ and $HZH = X$, from which it follows that CNOT can be made from H and CZ, and finally $Y = iXZ$. So we need only examine the terms as H, S, and CZ are added—none involves a constraint so there is no $\Upsilon$:

- H: $2u_i y_g$.
- S: $u_i$, but since $u_i$ is 0–1 valued we can add $u_i^2$ instead.
- CZ: $2u_i u_j$.

Thus $Q_C$ is a sum of monomials of the form $2xy$ or $x^2$. Modulo 4, both of these terms are invariant under replacing $x$ by $x + 2$. Hence solution counts in $\{0, 1\}^t$ where $t$ is the total number of variables and the count in $\mathbf{Z}_4^t$ are related by a fixed factor of $2^t$. We can thus use the theorem of [36] directly to count solutions in $\{0, 1\}^t$ to $Q_C - J$, $J = 0, 1, 2, 3$. $\qquad\square$

Now, however, notice that CS also produces an additive quadratic term, namely $u_i u_j$. Thus any circuit $C$ composed of H and CS (which simulate S and CZ) also has $Q_C$ of degree 2. If the theorem of [36,37] applied to counting *binary* solutions then BQP = P would follow. The nub is that the term $xy$ is not invariant under $x \mapsto x + 2$. Counting *0-1* solutions for quadratic polynomials with such terms is shown #P-complete in general by [38]. The difference between $u_i$ and $u_i u_j$ reflects the linear-versus-quadratic difference in [16], but here we have isolated the jump in complexity to the latter's coefficient being 1 not 2. This happens entirely within a setting where counting the number of solutions of quadratic polynomials modulo $K \geq 4$ is easy—but counting the number of *binary* solutions is hard.

Since our proof of Theorem 4 can yield amplitude information at any stage of the circuit we speak of simulation not just emulation here. The general algorithm in [36,37] does not run in $\tilde{O}(t)$ time. It remains to be seen whether its specialization to sums of $2xy$ or $x^2$ can be honed to rival the nearly linear running time of Jozsa [39]. The Toffoli, CS, and T gates all introduce terms of degree 3 into $Q_C$. It is interesting to ask whether circuits obtained by adding one of these gates have $Q_C$ with a simply-expressed structure that resists the "dichotomy" phenomenon (problems being either in P or #P-complete, nothing in-between) in these papers.

Note that we avoided the constraint $\Upsilon \cdot (\cdots)$ involved with CNOT. That or propagating the annotation $2u_i u_j - u_i - u_j$ along line $j$ would lead to terms of degree 3 or higher, while still giving polynomials that are functionally equivalent to the ones of degree 2 above. This leads to the broad question of recognizing such equivalence, and whether algebraic and Boolean solvers may even go beyond it by finding simplifications that do not have direct analogues at the level of quantum gates. The simplest identity involving a nondeterministic gate, namely HH = I, already shows some challenges. Substituting $x_1 = a$ and $z_1 = b$ gives the diagram:

The multiplicative polynomial of the left-hand circuit is

$$P_C = (1 - 2ay)(1 - 2yb) \mapsto 1 - 2ay - 2yb + 4ayb,$$

with a background factor of $R = 1/2$ from the two Hadamard gates. Why is this equivalent to the identity-gate polynomial? The latter is

$$P_I = E(a,b) = 1 - a - b + 2ab.$$

A clue is to look at what happens to $P_C$ under the "illegal" substitution $b = 1-a$, when it becomes

$$1 - 2ay - 2y + 2ay + 4ay - 4a^2y \mapsto 1 - 2y.$$

A multiplicative term $(1 - 2y)$ where this is the only occurrence of the interior variable $y$ behaves much like "$\Upsilon$" in the additive representations. It sets up a 1-1 correspondence between solutions for each $e(\omega)$ and $e(-\omega)$, which cancels everything to zero. Thus all assignments into $P_C$ that make $a \neq b$ contribute a net of zero to the complex amplitude. Substituting $a = b$ makes both polynomials reduce to 1. Interestingly, substituting $y = 1/2$ into $P_C$ yields $P_I$, but this is not a "legal" substitution.

For the additive representation over $\mathbf{Z}_4$ we get $Q_C = 2ay + 2yb = 2y(a + b)$. Again the legal paths with $b \neq a$ cancel, while those with $b = a$ make $2y(a + b)$ a multiple of 4, which yields 0 like the identity does. But how can we recognize this? The Boolean formula $\phi_C$ does $p_1 = p_0 \oplus (a \wedge y)$ and $p_2 = p_1 \oplus (y \wedge b)$, which combine to give $p_2 = p_0 \oplus (a \wedge y) \oplus (y \wedge b)$. For $y = 0$ this gives $p_2 = p_0 = 0$, whereas for $y = 1$ this makes $p_2 = p_0 \oplus (a \oplus b)$. Again we can infer that $a \neq b$ gives canceling phases while $a = b$ makes $p_2 = 0$ in this case too, so the net effect is the identity. But still, this already seems challenging to automate, let alone recognizing larger-scale circuit identities discussed previously. The nub is how well #SAT solvers can rearrange clauses so that variables like $y$ get "leveled off" in all cases, in the manner of eliminating rows in the *Tetris* video game.

Now we consider a much harder example of equivalence. A controlled gate CG deviates from the cases in Sect. 5 when G is nondeterministic. For example, the controlled Hadamard gate CH has the circuit notation and matrix shown at left below.

$$
\begin{array}{c}
\rule{0pt}{0pt} \\
\boxed{H}
\end{array}
=
\begin{pmatrix}
1 & 0 & 0 & 0 \\
0 & 1 & 0 & 0 \\
0 & 0 & \frac{1}{\sqrt{2}} & \frac{1}{\sqrt{2}} \\
0 & 0 & \frac{1}{\sqrt{2}} & -\frac{1}{\sqrt{2}}
\end{pmatrix}
=
\boxed{R_x(-\pi/2)}\!-\!\boxed{T^*}\!-\!\oplus\!-\!\boxed{T}\!-\!\boxed{R_x(\pi/2)}
$$

The matrix is not balanced. Letting $i$ be the control line and $j$ the target, we can introduce a new variable $y_g$ opposite $u_j$. The phase term $(1 - 2u_jy_g)$ for a free-standing Hadamard on line $j$ becomes $(1 - 2u_iu_jy_g)$ but the control gives a constraint: if $\neg u_i$ then $y_g = u_j$. So we could multiply $P$ by $(1 - 2u_iu_jy_g)(u_i + (1 - u_i)(1 + 2u_jy_g - u_j - y_g))$ and do analogously for $Q$ by

$$Q \mathrel{+}= (K/2)u_iu_jy_g + \Upsilon_\ell(1 - u_i)(u_j + y_g - 2u_iy_g).$$

The problem from the lack of balance, however, is a miscount in case $u_i = 0$. Then $y_g$ is forced to equal $u_j$ so, for instance, there is only one path from the input 00 to the output 00. We could patch this by introducing a new variable $v$, multiplying $P$ also by $(1 - u_i v)$, adding $u_i v \Upsilon_\ell$ to $Q$, and doing the following for $\phi$:

$$\phi \wedge \; = (p_\ell = p_{\ell-1} \oplus (u_i \wedge u_j \wedge y_g)) \wedge (y_g = u_j \oplus (u_i \wedge v))$$

The right-hand *pae* enforces the constraint when $u_i = 0$ and rectifies the count of satisfying assignments. However, $v$ needs to be treated as a new "virtual location" so that the paths for $v = 0$ and $v = 1$ do not amplify. This re-raises issues of sampling and *post-selection* that can be explored further. Alternately, one can use the equivalence of CH to a composition of five balanced gates shown at right. Let $y_1$ be the variable introduced by the $R_x(-\pi/2)$ and $y_2$ the one introduced by its conjugate. For $a = 00$, what happens is that the forced variable $v_f$ introduced by the CNOT gate is equated to $y_1$. The final quarter and half phases computed in four stages (besides the CNOT which changes no phase) are:

$$q_4 = q_3 \oplus v_f \oplus y_2 \quad = \quad y_1 \oplus y_1 \oplus y_2 \quad = \quad y_2$$
$$p_4 = p_3 \oplus ((v_f \oplus y_2) \wedge \bar{q}_3) \quad = \quad (y_1 \oplus y_2) \wedge \bar{y}_1 \quad = \quad \bar{y}_1 \wedge y_2.$$

The outcome $b = 00$ sets $y_2 = 0$ and hence gives both paths for $y_1$ a final phase of zero in a way that leaves the variable $y_1$ completely free in both equations. Thus $y_1$ acts like "$v$" above. The potential outcome $b = 01$ sets $y_2 = 1$, which fixes the quarter phase as 1 and makes the variable $y_1$ switch between $i$ and $-i$ in the top phase, which duly cancel to make $b = 01$ impossible. This leads to an operational verification of equivalence when the other values of $a$ are verified as well, but this is far from a simplification.

The challenge is to recognize such simplifications. The identity $\mathsf{HSH} = \mathsf{V}$ and its analogue using CS and CV may have intermediate difficulty. So may the equivalence of the Toffoli gate to two-qubit gates [20]:

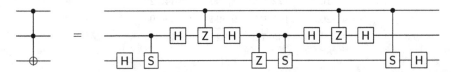

In our rendition there are six Hadamard gates to "level away." We have only opened the door to these questions about equivalence and efficacy by a crack. We conclude with only a very preliminary indication that there may be light through the crack from the performance and scaling of existing solvers.

## 8    A Few Experimental Results

We show the experimental results from the performance of solving the generated Boolean formulas using our brute-force (BF) method and current versions of the *Cachet* [12–14] and *sharpSAT* [11] solvers. All the circuits generated and tested begin with a bank of Hadamard-gates on every line applied to the input vector, and subsequently differ as follows:

- CNOT staircase: apply CNOT gates with control $n$ and target $n+1$ followed by a T-gate on line $n$ for $n = 1, \cdots, m-1$. Concretely, a sequence of applied gates would be $\mathsf{CNOT}(1,2), \mathsf{T}(2), \mathsf{CNOT}(2,3), \mathsf{T}(3), \ldots, \mathsf{T}(m), \mathsf{CNOT}(m,1)$.
- CNOT staircase with appended CZ and CV gates that alternate: After the bank of H gates and the above CNOT staircase, apply CV and CZ alternately to lines $n, n+1$ and $n+2$. Concretely, a sequence of applied gates would be:

$$\mathsf{CNOT}(1,2), \mathsf{T}(2), \mathsf{CNOT}(2,3), \mathsf{T}(3), \ldots, \mathsf{T}(m), \mathsf{CNOT}(m,1)$$
$$\mathsf{CV}(1,2), \mathsf{CZ}(2,3), \mathsf{CV}(3,4), \mathsf{CZ}(4,5), \cdots, \mathsf{CZ}(n-2,n-1), \mathsf{CV}(n-1,n).$$

- Initial segments of circuits proposed in [21] to be hard for classical simulations.

The following results were run from C++ code on one core thread of a Dell PowerEdge R720 server with 3.3 Ghz E5-2643 CPU. The experimental specification called for reading a description of the quantum circuit as described above, transcribing it into the standard ("DIMACS") format used by SAT solvers, and running ten trials each of our brute-force routine, *sharpSAT*, and *Cachet*. The latter two were compiled with optimization on the same machine as our solver. Our code uses pointers to unsigned integers to reference Boolean values; there does not seem to be any tangible gain from packing integers to represent multiple Boolean values or using a `bitset` implementation.

**Table 1.** CNOT staircase (microsecond (us))

| $m$ | BF | sharpSAT | Cachet |
|---|---|---|---|
| 4 | 35 | 7,409 | 35,870 |
| 8 | 618 | 8,021 | 36,245 |
| 12 | 12,239 | 8,292 | 35,245 |
| 16 | 122,063 | 8,100 | 34,120 |
| 20 | 2,101,034 | 9,594 | 39,994 |
| 24 | 62,935,720 | 9,024 | 42,994 |

Table 1 shows the results of solving the generated Boolean formulas for circuits consisting of a "staircase" of $m$ Hadamard and CNOT gates producing entanglements. While the brute-force (BF) running time grows exponentially in $m$ as expected, the running times of *sharpSAT* and *Cachet* change little. This suggests that the solvers are able to figuratively flatten the staircase so that the transformed solutions are easy to count. The next experiment tries to frustrate this by sprinkling controlled gates of non-binary phases amid the lines. The CV gates add extra nondeterminism in the standard basis.

In Table 2, the relations between them are similar to that in Table 1 until the line for $m = 16$. The BF running time balloons up even more owing to the extra nondeterministic variables. The *sharpSAT* solver seems to have special difficulty with the circuits of 20 and 24 qubits.

**Table 2.** CNOT staircase with CZ and CV (microsecond (us))

| $m$ | BF | sharpSAT | Cachet |
|-----|-----|---------|--------|
| 4 | 410 | 8,373 | 42,744 |
| 8 | 91,534 | 8,486 | 49,493 |
| 12 | 13.9 s | 10,400 | 64,300 |
| 16 | 14,588 s | 18,500 | 52,000 |
| 20 | $\gg$5 h | 145,700 | 106,000 |
| 24 | $\gg$5 h | 1,196,100 | 362,700 |

We also tried initial sets of layers from the circuits treated in [22] based on indications from [21] of their being hard to simulate classically. Those circuits had too much nondeterminism for BF but gave results within a few hours for *sharpSAT* and *Cachet* until the circuits reached 6 or 7 layers of 24 to 36 qubits—well short of the 40-layer simulations on massively parallel hardware announced by [22].

The results show that *sharpSAT* and *Cachet* give better scalability on these circuits. They as yet do not, however, even "recognize" the identity $HH = I$ in the sense of having similarly close running times when extra $HH$ pairs are added to these circuits. Of course, our BF method has its time compounded by a factor of 4 for each pair since it blindly tries all combinations. This points to the goal is tuning the solvers for a repertoire of basic quantum simplifications, in the hope that this will boost the heuristics already employed.

The final preliminary experiment, just at press time, emulated the circuits for Shor's algorithm that are constructed by libquantum [2–4]. The libquantum package and its shor routine are distinguished among quantum simulation software by being part of the SPEC CPU2006 benchmark suite [40]. We modified the v1.1.1 release code so that it prints out each quantum gate in the readable format of our emulator. The circuits are generated specially for each $M$ and choice of random seed $a$. For $M = 2021$ and $a = 7$ the circuit built by the shor routine uses 22 principal qubits, 35 ancillas, and has 98,135 elementary gates. By far the largest block is for the modular exponentiation step which consists entirely of deterministic gates (only NOT, CNOT, and Toffoli). They are somewhat larger than the original circuits for Shor's algorithm detailed in [41]. They are far from optimal; indeed, Markov and Saeedi [31,42] showed 6-to-8-fold improvements by high-level means and other gate-level improvements have been made [32,43,44].

The SPEC CPU2006 benchmark consists of one run of shor on $M$ and $a$, which does just one iteration of the quantum circuit—no restarts in case it doesn't succeed. It uses a numerical gate-by-gate simulation. For $M$ approaching 10,000 our compile of shor overflows its hash table of over 500 MB. It functioned correctly on $M = 2021 = 43 * 47$, which is just under $2^{11}$. Our emulator's brute-force routine reaches its limit for numbers larger than $2^9 = 512$, which entails running through $2^{36} = 64$ billion assignments for each of 9 sampled bits. Optimizing the initial modular exponentiation stage would make very little difference in our brute-force routine because only one in every $2^{18}$ assignments backtracks beyond the final QFT step which has 18 Hadamard gates of its own. Runs with the #SAT solvers succeeded for $M = 15$ and $M = 21$ but bogged down for $M = 55$, with *sharpSAT* expanding to over 34 GB of system resources. This evidently owes to the second copy of $\phi$ in the proof of Theorem 2 doubling the count of Hadamard gates again. The brute-force compilation needed only the single copy and stayed within 71 MB, under 0.1% of system memory, per billion assignments tried.

## 9    Conclusions and Research Directions

We have defined a natural *emulator* in the sense of [8]. It has no explicit representation of matrices or quantum states or any physical elements and loses no precision while needing only whole integer arithmetic. Preliminary experimental work shows that it is competent even in brute-force simulation and enables distinctly high performance through #SAT solvers in several instances. It has a high memory footprint only in the accumulation of final results. The sampling procedure of Sect. 6 essentially eliminates that footprint but at double the cost in nondeterminism and a squaring of brute-force simulation time. Overall the architecture is markedly different from that of commonly employed systems. It is so fine-grained as to escape limitations of more-structured systems including [45–49], but eschews explicit benefit from such structures. We showed its capability to work with quantum circuits of thousands of gates, though also where it is lagging by a factor of about 20 in the magnitude of numbers $M$ that it can handle compared to `libquantum` and that the #SAT solvers lagged by another factor of 10.

Higher performance may come from software advances in #SAT solvers. These might be tailored to leverage the special "parity-of-AND" form of the equational clauses before conversion to conjunctive normal form. At the very least, our work has supplied a new class of natural instances by which to challenge these solvers. One natural metric will come from the work in progress of emulating Shor's algorithm. We have shown all the ingredients except for concretely optimizing the deterministic layer for modular exponentiation—which may make a greater difference for #SAT solvers than it does for our brute-force routine. Research progress will need to center on the details of the solvers and their heuristics, to tune them more to recognizing symmetries and identities arising in quantum circuits. Most in particular, it would be interested to test the direction-of-flow arguments made at the end of Sect. 5 on a set of natural instances.

Another question is whether solvers can be tailored to the algebraic forms, the low-degree $Q_C$ polynomials in particular. Comparison of the efficacy of our algebraic and logical representations is hampered by the relative lack of dedicated symbolic polynomial equation solvers compared to SAT solvers. On the theoretical side, our own proof of Theorem 4 shows a new level of fineness in the demarcation between cases of counting problems that are polynomial-time solvable and those that are #P-complete.

A further research direction suggested by the obstacles to exact emulation of Shor's algorithm is to use approximation. In the context of simulators typified by libquantum and much research on perturbations of Shor's algorithm, *approximation* has its standard numerical meaning, as exemplified by [50–53]. In logic, we can approximate a complex predicate by a simple one that gives the correct answer on all but a sparse set of instances. This suggests looking for a sparse approximation to the modular exponentiation relation.

We close with an analogy to elaborate the main issue with our architecture. Solvers that represent whole state vectors in some form and emulate circuit levels sequentially figuratively have the memory footprint of a giant. Once the giant gets going, however, it walks with a steady gait. Our model instead employs an army of fleet-footed mice and can send one 'mouse' (i.e., evaluate one Feynman path) at a time with zero footprint—except for housing the results of the mice at the end. The issue is that each intermediate nondeterministic gate doubles the size of the mouse army. Of course the brute-force simulation doesn't reduce it but all heuristics must grapple with the initial condition that multiple mice are still "there" before any cancellations or Tetris-style blocking are applied. Aaronson and Chen [54] have recently shown a simple tradeoff between the "path" and "whole-state" extremes, but it still pays some exponential factor (they state what in our notation would be $2^n$ versus $2^s$, but in our setup it is more like $2^m$ versus $2^h$) up front.

The formulas manipulated by SAT and #SAT solvers, insofar as they expand via resolution and other techniques, are between the mice and the giant. The further success of this approach may depend on how much implicit combination they can achieve. For some sampling steps of quantum algorithms, certain trade-offs between accuracy of the counting and size can be tolerated. How this can possibly interact with the deep tradeoff of approximation and hardness in sampling, over which the argument over "quantum supremacy" is currently centered, remains to be seen.

**Acknowledgments.** Most of the initial work on this paper was done while the first author was a sabbatical visitor to the Universitié de Montreal, partly supported by the UdeM Département d'informatique et de recherche opérationnelle, and by the University at Buffalo Computer Science Department. We thank especially Professors Pierre McKenzie, Alain Tapp, and Jin-Yi Cai for insightful discussions, and Igor Markov for further pointers to the literature and a press-time tip that libquantum could be modified to output the entire quantum circuits of thousands of gates for Shor's algorithm in a format readable by our emulator. We thank the referees and also Michael Nielsen, John Sidles, Wim van Dam, Alex Russell, and Ronald de Wolf for helpful comments.

# References

1. Dawson, C., Haselgrove, H., Hines, A., Mortimer, D., Nielsen, M., Osborne, T.: Quantum computing and polynomial equations over the finite field $Z_2$. Quantum Inf. Comput. **5**, 102–112 (2004)
2. Butscher, B., Weimer, H.: Simulation eines Quantencomputers (2003). http://www.libquantum.de/files/libquantum.pdf
3. Weimer, H., Müller, M., Lesanovsky, I., Zoller, P., Büchler, H.: A Rydberg quantum simulator. Nature Phys. **6**, 382–388 (2010)
4. Weimer, H., Butscher, B.: libquantum 1.1.1: the C library for quantum computing and quantum simulation (2003–2013 (v. 1.1.1)). http://www.libquantum.de/
5. Wybiral, D., Hwang, J.: Quantum circuit simulator (2012). http://www.davyw.com/quantum/
6. Shor, P.W.: Algorithms for quantum computation: discrete logarithms and factoring. In: Proceedings of the 35th Annual IEEE Symposium on the Foundations of Computer Science, pp. 124–134 (1994)
7. Boneh, D.: Twenty years of attacks on the RSA cryptosystem. Notices Am. Math. Soc. **46**, 203–213 (1999)
8. Häner, T., Steiger, D., Smelyanskiy, M., Troyer, M.: High performance emulation of quantum circuits. In: Proceedings of the International Conference for High Performance Computing, Networking, Storage and Analysis, Salt Lake City, Utah. IEEE Press, November 2016. Article 74 in e-volume
9. Greuel, G.M., Pfister, G., Schönemann, H.: Singular version 1.2 user manual. In: Reports on Computer Algebra, vol. 21. Centre for Computer Algebra, University of Kaiserslautern (1998). http://www.singular.uni-kl.de/
10. Greuel, G.M., Pfister, G., Schönemann, H.: Singular 3.0. A Computer Algebra System for Polynomial Computations, Centre for Computer Algebra, University of Kaiserslautern (2005). http://www.singular.uni-kl.de
11. Thurley, M.: sharpSAT – counting models with advanced component caching and implicit BCP. In: Biere, A., Gomes, C.P. (eds.) SAT 2006. LNCS, vol. 4121, pp. 424–429. Springer, Heidelberg (2006). https://doi.org/10.1007/11814948_38
12. Sang, T., Bacchus, F., Beame, P., Kautz, H., Pitassi, T.: Combining component caching and clause learning for effective model counting. In: Seventh International Conference on Theory and Applications of Satisfiability Testing, Vancouver (2004)
13. Sang, T., Beame, P., Kautz, H.: Heuristics for fast exact model counting. In: Eighth International Conference on Theory and Applications of Satisfiability Testing, Edinburgh, Scotland (2005)
14. Sang, T., Beame, P., Kautz, H.: Performing Bayesian inference by weighted model counting. In: Proceedings of the Twentieth National Conference on Artificial Intelligence (AAAI 2005), Pittsburgh, PA (2005)
15. Gerdt, V., Severyanov, V.: A software package to construct polynomial sets over $Z_2$ for determining the output of quantum computations. Nucl. Instrum. Methods Phys. Res. A **59**, 260–264 (2006)
16. Bacon, D., van Dam, W., Russell, A.: Analyzing algebraic quantum circuits using exponential sums (2008). http://www.cs.ucsb.edu/vandam/LeastAction.pdf
17. Adleman, L., DeMarrais, J., Huang, M.: Quantum computability. SIAM J. Comput. **26**, 1524–1540 (1997)
18. Fortnow, L., Rogers, J.: Complexity limitations on quantum computation. In: Proceedings of the 13th Annual IEEE Conference on Computational Complexity, pp. 202–206 (1998)

19. Barenco, A., Deutsch, D., Ekert, A., Jozsa, R.: Conditional quantum dynamics and logic gates. Phys. Rev. Lett. **74**(20), 4083–4086 (1995)
20. Barenco, A., Bennett, C., Cleve, R., DiVincenzo, D., Margolus, N., Shor, P., Sleator, T., Smolin, J., Weinfurter, H.: Elementary gates for quantum computation. Phys. Rev. A **52**(5), 3457–3467 (1995)
21. Boixo, S., Isakov, S.V., Smelyanskiy, V.N., Babbush, R., Ding, N., Jiang, Z., Bremner, M.J., Martinis, J.M., Neven, H.: Characterizing quantum supremacy in near-term devices (2016). https://arxiv.org/pdf/1608.00263.pdf
22. Häner, T., Steiger, D.: 0.5 petabyte simulation of a 45-qubit quantum circuit (2017). arXiv:1704.01127v1
23. Feynmann, R.: Simulating physics with computers. Int. J. Theor. Phys. **21**, 467–488 (1982)
24. Feynmann, R.: Quantum mechanical computers. Found. Phys. **16**, 507–531 (1986)
25. Deutsch, D.: Quantum theory, the Church-Turing principle, and the universal quantum computer. Proc. Royal Soc. A **400**, 97–117 (1985)
26. Deutsch, D.: Quantum computational networks. Proc. R. Soc. Lond. A **425**(1868), 73–90 (1989)
27. Yamashita, S., Markov, I.: Fast equivalence-checking for quantum circuits. In: Proceedings of the 2010 IEEE/ACM Symposium on Nanoscale Architectures, Anaheim, CA, USA (2010). May 2013 update at https://arxiv.org/pdf/0909.4119.pdf
28. Eggersglüß, S., Wille, R., Drechsler, R.: Improved SAT-based ATPG: more constraints, better compaction. In: Proceedings of the 2013 International Conference on Computer-Aided Design, San José, CA, USA, pp. 85–90 (2013)
29. Schönhage, A., Strassen, V.: Schnelle Multiplikation grosser Zahlen. Comput. Arch. Elektron. Rechnen **7**, 281–292 (1971)
30. van Meter, R., Itoh, K.: Fast quantum modular exponentiation. Phys. Rev. A **71**, 052320 (2005)
31. Markov, I., Saeedi, M.: Constant-optimized quantum circuits for modular multiplication and exponentiation. Quantum Inf. Comput. **12**, 361–394 (2012)
32. Pavlidis, A., Gizopoulos, D.: Fast quantum modular exponentiation architecture for shor's factoring algorithm. Quantum Inf. Comput. **14**, 649–682 (2014)
33. Cao, Z., Cao, Z., Liu, L.: Remarks on quantum modular exponentiation and some experimental demonstrations of Shor's algorithm (2014). https://arxiv.org/abs/1408.6252
34. Gottesman, D.: The Heisenberg representation of quantum computers (1998). http://arxiv.org/abs/quant-ph/9807006
35. Aaronson, S., Gottesman, D.: Improved simulation of stabilizer circuits. Phys. Rev. A **70** (2004)
36. Cai, J.-Y., Chen, X., Lipton, R., Lu, P.: On tractable exponential sums. In: Lee, D.-T., Chen, D.Z., Ying, S. (eds.) FAW 2010. LNCS, vol. 6213, pp. 148–159. Springer, Heidelberg (2010). https://doi.org/10.1007/978-3-642-14553-7_16
37. Cai, J.-Y., Chen, X., Lu, P.: Graph homomorphisms with complex values: a dichotomy theorem. SIAM J. Comput. **42**, 924–1029 (2013)
38. Cai, J.Y., Lu, P., Xia, M.: The complexity of complex weighted Boolean #CSP. J. Comp. Syst. Sci. **80**, 217–236 (2014)
39. Jozsa, R.: Invited Talk: embedding classical into quantum computation. In: Calmet, J., Geiselmann, W., Müller-Quade, J. (eds.) Mathematical Methods in Computer Science. LNCS, vol. 5393, pp. 43–49. Springer, Heidelberg (2008). https://doi.org/10.1007/978-3-540-89994-5_5. arXiv:0812.4511 [quant-ph]
40. Spec.org, Butscher, B., Weimer, H.: 462.libquantum SPEC CPU2006 benchmark description (2006). https://www.spec.org/cpu2006/Docs/462.libquantum.html

41. Beckman, D., Chari, A., Devabhaktuni, S., Preskill, J.: Efficient networks for quantum factoring. Phys. Rev. A **54**, 1034–1063 (1996)
42. Markov, I., Saeedi, M.: Faster quantum number factoring via circuit synthesis. Phys. Rev. A **87**(012310), 1–5 (2013)
43. Beauregard, S.: Circuit for shor's algorithm using 2n + 3 qubits. Quantum Inf. Comput. **3**, 175 (2003)
44. Häner, T., Roetteler, M., Svore, K.: Factoring using 2n + 2 qubits with toffoli based modular multiplication. Quantum Inf. Comput. **17**, 673–684 (2017)
45. Viamontes, G., Rajagopalan, M., Markov, I., Hayes, J.: Gate-level simulation of quantum circuits. In: Proceedings of the ACM/ IEEE Asia and South-Pacific Design Automation Conference (ASPDAC), Kitakyushu, Japan, pp. 295–301, January 2003
46. Viamontes, G., Markov, I., Hayes, J.: Improving gate-level simulation of quantum circuits. Quantum Inf. Process. **2**, 347–380 (2003)
47. Greve, D.: QDD: a quantum computer emulation library (1999–2007). http:// thegreves.com/david/QDD/qdd.html
48. Patrzyk, J., Patrzyk, B., Rycerz, K., Bubak, M.: Towards a novel environment for simulation of quantum computing. Comput. Sci. **16**, 103–129 (2015)
49. Lee, Y., Khalil-Hani, M., Marsono, M.: An FPGA-based quantum computing emulation framework based on serial-parallel architecture. J. Reconfigurable Comput. **2016**, 18 pages (2016)
50. Barenco, A., Ekert, A., Suominen, K.A., Törmä, P.: Approximate quantum Fourier transform and decoherence. Phys. Rev. A **54**, 139–146 (1996)
51. Zilic, Z., Radecka, K.: Scaling and better approximating quantum fourier transform by higher radices. IEEE Trans. Comp. **56**, 202–207 (2007)
52. Rötteler, M., Beth, T.: Representation-theoretical properties of the approximate quantum Fourier transform. Appl. Algebra Eng. Commun. Comput. **19**, 117–193 (2008)
53. Prokopenya, A.N.: Approximate quantum fourier transform and quantum algorithm for phase estimation. In: Gerdt, V.P., Koepf, W., Seiler, W.M., Vorozhtsov, E.V. (eds.) CASC 2015. LNCS, vol. 9301, pp. 391–405. Springer, Cham (2015). https://doi.org/10.1007/978-3-319-24021-3_29
54. Aaronson, S., Chen, L.: Complexity-theoretic foundations of quantum supremacy experiments (2016). https://arxiv.org/abs/1612.05903

# Advanced Monitoring Based Intrusion Detection System for Distributed and Intelligent Energy Theft: DIET Attack in Advanced Metering Infrastructure

Manali Chakraborty[⊠]

Department of Computer Science and Engineering,
University of Calcutta, Kolkata, India
manali4mkolkata@gmail.com

**Abstract.** Power grid and energy theft has an eternal relationship. Though we moved towards Smart Grid, with an expectation for a more efficient, reliable and secure service, so does the attackers. Smart Grid and AMI systems incorporate a good number of security measures, still it is open to various threats. Recent attacks on Smart Grids in U.S., Gulf State and Ukraine proved that the attacks on the grid have become more sophisticated. In this paper we have introduced a new, distributed and intelligent energy theft: DIET attack and proposed an advanced Intrusion Detection System to protect AMI system. The proposed IDS can perform a passive monitoring on the system as well as detect attackers. This features make this IDS more robust and reliable.

**Keywords:** Intrusion detection system · Non technical loss
Energy theft · AMI · Smart Grid · Trust

## 1 Introduction

Smart Grid is meant to modernize traditional power grids with the two-way data communication along with energy supply. In order to enhance the functionalities of the network, Smart Grid offers several applications to help both customers and utilities to optimize the energy usage and billing. Advanced Metering Infrastructure or AMI is one of the most important features of Smart Grid [1]. It establishes a direct communication between customers and utilities, including, meter readings at periodic intervals (sometimes on demand) to the Data Collection Units or DCUs, updated electricity tariffs at regular intervals to smart meters, electricity outage alert messages and sometimes it upgrades the meter firmware [2]. However, due to the unique characteristics of AMI, such as complex network structure, resource-constrained smart meter, and privacy-sensitive data, it is an especially challenging issue to make AMI secure. Energy theft is one of the most important concerns related to the smart grid implementation. It is estimated that utility companies lose more than $25 billion every year due

© Springer-Verlag GmbH Germany, part of Springer Nature 2018
M. L. Gavrilova et al. (Eds.): Trans. on Comput. Sci. XXXI, LNCS 10730, pp. 77–97, 2018.
https://doi.org/10.1007/978-3-662-56499-8_5

to energy theft around the world [1]. Energy theft may become an even more serious problem since the smart meters used in smart grids are vulnerable to more types of attacks compared to traditional mechanical meters. The unique challenges for energy theft in AMI call for the development of effective detection techniques.

Generally, energy theft can be accomplished using three ways [1,3]. Firstly, by interrupting smart meters from recording correct electricity usages, secondly, by forging demand information in smart meters and lastly by injecting false/bad data in the communication line. Now, the first attack is the only one that exists for the traditional meters, the other two attacks are exclusively for smart meters. Besides, premise of energy theft in AMI can also be classified in three categories:

- Type-1: where the attacker modifies its own smart meter to maximize its individual gain.
- Type-2: where the attacker modifies numerous smart meters in his neighborhood to either maximize its personal gain or penalize the utilities.
- Type-3: the cooperative attack, where a bunch of attackers create a chain of attacks on a large scale to immobilize the system in a short time interval.

In the first scenario, it is quite easy to detect the attack by analyzing the electricity usage pattern. Classification based detection schemes are quite suitable for these types of attacks. Besides, there exist several works to detect energy thefts which belong into the first two category. However, these types of attacks can be made more intelligent and difficult to detect, if implemented wisely. In this paper, we have proposed an attack model for distributed and intelligent electricity theft and proposed a two tier trust based intrusion detection system. The third part: collaborative attack is much complicated to implement as well as detect. We have considered these types of attacks as a part of our future extension of this paper.

There exist a good number of research works addressing solutions towards energy theft problem in Smart Grid. In [8] authors proposed a Support Vector Machine (SVM) based detection model to construct users' load profile pattern and then detect deviations from the standard pattern in order to identify abnormal behavior. Besides, to improve the performance of this model, authors incorporate fuzzy systems. The complete detection model identifies abnormal behaviors in the grid by comparing current load with recorded load profile and other additional information. Authors in [19] proposed an Auto Regressive Moving Average (ARMA) based model to analyze the probability distributions of the normal and malicious consumption patterns of users. They have applied the generalized likelihood ratio (GLR) test to detect energy theft attacks. The proposed work is heavily dependent on the data capturing accuracy of the ARMA model. Besides, it is based on the assumption that the attacker would always choose to decreases the mean value of the real consumption. Works presented in [9,10] also proposed a detection mechanism based on pattern matching and data classification. First, they proposed an classification method based on SVM and Rule based systems [9]. Then in [10], they introduce High Performance Computing (HPC) based algorithms to enhance the performance of their previous model. They have implemented some parallelized encoding algorithms to speed up the data classification, analyze and detection process. They have been able to differentiate the behavior of fraud customers from genuine users, using this model. AMIDS [11] is another AMI Intrusion Detection model, where a data mining technique based Non Intrusive Load Monitoring (NILM) system can collect data from three different sensors. These sensors gather data to identify cyber attacks, physical attacks and power measurement based anomaly. Authors of this paper claim that the proposed intrusion detection system (IDS) can detect several attacks by using information fusion from different sensors and correlation of different alert triggers. A Radio Frequency IDentification (RFID) based theft detection technique is proposed in [12]. The proposed system is divided in two parts: ammeter inventory management and ammeter verification control. RFID tags are attached with meters and used to detect energy theft. In addition, the reader acquires the information transmitted from the tag and sends it to the company's ERP system through the network to determine whether it is the approved tag or a different one placed by electricity thieves. Although the RFID technology can be used to detect energy theft, the utility companies have to pay extra cost to install the system. In order to find out whether implementing RFID technology is beneficial for the utility company, cost-benefit theory is used to analyze different value changes caused by the proposed system. Authors of paper [13] proposed a rather simple approach. They compare the meter readings of users with utilities reading. If the difference exceeds a threshold value, then that meter is marked as malicious and the connection will be terminated immediately.

The detection methods for energy theft can be broadly categorize into three types [1, 20]: classification or statistical methods based detection techniques, monitoring based detection techniques and game theory based detection techniques. Classification based methods apply data mining methods and machine learning to energy usage patterns, collected from smart meters. They detect attacks by finding the deviation from the original data. These methods are cost effective and can be implemented easily. However, due to its lack of consideration for innovative and adaptive attack techniques, often some intelligent and minute attacks remain undetectable. Besides the false positive rates are on a higher side for these type of methods. Monitoring based techniques use sensor nodes, RFIDs and sometimes other smart meters to monitor the state of the network to detect the attack. This method has a better detection rate and lower false positive rate than the previous one. Continuous monitoring ensures the detection of very minute changes in the system. However, the implementation and maintenance cost of such system can become a disadvantage for implementation. Lastly, game theory based methods [14, 15] are new in this domain, very few works have been done to detect energy theft. Planning the strategies for each player and formulated their goals can be a bit tricky in Smart Grid environment. The rules of the games should update simultaneously according to the change of situations in network and characteristics of players. Besides, these types of methods have greater false positive rates than monitoring based methods. It may be summarized that the monitoring based methods are best suitable to detect intelligent and minute attacks, providing the implementation and maintenance costs are minimized. Thus the main goal is to propose an effective monitoring system which ensures the trade-off between cost optimization and detection efficiency.

In this paper, we have introduced a new attack type specific to Smart Power Grid. We propose to call it Distributed and Intelligent Energy Theft (DIET) attack. Further, we have proposed a two-tier solution to detect the proposed DIET attack and perform a passive monitoring on the system, to provide an additional level of security. We have simulated DIET attack and the proposed detection mechanism using Qualnet 5.2 simulator [16].

The rest of the paper is organized as follows: Sect. 2 describes the network infrastructure for our proposed solution, Sect. 3 elaborates the proposed attack scenario, the working mechanism of our proposed IDS is described in Sect. 4, whereas, the simulation results and performance analysis is presented in Sect. 5, and finally Sect. 6 concludes this work.

## 2    Smart Infrastructure for Communication

Figure 1 shows the communication architecture of Smart Grid. Smart-energy Utility Network (SUN) hierarchically consists of three components: Home Area

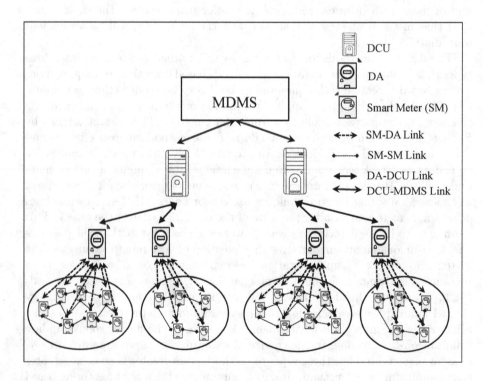

**Fig. 1.** Communication architecture of AMI in smart grid.

Network (HAN), Neighborhood Area Network (NAN), and Wide Area Network (WAN) [17]. The HAN provides the communication between the Smart Meters in a home and other appliances in that home. The NAN connects SMs to the Data Aggregators (DAs) and Data Collection Units (DCUs), and WAN provides access between the DCUs and Meter Data Management System (MDMS). DAs collect data from hundred of SMs registered under it and send them to DCUs. DCUs are responsible for communication with MDMS. Smart Grid has a quasi hierarchical structure, where the number of intermediate levels in the network varies with demographic and socio-economic condition of any particular region [7]. The smart meters act as hosts in a network, DCUs are the routers of the network and DAs are intermediate connectors. We assume that Smart Meters are managed by its immediate upper level DA or DCU, depending on the hierarchy. We assume that Smart Grid is a cluster based network, where each DA acts as a cluster head and can accommodate utmost 1000 of Smart meters. When a SM X is installed in a grid, it should find a DA to bind with. X will continue to communicate through DA in the network.

Firstly, we propose Near Term Digital Radio architecture [21] for the Clustering scheme used by our IDS. In this specific architecture, the cluster is divided into several physical subnets. Each subnet consists of the Cluster Head or DA and the Cluster Members or SMs which are at one - hop distance from the DAs. All SMs within a cluster can communicate with the DA using the same frequency and can communicate with other SMs within the same subnet using another frequency. These two channels are assumed to have different frequencies, so that there is no interference. DAs can also communicate with its upper level DCUs and DCUs with MDMS. The MDMS sends its messages to the DCUs, which then propagates the information through other DAs and finally it reaches to SM.

Communication between DAs, DCUs and MDMSs are supposed to be secure. However, SM to SM communication link may be compromised by attacker. In this paper, we have proposed a new Smart Grid specific energy theft (DIET) attack. In order to model this attack scenario we have used several network attacks, such as, extracting meter credentials and Man in the Middle (MITM) attack.

## 2.1 Information Stored at Smart Meters

The basic job of a smart meter is to track the energy usage of its customer and communicate with a DA. Generally a SM send their electricity usage after every 15 min of interval to the cluster head (DA) and receives various instructions from the DA. Now, in order to implement our IDS, we assume that,

- Every SM has an unique MAC address within its cluster.
- A smart meter can acquire its neighbor SMs' address through Neighbor Discovery procedure and can communicate with them over a wireless medium.

- A SM send a Electricity Usage (EU) message to the DA after every 15 min and broadcasts the same message at the same interval so that all of its neighbors can keep a tab of its electricity usage.
  $EU_{i,t}$ denotes the energy usage of SM $i$ at time interval $t-(t-1)$, where $i$ denotes it unique MAC address.
- Every SM maintains an array, Neighbor's Electricity Usage (NEU) for storing the information about the energy usage of its neighbors. $NEU_{i,t}[j]$ denotes the electricity usage of SM with unique MAC address $j$, at time $t$ as stored at smart meter $i$.

Every time when a $SM_i$ receives a broadcasted message from its neighbor $SM_j$ at time $t$ it adds the value of its electricity usage with the previously stored value for $SM_j$ in the array, and updated its NEU as,

$$NEU_{i,t}[j] = NEU_{i,t-1}[j] + EU_{j,t}$$

Where, $t-(t-1) = 15$ min.
Thus, a SM stores its neighbor SMs' electricity usage in a cumulative array.

## 2.2   Information Stored at Cluster Heads

Cluster heads acts as a bridge between customers and utility. The main function of cluster heads, or DAs, or DCUs (depending on the hierarchical structure of the Grid) is to receive the electricity usage information of its SMs and provide billing information, electricity pricing and various informations to the SMs, depending on the applications. Besides cluster heads are also responsible for analyzing the data and detect any anomalies or abnormal behaviors in its cluster and report to the MDMS. We assume that,

- Each cluster head maintains a Smart Meter Connection (SMC) graph to store the topological information about its cluster. The graph is represented by an array of linked lists, where the size of the array defines the total number of SMs in the cluster and the size of each individual list represents the number of neighbors of that SM.
- Besides, every DA, i.e., cluster head will maintain a 2-D array ES(N,T) of energy supplied to each smart meters in its cluster, Where N is the total number of smart meters, registered with the cluster head and T denotes time. ES[i][t] denotes the energy supplied to the smart meter with MAC address i at $t$ time-stamp.

Each cluster head communicates with the SMs within its cluster, and then transmits the aggregated data to its upper level DCU or MDMS.

Data structures, EU, NEU and ES are initialized after every 4 h. And the Smart meter Connection (SMC) graph is updated after the joining of every new SM in the cluster.

# 3  Proposed DIET Attack Model

In [3], the authors have addressed the issue of energy theft in smart grids using AMI. However, the authors elaborate on Type-1 attacks only and how they can be achieved in the AMI. The implementation of such attacks requires the attacker to hack into his Smart Meter using a Man-in-the-Middle attack. Once the attacker has his Smart Meter credentials, he can drop packets, inject new packets, as well as modify the usage information stored within the Smart Meters.

However, the situation is quite different for Type-2 attacks. Here, the attacker tries to hack and modify the data packets of its neighboring smart meters and then forward those malicious packets to DCU. Now, the first level of security can be easily provided by the AMI by implementing a modified version of the Needham Schroeder protocol [18] (like the Kerberos protocol or the Needham-Schroeder-Lowe protocol) to prevent replay attacks and Man-in-the-middle attacks. This prevents any eavesdropper from spoofing its neighboring Smart Meters during mutual authentication. Once this is ensured our only concern remains in securing the network communication. Whenever a Smart Meter tries to send a periodic update to the DCU about it's usage, the attacker may intercept this packet, drop it from the network and inject a new packet (with the neighbors credentials) with modified usage statistics.

In this paper, we have considered a special case of Type-2 energy theft attack. The Type-2 energy theft attack can be made quite difficult, if the attacker modifies the energy usage of a meter with a very negligible amount. 6% to 8% Technical Loss (TL) in transmission and distribution (T&D) is considered as normal in traditional power grid [4], but with Smart Grid the TL in T&D is reduced to 4% to 6% [5], i.e., if the allocated energy is 10 kW for a particular smart meter, then 9.4–9.6 kW of electricity is expected to be used by the smart meter. Now, suppose a smart meter registered 9.55 kW of electricity usage and sends it to the DCU. The attacker captures the packet and modifies the data to 9.45 kW. Apparently, the modified amount is so negligible to the customer that it would not bother him while billing. The DCU would also not be able to detect any anomaly. On the other hand, if the attacker modifies 100 smart meters like this, then it would create a 10 kW Non-Technical Loss (NTL) in the system.

There can be two intentions behind this type of attack: the attacker can either maximize its personal gain by reducing its electricity usage by the same amount as stole from the neighboring meters, or just minimize utility's gain by introducing a generous amount of NTL in the system.

- Personal Gain: The attacker may reduce its usage statistics by X% and uniformly distribute this power consumption value among its neighboring Smart Meters. From the DCU's perspective, the total power consumed by the Smart Meters appears to be proportional to the Power allocated to that DCU. The energy theft goes undetected. Here, the utility company does not bear the brunt of the attack.
- Utility Loss: In this other type of attack, the attacker does not look for personal gains; but is rather motivated by a more malicious intent of inflicting

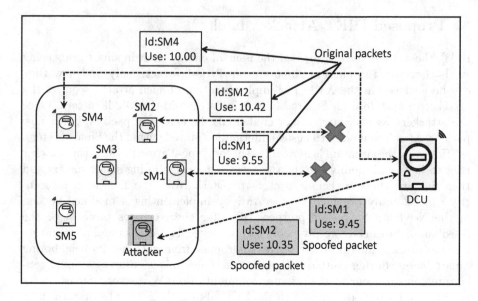

**Fig. 2.** DIET attack model.

financial losses to the utility. The attacker achieves this by considering the Technical Loss during Transmission and Distribution. It drops all packets from neighboring Smart Meters containing usage statistics and injects new packets having usage statistics slightly less than the original (within the TL threshold). The DCU interprets this as TL during T&D although consumers have consumed this power but have not been billed for the same.

Figure 2 explains our DIET attack scenario. Here, the attacker captures the data packets from SM 1 and 2, and modifies them slightly, so that it lies within the TL threshold and send them to the DCU. The transmission between SM 4 and DCU remains secure.

This attack will proved to be more effective in densely populated areas, where the attacker can have a huge number of smart meters as its neighbors Implementation of this attack become easier in a urban locality with numerous multi storied buildings, where a huge number of smart meters are placed across a long vertical line, but in a small horizontal section. As the attacker can access numerous SMs within its neighbor proximity, the scale of attack can be made more devastating in such scenarios.

## 4    Description of the Proposed IDS

In order to detect the DIET attack, we have proposed an IDS model. The detection mechanism will be performed in the cluster heads after certain time intervals. The IDS can detect Type-1 and Type-2 energy theft attacks. We assume that the Intrusion Detection System (IDS) will be running periodically with a time interval of 4 h.

## 4.1   Used Parameters in the IDS

We would first like to define the parameters used in the proposed IDS before explaining the working principle of our algorithm.

1. CH = Cluster Head.
2. SM = Smart Meter, $SM_i, SM_j$ denotes smart meters with MAC address i and j respectively.
3. $EU_{i,t}$ denotes the electricity usage of $SM_i$ at time $t$.
4. $\delta$ defines the allowed technical loss margin for each SM.
5. $EURec_t[i]$ defines the total electricity usage of $SM_i$ at time $t$ as recorded by the CH.
6. $NEU_{i,t}[j]$, denotes the electricity usage of SM with unique MAC address $j$, at time $t$ as stored at smart meter $i$.
7. $DEP\_VL_i$ denotes the *Dependability Factor* of $SM_i$.
8. DEP_TH denotes the threshold value for the *Dependability Factor*.
9. *Attacked Nodes* defines a list to store the SMs which have been attacked by the attacker.
10. *Negative Neighbors* of $SM_i$ is the list of neighbour nodes which causes an anomaly in the detection phase of the IDS.
11. *Possible attacker Node* holds the MAC address of those SMs which show abnormal behaviour in terms of stored information of its neighbor SMs.
12. *Attacker Nodes* contains the nodes which are detected as attacker.

## 4.2   Working Principle of Proposed IDS

The working principle of our algorithm can be divided into two phases: Data processing phase and Detection phase.

**Data Processing Phase:** In data processing phase, each SM in a cluster send its electricity usage data to the cluster head at 15 min interval. Besides, they also broadcast the same message over a separate channel, meant for only SMs in a cluster. Upon receiving this messages, each SM update itself regarding its neighbors' usage history. Cluster heads perform a preliminary detection at every 15 min, to detect type-1 attacks. Besides, CH also stores this periodic usage values in order to maintain a consistent usage log of each SM. The flow diagram of information for data processing phase of IDS, among various components in the AMI communication hierarchy is depicted in Fig. 3.

**Detection Phase:** We assume that the detection phase will execute at every 4 h instead of 15 min. The reason behind this is to reduce the packet transmission overhead and network congestion. At every 4th hour CH will request its SMs to send their $NEU_{i,t}[j]$ array. Upon receiving this packets from all the SMs, CH

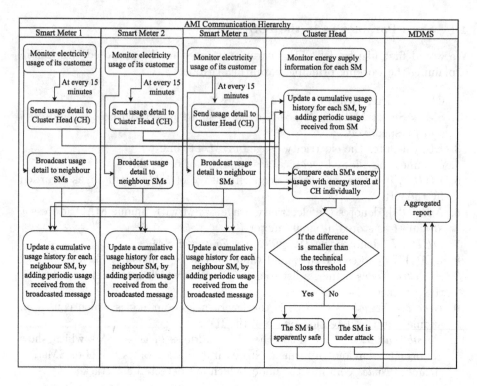

**Fig. 3.** Flow diagram for data processing phase of the proposed IDS.

extracts the neighbor information for each $SM_i$, and compares those values with $EURec_t[i]$. If all the neighbors' information match with $EURec_t[i]$, then $SM_i$ is marked as safe, otherwise, the CH marks $SM_i$ as *Attacked Node*. The CH then identifies the neighbors whose information matched with the stored information for $SM_i$ and marks those as *Matched Nodes*, and the other neighbors of $SM_i$ as, *Mismatched Nodes*. Now, the main idea of DIET attack is that the attacker is working alone. So, in case of an attack, the attacker's information will match with the recorded usage of $SM_i$, while the other neighbors will have a different information, but same collectively. Thus, the CH then compares the total numbers of *Matched Nodes* and *Mismatched Nodes* of $SM_i$ and marks the minority group as *Negative Neighbors*. The intersection of *Negative Neighbors* of all SMs in a cluster is detected as *Attacker Nodes*. Whereas, the other *Negative Neighbors* are marked as *Possible Attacker Nodes* and the CH decreases the *Dependability Value* of these nodes at each detection cycle. These nodes can unmark themselves by showcasing good behavior and gaining *Dependability Value* at next detection cycles, or can be marked as *Attacker Nodes* if the *Dependability Value* goes under the threshold level.

The detailed procedure for attack detection is described in Fig. 4.

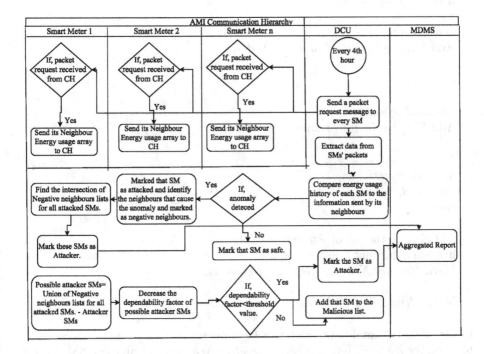

**Fig. 4.** Flow diagram for detection phase of the proposed IDS.

## 4.3 Algorithm for the Proposed IDS

The algorithm for both the phases of our proposed algorithm is described in this section. Step 1 of this algorithm defines the data processing phase and the rest of the part is used to detect DIET attack. Here $n$ is the total number of SMs under a Cluster Head and $m$ is the maximum number of neighbors for each individual SMs among $n$ SMs in the cluster

1. At every 15 min, when CH receives a $EU_{i,t}$ message from $SM_i$, it checks
   if $(ES_{i,t-1} - \delta <= EU_{i,t} <= (ES_{i,t-1}))$
   {
   then, apparently $SM_i$ is safe;
   $EURec_t[i] = EURec_{t-1}[i] + EU_{i,t}$;
   }
   else, $SM_i$ is under attack;
2. After every 4 h, CH will ask its SMs to send their NEU array;
3. After receiving all the arrays, CH checks
   for(i = 1 to n)
   for(j = 1 to m)

{
if $(EURec_t[i] == NEU_{j,t}[i])$
{
match_count++;
Add $SM_j$ to the list of *Matched Nodes*;
}
else
{
mismatch_count++;
Add $SM_j$ to the list of *Mismatched Nodes*;
}
}

4. if(match_count==m)
   then, $SM_i$ is safe;
   else,
   {
   add $SM_i$ to the list of *Attacked Nodes*;
   if(mismatch_count > match_count)
   Mark *Matched Nodes* as *Negative Neighbors*;
   else
   Mark *Mismatched Nodes* as *Negative Neighbors*;
   }

5. Let, $r$ be the total number of attacked nodes;

6. *Attacker Nodes* = Intersection of *Negative Neighbors* for all the $r$ SMs in the list *Attacked Nodes*;

7. *Possible Attacker Node* = Union of *Negative Neighbors* for all the $r$ SMs in the list *Attacked Nodes* − *Attacker Nodes*;

8. Decrease the DEP_VL of every SMs in *Possible Attacker Node* list.
   if, $DEP\_VL_x <$ DEP_TH
   Mark $SM_x$ as *Attacker Node*;
   else
   Add $SM_x$ to the list of *Malicious Nodes*;

9. End.

Once, the algorithm detects the attacker nodes and put them in *Attacker Nodes* list, the CH, then checks the *Attacked Nodes* list and replace their forged energy usage values by the original usage statistics with the help of its neighbors' information.

## 5   Simulation Results

We have implemented The DIET attack and the proposed IDS in Qualnet 5.2. The simulation settings and the used scenario are described in Table 1.

**Table 1.** Parameter settings for simulation environment

| Parameter | Value |
|---|---|
| Experimental area | $1500 * 1500m^2$ |
| Running time for each simulation | 100 s |
| Mac layer protocol | DCF of IEEE 802.11b standard |
| Network layer protocol | AODV |
| Traffic model | CBR |
| Number of CBR traffics | 10% of the total number of nodes |
| Cluster head : Smart meter | 1 : 10 |

## 5.1 DIET Attack Simulation

Firstly, the DIET attack is implemented and the results are analyzed. We have considered varying node density of 11 to 55 nodes for our experiment. Data has been collected for every variation and then the averaged values are plotted in the graph. In order to implement DIET attack, we assumed that each Cluster Head can have atmost 10 SMs under its surveillance, and the energy supplied to these SMs is remained fixed at 10 kW. $\delta$ is defined as 5% of supplied energy, i.e., 0.5 kW.

Figure 5 depicts the allowed, original and registered TL for implemented DIET attack. Energy theft = (registered TL − original TL). Now, the registered TL is still under the threshold of allowed TL, thats why the theft can not be detected by the system.

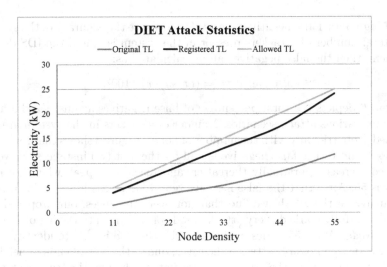

**Fig. 5.** Original technical loss and registered technical loss for DIET attack with varying node density.

## 5.2   IDS Implementation

In order to evaluate the performance of our proposed algorithm, we have considered three metrics: false positive, false negative and detection efficiency. False negative and false positive are both very important metric towards Smart Grid. Identify a legitimate SM as an attacker (false positive) can harm the customers', as well as utility's reputation and cause for temporarily disruption of service for that innocent customer. On the other hand, not being able to identify an attacker can lead to financial loss, malicious billing and can even cause havoc devastation.

We have considered four different attack scenarios to evaluate our algorithm.

- **Attack Scenario A** has 100% of DIET attacks, i.e., where an attacker modifies its neighbor SMs usage data, but within the TL threshold. We assume that typical Type-1 and Type-2 attacks are not present for this situation.
- **Attack Scenario B** has 50% of DIET attackers and another 50% of both Type-1 and Type-2 attackers.
- **Attack Scenario C** has 25% of DIET attackers and another 75% of both Type-1 and Type-2 attackers.
- **Attack Scenario D** has equal share of all the three attackers, i.e., 33.33% of DIET, Type-1 and Type-2 attackers.

**False Positive:** Our proposed algorithm does not identify any false positives for our entire simulation time with various node density and number of attackers It only detects genuine attackers and put them in *Attacker Nodes* list. However, it adds some genuine SMs in *Possible Attacker Nodes* list and decreases the DEP_VL for those nodes at some iterations.

**False Negative:** False negatives are used to measure the accuracy of the system. If the total number of attackers present in the system is $x$, and the IDS detects $y$ of them, then the false negative can be calculated as:

$$\text{False Negative} = ((x-y)/x) * 100\%$$

Figure 6 depicts the total percentage of false negatives against varying node density for various attack scenarios. Number of attackers in the system are also increased proportionally with the number of nodes. Figure 6 shows that for attack scenario A and C, the false negative is null for the first two instances. However, it started increasing gradually thereafter, and reaches its peak when the node density is 55. After that the false negative tend to decrease in scenario A. Now, while analyzing the graph, we find that, for every instances, our proposed IDS either successfully marked every attacker node or add them to the list of *Possible attacker Nodes*. With 55 nodes in the scenario, the IDS is able to identify every attacker node as a possible attacker, however, due to the lack of enough neighbor support, it cannot mark the attackers immediately Though, the trust evaluation process will help them detect gradually. Thus, we can confirm that our proposed system can eventually detect all the attackers.

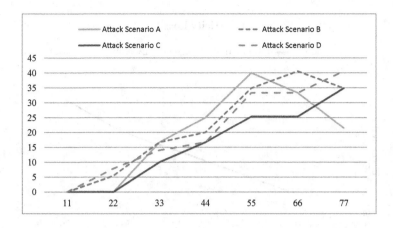

**Fig. 6.** False negatives vs Node density for different attack scenarios.

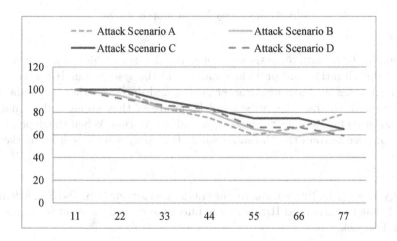

**Fig. 7.** Detection efficiency vs Node density for different attack scenarios.

**Detection Efficiency:** Detection efficiency can simply be calculated as, (100 - false negative), provided there is no false positives in the system.

Figure 7 shows the detection efficiency of our IDS. Since there is no false positives in our IDS, the graph for detection efficiency is simple reciprocal of false negative.

The detection efficiency for our proposed IDS remains 100% for smaller number of nodes (i.e., up to 22 nodes for our simulation scenario.). However, with increasing number of nodes and attackers, the detection efficiency tends to decrease gradually. The detection mechanism of our proposed IDS depends heavily on the anomalies in the data provided by SMs in a neighborhood. With fewer nodes in the scenario, it will be easier to analysis the data and hence the detection of an attacker. On the contrary, when the node density increases, it affects

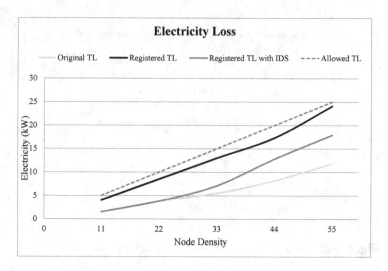

**Fig. 8.** Electricity loss in proposed IDS.

the complexity of data analysis and hence the detection efficiency. However, to address this situation and provide a stability in the system, our IDS marked all suspicious nodes as *Possible Attacker Nodes*, and decreases their dependability factor as well, so that the system can be aware of that nodes and do not let those nodes to further affect the decision making process. When the dependability factor goes beyond the threshold value, then only a node will be marked as attacker.

**Energy Loss:** Finally we measure the energy loss for our IDS, and Fig. 8 demonstrated that the proposed IDS is successfully able reduce the electricity loss due to DIET attack.

**Comparison with Existing Works:** In this section, we have done a detailed comparative analysis of our proposed IDS with a specification based IDS proposed in [22]. In this paper, authors deployed sensors in NAN to monitor the communication network and detect malicious activities in the AMI based on formal verification of the specifications and monitoring operations. Authors claimed that the proposed IDS can detect both known and unknown attacks in network level, including MITM, black hole attack etc. Since, our proposed IDS handles DIET attack, which in turn associates with MITM and stealing of meter data credential attacks, we consider the IDS, proposed in [22] as an appropriate choice for comparison. We have implemented the IDS of [22] for different attack scenarios, as mentioned in Sect. 5.2.

Figure 9 provides the comparative analysis of our proposed IDS and specification based IDS proposed in [22]. We have considered the performance of both the algorithms for four different attack scenarios and with seven different node

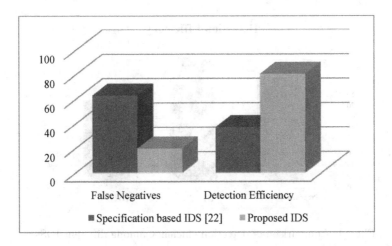

**Fig. 9.** Comparative results of false negatives and detection efficiency.

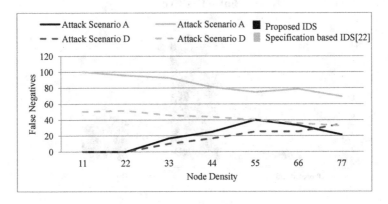

**Fig. 10.** Comparative analysis for different attack scenarios.

densities over 11 nodes to 77 nodes, and then averaged the results. The IDS in [22] monitors the state of communication network and verifies with existing specification rules. It does not consider the content of packets transmitted over the network, rather it keeps tab of total packet received and sent, time stamps of different events, frequency of packet transmission etc. Thus, it cannot detect Type-I attack, as in this case, a SM modifies its own packets and transmits them. On the other hand, in DIET attack, a SM steals its neighbor SMs' credentials, manipulates their meter data within tolerance level and retransmits to the DA. Thus, at the end points, the packet received and sent metrics for a particular SM will remain unaltered. Hence the attack will remain undetected. However, when node density increases, so does the traffic and if the sensors detect an abnormally large number of packet transmission on a particular channel, then it can detect the attack sometimes. However, for typical Type-II attack, the attack can be detected by considering cumulative energy usage parameters.

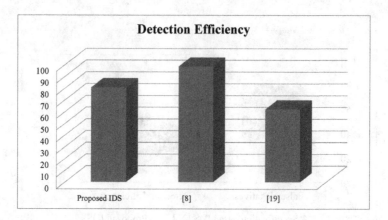

**Fig. 11.** Comparison of detection efficiency among different IDSs.

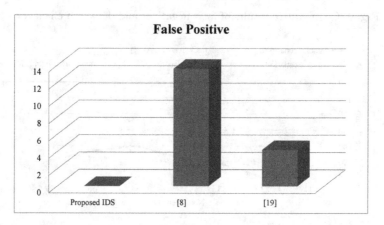

**Fig. 12.** Comparison of false positives among different IDSs.

Figure 10 gives the performance of two IDSs for attack scenario A and D. In attack scenario A, our proposed IDS performs much better than the other one. Specification based IDS [22] performs better with increased node density. Still it never performs like our proposed IDS. However, for attack scenario D, the IDS of [22] performs much better, but still the false negatives are much higher than our proposed IDS.

We have compared the performance our IDS with other existing IDSs. Figures 11 and 12 provide comparative analysis of our proposed IDS and two existing IDSs based on SVM [8] and ARMA-GLR [19] models respectively. Now, our proposed IDS offers better detection efficiency than [8], however, Fig. 11 shows that the [19] performs much better than our IDS. On the other hand Fig. 12 shows that both [8,19] have false positives, where our IDS has none.

As we already mentioned, false positives and false negatives are two important metrics to evaluate the performance of any IDS. Now, energy theft is an attack scenario which involves the customers directly. The attackers disguised themselves as customers. So we have to give extra care to detect attackers. False positives may harm the reputation of genuine customers, which incurs in bad reputation for the utilities. Thus, while dealing with energy theft attack, false positives are much more important than false negatives. Thus we designed our IDS in such a manner that it marks a node as attacker only after being 100% sure of that. Otherwise, it can mark suspicious nodes as possible attackers, and monitor their further behavior. This in turn justifies the results of Figs. 11 and 12.

# 6  Conclusions

Smart grid and especially AMI system enhances the efficiency, reliability, stability, security and economic facilities of traditional power grid systems. Advanced metering infrastructure (AMI) is arguably the most important and critical part of Smart Grid. AMI deals with the most sensitive informations in the Grid and transmits them through the network. There already exist a good number of security solutions for AMI. However the percentage of security attacks are also increasing day by day, and so does the innovative and intelligent ideas behind those attacks.

Energy theft is always a serious concern for power industry. With traditional power grid, tapping, physical tampering of meters are the common sources to theft. Smart Grid and AMI can mitigate these attacks, however, with the recent advancement in the technology, the attackers also invent newer and sophisticated ideas to attack the grid. In this paper, we have proposed a new attack situation named, DIET attack. Simultaneously, we have simulated this attack in QUALNET and analyze the effect on the grid. In order to detect DIET attack, we have proposed an advanced IDS.

Our IDS can successfully detect Type-1 and Type-2 attacks. Moreover, for some scenarios, the IDS cannot detect the attacker primarily, but it is been able to mark all of them as *Possible Attacker* and take precautionary measures against them. If those nodes continue to being malicious, then eventually the proposed IDS detect that node as attacker, otherwise, in case of a genuine node, the dependability factor will be increased with positive behavior. Besides, there exists lots of works for detecting energy theft, many of them are only capable to detect whether a theft happened or not. On the contrary, the proposed IDS can not only identify an intelligent theft situation, but can detect the attackers and mark possible attackers in the network as well.

As a future extension of this paper, we would like to merge our idea with some secure routing protocols like [6], where trust based evolution of nodes are performed for route selection to ensure a secure communication system. The collaboration of the proposed IDS with this type of routing protocols will confirm security from DIET attack at transmission time and improve the performance of the system, in terms of detection efficiency and false negatives.

**Acknowledgments.** This work is a part of the Ph.D. work of the author, a Senior Research Fellow of Council of Scientific & Industrial Research (CSIR), Government of India. We would like to acknowledge CSIR, for providing the support required for carrying out the research work.

# References

1. Jiang, R., Lu, R., Wang, Y., Luo, J., Shen, C., Shen, X.S.: Energy-theft detection issues for advanced metering infrastructure in smart grid. Tsinghua Sci. Technol. **19**(2), 105–120 (2014)
2. Grochocki, D., Huh, J.H., Berthier, R., Bobba, R., Sanders, W.H., Crdenas, A.A., Jetcheva, J.G.: AMI threats, intrusion detection requirements and deployment recommendations. In: Smart Grid Communications (SmartGridComm), pp. 395–400. IEEE (2012)
3. McLaughlin, S., Podkuiko, D., McDaniel, P.: Energy theft in the advanced metering infrastructure. In: Rome, E., Bloomfield, R. (eds.) CRITIS 2009. LNCS, vol. 6027, pp. 176–187. Springer, Heidelberg (2010). https://doi.org/10.1007/978-3-642-14379-3_15
4. ABB Inc.: Energy Efficiency in the Power Grid. ABB Inc., Fort Smith (2007)
5. U.S. Energy Information Administration. www.eia.gov
6. Chakraborty, M., Deb, N., Chaki, N.: POMSec: Pseudo-opportunistic, multipath secured routing protocol for communications in smart grid. In: Saeed, K., Homenda, W., Chaki, R. (eds.) CISIM 2017. LNCS, vol. 10244, pp. 264–276. Springer, Cham (2017). https://doi.org/10.1007/978-3-319-59105-6_23
7. Chakraborty, M., Chaki, N.: An IPv6 based hierarchical address configuration scheme for smart grid. In: Applications and Innovations in Mobile Computing (AIMoC), Kolkata, pp. 109–116 (2015). https://doi.org/10.1109/AIMOC.2015.7083838
8. Nagi, J., Yap, K.S., Tiong, S.K., Ahmed, S.K., Mohamad, M.: Nontechnical loss detection for metered customers in power utility using support vector machines. IEEE Trans. Power Deliv. **25**(2), 1162–1171 (2010)
9. Depuru, S., Wang, L., Devabhaktuni, V.: Support vector machine based data classification for detection of electricity theft. In: IEEE/PES Power Systems Conference and Exposition (PSCE), pp. 1–8 (2011)
10. Depuru, S., Wang, L., Devabhaktuni, V., Green, R.C.: High performance computing for detection of electricity theft. Int. J. Electr. Power Energy Syst. **47**, 21–30 (2013)
11. McLaughlin, S., Holbert, B., Zonouz, S., Berthier, R.: AMIDS: A multi-sensor energy theft detection framework for advanced metering infrastructures. In: IEEE Third International Conference on Smart Grid Communications (SmartGridComm), pp. 354–359 (2012)
12. Khoo, B., Cheng, Y.: Using RFID for anti-theft in a Chinese electrical supply company: A cost-benefit analysis. In: IEEE Wireless Telecommunications Symposium (WTS), pp. 1–6 (2011)
13. Xiao, Z., Xiao, Y., Du, D.H.C.: Non-repudiation in neighborhood area networks for smart grid. IEEE Commun. Mag. **51**(1), 18–26 (2013)
14. Amin, S., Schwartz, G.A., Tembine, H.: Incentives and security in electricity distribution networks. In: Grossklags, J., Walrand, J. (eds.) GameSec 2012. LNCS, vol. 7638, pp. 264–280. Springer, Heidelberg (2012). https://doi.org/10.1007/978-3-642-34266-0_16

15. Cardenas, A.A., Amin, S., Schwartz, G., Dong, R., Sastry, S.: A game theory model for electricity theft detection and privacy-aware control in AMI systems. In: IEEE 50th Annual Allerton Conference on Communication, Control, and Computing (Allerton), pp. 1830–1837 (2012)
16. QualNet 5.2 Simulator: Scalable network technologies Inc.
17. Kim, M.: A survey on guaranteeing availability in smart grid communications. In: Advanced Communication Technology (ICACT), pp. 314–317 (2012)
18. Stallings, W.: Cryptography and Network Security: Principles and Practice, 5th edn. Prentice Hall Press, Upper Saddle River (2010). ISBN: 0136097049 9780136097044
19. Mashima, D., Cárdenas, A.A.: Evaluating electricity theft detectors in smart grid networks. In: Balzarotti, D., Stolfo, S.J., Cova, M. (eds.) RAID 2012. LNCS, vol. 7462, pp. 210–229. Springer, Heidelberg (2012). https://doi.org/10.1007/978-3-642-33338-5_11
20. Jokar, P., Arianpoo, N., Leung, V.C.M.: Electricity theft detection in AMI using customers consumption patterns. IEEE Trans. Smart Grid 7(1), 216–226 (2016)
21. Ruppe, R., Griswald, S., Walsh, P., Martin, R.: Near Term Digital Radio (NTDR) system. In: MILCOM 1997, pp. 1282–1287 (1997)
22. Berthier, R., Sanders, W.H.: Specification-based intrusion detection for advanced metering infrastructures. In: IEEE 17th Pacific Rim International Symposium on Dependable Computing, pp. 184–193 (2011)

# Combining Symbolic and Numerical Domains
# for Information Leakage Analysis

Agostino Cortesi[1]([⊠]) [iD], Pietro Ferrara[2], Raju Halder[3], and Matteo Zanioli[4]

[1] Ca' Foscari University, Venice, Italy
cortesi@unive.it
[2] Julia srl, Verona, Italy
[3] Indian Institute of Technology Patna, Patna, India
[4] Alpenite srl, Venice, Italy

**Abstract.** We introduce an abstract domain for information-flow analysis of software. The proposal combines variable dependency analysis with numerical abstractions, yielding to accuracy and efficiency improvements. We apply the full power of the proposal to the case of database query languages as well. Finally, we present an implementation of the analysis, called Sails, as an instance of a generic static analyzer. Keeping the modular construction of the analysis, the tool allows one to tune the granularity of heap analysis and to choose the numerical domain involved in the reduced product. This way the user can tune the information leakage analysis at different levels of precision and efficiency.

## 1 Introduction

Protecting the confidentiality is a relevant problem when sensitive information flows through computing systems or transmits over public networks. Standard protection mechanisms, such as encryption, access control, etc. can suitably be applied at source level, but they are unable to protect the confidentiality once the information is released from the source and is allowed to flow through the computing systems.

The starting point of secure information flow analysis in software applications is the classification of program variables into different security levels. In the simplest case, two levels are commonly used: public (or low, $L$) and secret (or high, $H$). The main purpose is to prevent the leakage of sensitive information when flowing (implicitly or explicitly) from a high variable $h$ to a lower one $l$. An explicit flow from $h$ to $l$ occurs when the content of $h$ directly affects (e.g., through an assignment operator) $l$. On the other hand, an implicit flow from $h$ to $l$ occurs when the content of $l$ gets affected indirectly (e.g., through a boolean condition in an if statement) by $h$, as stated in [16].

There is a widespread literature on methods and techniques for checking secure information flows in software. Generally, works on information flow fall into two categories: ($i$) dynamic, instrumentation based approaches (*e.g.*, tainting), and ($ii$) static, language-based approaches (*e.g.*, type systems). The dynamic approaches

M. L. Gavrilova et al. (Eds.): Trans. on Comput. Sci. XXXI, LNCS 10730, pp. 98–135, 2018.
https://doi.org/10.1007/978-3-662-56499-8_6

introduce significant run-time overhead [10,31]. The static approaches typically require some changes to the language and the run-time environment as well as non-trivial type annotations [36], making their adoption too expensive in practice.

Nevertheless, despite of these deep and extensive works, their practical applications have been relatively poor. Usually these approaches work on an ad-hoc programming language [4], and they do not support mainstream languages. This means that one should completely rewrite a program in order to apply them to some existing code.

Recently a new generic static analyzer (Sample[1]) based on the Abstract Interpretation theory has been developed and applied to many different contexts and analysis. Roughly, this analyzer splits and combines the abstraction of the heap and the approximation of other semantic information, e.g. string [12], type [18] abstractions.

In this paper[2], we introduce a language-based information-flow analysis of imperative and database query languages based on the Abstract Interpretation framework, by combining symbolic and numerical domains; we present the tool Sails (Static Analysis of Information Leakage with Sample); finally, we show experimental results applying Sails on security benchmark programs.

In particular,

1. we represent variables' dependences in the form of propositional formula $\psi = x \rightarrow y$, where $x$, $y$ are variables and value of $y$ possibly depend on the value of $x$; in order to detect possible information leakage, we check the satisfiability of $\psi$ when assigning each variable the truth value corresponding to its sensitivity level;
2. we define abstract semantics of ($i$) imperative and ($ii$) database query languages in the domain of propositional formulae, by considering an over-approximation of variables' dependences at each program point;
3. we enhance the accuracy of the technique by analysing programs over numerical abstract domains, using reduced product of the symbolic propositional formulae domain and numerical abstract domains;
4. finally, we show encouraging experimental results on a set of security benchmarks using the tool Sails which is implemented based on our proposal.

The overall analysis combines a symbolic variable dependency analysis, based on the propositional formulae domain [11], and a variable value dependency analysis using numerical abstractions (e.g., intervals or polyhedra). Unlike other works, our proposal provides an information flow analysis without any major constraint on the target language, since it tracks information flows between variables and heap locations over programs written in mainstream object-oriented languages like Java and Scala.

The rest of the paper is organized as follows. Section 2 introduces the dependency analysis through the propositional formulae domain. Section 3 combines the dependency analysis with numerical domains through a reduced product.

---

[1] http://www.pm.inf.ethz.ch/research/semper/Sample.

[2] The paper is a revised and extended version of [24,45,46].

An extension to the case of database query languages is discussed in Sect. 4. Section 5 presents the main issues we solved in order to plug this information flow analysis into Sample while developing Sails. Section 6 presents the experimental results when applying Sails to a complex case study and to the SecuriBench-micro suite. Finally, Sect. 7 presents the related work and Sect. 8 concludes.

## 2    Dependency Analysis

This section formalizes the dependency analysis and proves its soundness following the abstract interpretation framework.

### 2.1    The Language

For the sake of simplicity, we consider a simple imperative language where programs consist of labeled commands (similar to [25]). The syntax is defined in Table 1[3].

Table 1. Syntax of the language

| Expressions | | | |
|---|---|---|---|
| exp | $\in$ | E | |
| exp | ::= | $n$ | where $n \in \mathbb{N}$ |
| | \| | v | |
| | \| | $exp_1 \oplus exp_2$ | where $\oplus = \{+, -, *, /\}$ |
| **Conditions** | | | |
| b | $\in$ | B | |
| b | ::= | true | |
| | \| | false | |
| | \| | $b_1 \otimes b_2$ | where $\otimes = \{\vee, \wedge\}$ |
| | \| | $\neg b$ | |
| | \| | $exp_1 \oslash exp_2$ | where $\oslash = \{\leq, >, =\}$ |
| **Labeled commands** | | | |
| $\ell$ | $\in$ | L | set of labels |
| c | $\in$ | C | |
| c | ::= | $^\ell$skip | |
| | \| | $^\ell$v := exp | |
| | \| | if $^\ell$b then $c_1$ else $c_2$ $^{\ell'}$endif | |
| | \| | $c_1 ; c_2$ | |
| | \| | while $^\ell$b do c $^{\ell'}$done | |
| $\mathcal{P}$ | ::= | $c^\ell$ | program that ends with label $\ell$ |

---

[3] In the rest of the paper, we will omit the initial and final labels of statements when not required.

**Table 2.** Initial label function

$$in[\![^\ell\text{skip}]\!] \stackrel{\text{def}}{=} \ell$$
$$in[\![^\ell\text{v} := \text{exp}]\!] \stackrel{\text{def}}{=} \ell$$
$$in[\![\text{if } ^\ell\text{b then } c_1 \text{ else } c_2 \; ^{\ell'}\text{endif}]\!] \stackrel{\text{def}}{=} \ell$$
$$in[\![c_1; c_2]\!] \stackrel{\text{def}}{=} in[\![c_1]\!]$$
$$in[\![\text{while } ^\ell\text{b do } c \; ^{\ell'}\text{done}]\!] \stackrel{\text{def}}{=} \ell$$

**Table 3.** Final label function

| $\mathcal{P} ::= c^\ell$ | $fin[\![\mathcal{P}]\!] \equiv \ell$ |
|---|---|
| | $fin[\![c]\!] \equiv fin[\![\mathcal{P}]\!]$ |
| $c ::= {}^\ell\text{skip}$ | $fin[\![^\ell\text{skip}]\!] \equiv fin[\![c]\!]$ |
| $\quad\mid\; {}^\ell\text{v} := \text{exp}$ | $fin[\![^\ell\text{v} := \text{exp}]\!] \equiv fin[\![c]\!]$ |
| $\quad\mid\; \text{if } ^\ell\text{b then } c_1 \text{ else } c_2 \; ^{\ell'}\text{endif}$ | $fin[\![\text{if } ^\ell\text{b then } c_1 \text{ else } c_2 \; ^{\ell'}\text{endif}]\!] \equiv fin[\![c]\!]$ |
| | $fin[\![c_1]\!] \equiv \ell'$ |
| | $fin[\![c_2]\!] \equiv \ell'$ |
| $\quad\mid\; c_1; c_2$ | $fin[\![c_1; c_2]\!] \equiv fin[\![c]\!]$ |
| | $fin[\![c_1]\!] \equiv in[\![c_2]\!]$ |
| | $fin[\![c_2]\!] \equiv fin[\![c]\!]$ |
| $\quad\mid\; \text{while } ^\ell\text{b do } c \; ^{\ell'}\text{done}$ | $fin[\![\text{while } ^\ell\text{b do } c \text{ done}]\!] \equiv fin[\![c]\!]$ |
| | $fin[\![c]\!] \equiv \ell$ |

**Table 4.** Action function

$$a[\![^\ell\text{skip}]\!] \stackrel{\text{def}}{=} \{^\ell skip\}$$
$$a[\![^\ell\text{v} := \text{exp}]\!] \stackrel{\text{def}}{=} \{^\ell\text{v} := \text{exp}\}$$
$$a[\![\text{if } ^\ell\text{b then } c_1 \text{ else } c_2 \; ^{\ell'}\text{endif}]\!] \stackrel{\text{def}}{=} \{^\ell b, \; ^\ell\text{not b}, ^{\ell'} \text{endif}\} \cup a[\![c_1]\!] \cup a[\![c_2]\!]$$
$$a[\![c_1; c_2]\!] \stackrel{\text{def}}{=} a[\![c_1]\!] \cup a[\![c_2]\!]$$
$$a[\![\text{while } ^\ell\text{b do } c \; ^{\ell'}\text{done}]\!] \stackrel{\text{def}}{=} \{^\ell b, ^\ell \text{not b}, ^{\ell'} \text{done}\} \cup a[\![c]\!]$$

Let $in : \mathsf{C} \to \mathsf{L}$ and $fin : \mathsf{C} \to \mathsf{L}$ be two functions. By $in[\![c]\!]$ and $fin[\![c]\!]$ we denote the *initial* and *final label* of command $c \in \mathsf{C}$ respectively. These two functions are formally defined in Tables 2 and 3.

Each command corresponds to one or more *actions*. The set of actions, denoted by $\mathsf{A}$, consists of $\{^\ell\text{skip}, {}^\ell\text{v} := \text{exp}, {}^\ell b, {}^\ell\neg b, {}^\ell\text{endif}, {}^\ell\text{done}\}$. Let $a : \mathsf{C} \to \wp(\mathsf{A})$ be a function that, given a command, returns the set of actions involved in it. The function $a$ for various commands is defined in Table 4.

Without loss of generality, we assume that the variables appearing in a program are implicitly declared. We denote by $\mathsf{V}(\mathcal{P})$ the set of variables in program $\mathcal{P}$ and, similarly, by $\mathsf{V}(\text{exp})$ and $\mathsf{V}(b)$ the variables contained in expression exp and condition $b$ respectively. The definition of $\mathsf{V}$ is reported in Table 5.

**Table 5.** Variables functions

| |
|:---:|
| $V(n) \stackrel{\text{def}}{=} \emptyset$ |
| $V(v) \stackrel{\text{def}}{=} \{v\}$ |
| $V(\exp_1 \oplus \exp_2) \stackrel{\text{def}}{=} V(\exp_1) \cup V(\exp_2)$ |
| $V(\text{true}) \stackrel{\text{def}}{=} \emptyset$ |
| $V(\text{false}) \stackrel{\text{def}}{=} \emptyset$ |
| $V(b_1 \otimes b_2) \stackrel{\text{def}}{=} V(b_1) \cup V(b_2)$ |
| $V(\exp_1 \oslash \exp_2) \stackrel{\text{def}}{=} V(\exp_1) \cup V(\exp_2)$ |
| $V(\text{skip}) \stackrel{\text{def}}{=} \emptyset$ |
| $V(v := \exp) \stackrel{\text{def}}{=} \{v\} \cup V(\exp)$ |
| $V(\text{if } b \text{ then } c_1 \text{ else } c_2 \text{ endif}) \stackrel{\text{def}}{=} V(b) \cup V(c_1) \cup V(c_2)$ |
| $V(c_1; c_2) \stackrel{\text{def}}{=} V(c_1) \cup V(c_2)$ |
| $V(\text{while } b \text{ do } c \text{ done}) \stackrel{\text{def}}{=} V(b) \cup V(c)$ |

**Table 6.** Evaluation of expressions

| |
|:---:|
| $E \in E \rightarrow (\mathcal{E} \rightarrow \mathbb{N})$ |
| $E[\![n]\!]\rho \stackrel{\text{def}}{=} n$ |
| $E[\![v]\!]\rho \stackrel{\text{def}}{=} \rho(v)$ |
| $E[\![\exp_1 \oplus \exp_2]\!]\rho \equiv v_1 \oplus v_2$ (such that $v_1 = E[\![\exp_1]\!]\rho \wedge v_2 = E[\![\exp_2]\!]\rho$) |

**Table 7.** Evaluation of boolean conditions

| |
|:---:|
| $B \in B \rightarrow (\mathcal{E} \rightarrow \{\text{true}, \text{false}\})$ |
| $B[\![\text{true}]\!]\rho \stackrel{\text{def}}{=} \text{true}$ |
| $B[\![\text{false}]\!]\rho \stackrel{\text{def}}{=} \text{false}$ |
| $B[\![b_1 \otimes b_2]\!]\rho \stackrel{\text{def}}{=} b_1 \otimes b_2$ (such that $b_1 = B[\![b_1]\!]\rho \wedge b_2 = B[\![b_2]\!]\rho$) |
| $B[\![\exp_1 \oslash \exp_2]\!]\rho \stackrel{\text{def}}{=} \text{true if } \exists v_1 = E[\![\exp_1]\!]\rho : v_2 = E[\![\exp_2]\!]\rho : v_1 \oslash v_2$ |
| $\text{false if } \exists v_1 = E[\![\exp_1]\!]\rho : v_2 = E[\![\exp_2]\!]\rho : \text{not}(v_1 \oslash v_2)$ |

## 2.2 The Concrete Domain

An *environment* $\rho \in \mathcal{E}$ is a function $\rho : V \rightarrow \mathbb{N}$ which assigns a value to each variable. A *state* $\sigma \in \Sigma = (L \times \mathcal{E})$ is a pair $\langle \ell, \rho \rangle$ where the program label $\ell$ is the label of the action to be executed and the environment $\rho$ defines the values of program variables at $\ell$.

We denote by $E[\![\exp]\!]\sigma$ and $B[\![b]\!]\sigma$ the evaluation of expression $\exp \in E$ and condition $b \in B$ respectively on the state $\sigma$. The details can be found in Tables 6 and 7 respectively.

Given a program $\mathcal{P}$, the set of possible initial and final states are defined as $I[\![\mathcal{P}]\!] \equiv \{ \langle in[\![\mathcal{P}]\!], \rho \rangle \mid \rho \in \mathcal{E} \}$ and $F[\![\mathcal{P}]\!] \equiv \{ \langle fin[\![\mathcal{P}]\!], \rho \rangle \mid \rho \in \mathcal{E} \}$.

**Table 8.** The transition function

$$T[\![^\ell skip^{\ell_1}]\!] = \{\langle\ell,\rho\rangle \xrightarrow{\ell skip^{\ell_1}} \langle fin[\![^\ell skip^{\ell_1}]\!],\rho\rangle \mid \rho \in \mathcal{E}\}$$

$$T[\![^\ell v := exp^{\ell_1}]\!] = \{\langle\ell,\rho\rangle \xrightarrow{\ell v:=exp^{\ell_1}} \langle fin[\![^\ell v := exp^{\ell_1}]\!],\rho[v \leftarrow v]\rangle \mid \rho \in \mathcal{E} \wedge v = E[\![exp]\!]\rho\}$$

$$T[\![if\ ^\ell b\ then\ c_1\ else\ c_2\ ^{\ell'}endif^{\ell_1}]\!] = T[\![c_1]\!] \cup T[\![c_2]\!]\cup$$

$$\{\langle\ell,\rho\rangle \xrightarrow{\ell b} \langle in[\![c_1]\!],\rho\rangle \mid \rho \in \mathcal{E} \wedge true = B[\![b]\!]\rho\}\cup$$

$$\{\langle\ell,\rho\rangle \xrightarrow{\ell not\ b} \langle in[\![c_2]\!],\rho\rangle \mid \rho \in \mathcal{E} \wedge false = B[\![b]\!]\rho\}\cup$$

$$\{\langle\ell',\rho\rangle \xrightarrow{\ell' endif^{\ell_1}} \langle fin[\![if\ ^\ell b\ then\ c_1\ else\ c_2\ ^{\ell'}endif^{\ell_1}]\!],\rho\rangle \mid \rho \in \mathcal{E}\}$$

$$T[\![c_1;c_2]\!] = T[\![c_1]\!] \cup T[\![c_2]\!]$$

$$T[\![while\ ^\ell b\ do\ c\ ^{\ell'}done^{\ell_1}]\!] = \{\langle\ell,\rho\rangle \xrightarrow{\ell not\ b} \langle\ell',\rho\rangle \mid \rho \in \mathcal{E} \wedge false = B[\![b]\!]\rho\}\cup$$

$$\{\langle\ell,\rho\rangle \xrightarrow{\ell b} \langle in[\![c]\!],\rho\rangle \mid \rho \in \mathcal{E} \wedge true = B[\![b]\!]\rho\} \cup T[\![c]\!]\cup$$

$$\{\langle\ell',\rho\rangle \xrightarrow{\ell' done} \langle fin[\![while\ ^\ell b\ do\ c\ ^{\ell'}done^{\ell_1}]\!],\rho\rangle \mid \rho \in \mathcal{E}\}$$

The *labeled transition semantics* $T[\![c]\!]$ of a command $c \in \mathcal{P}$ is a set of transitions $\langle\sigma_1, a, \sigma_2\rangle$ between a state $\sigma_1$ and its next states $\sigma_2$ by an action $a \in a(c)$. The triple $\langle\sigma_1, a, \sigma_2\rangle$ is also denoted by $\sigma_1 \xrightarrow{a} \sigma_2$. The transition function $T : C \to \wp(\Sigma \times A \times \Sigma)$ in Table 8 tracks all reachable states.

A *labeled transition system* is a tuple $\langle\Sigma, I, F, A, T\rangle$, where $\Sigma$ is the set of states, $I \subseteq \Sigma$ is a nonempty set of initial states, $F \subseteq \Sigma$ is a set of final states, $A$ is a nonempty set of actions, and $T \in \wp(\Sigma \times A \times \Sigma)$ is the labeled transition relation.

We define the *partial trace semantics* of a transition system, similarly to [25], as the set of all possible traces of elements in $\Sigma$ (denoted by $\Sigma^\star$), recording the observation of executions starting from initial states and possibly reaching final states in finite time.

$$\Sigma^\star \in \wp(\Sigma \times A \times \Sigma)$$

$$\Sigma^\star = \{\sigma_0 \xrightarrow{a_0} \dots \xrightarrow{a_{n-1}} \sigma_n \mid n \geq 1 \wedge \sigma_0 \in I \wedge \forall i \in [0, n-1] : \sigma_i \xrightarrow{a_i} \sigma_{i+1} \in T^\ell\}$$

Let $\pi_0, \pi_1 \in \Sigma^\star$ be two partial traces. We define the following lattice operators:

- $\pi_0 \preceq \pi_1$ if and only if $\pi_0$ is a subtrace of $\pi_1$,
- $\pi_0 \curlywedge \pi_1 = \pi$ such that $(\pi \preceq \pi_1) \wedge (\pi \preceq \pi_2)$ and $(\forall\pi' : (\pi' \preceq \pi_1) \wedge (\pi' \preceq \pi_2)).\pi' \preceq \pi$.

$\Sigma^\star$ equipped with the order relation "$\preceq$" and the meet operator "$\curlywedge$", forms the meet semi lattice $\langle\Sigma^\star, \preceq, \curlywedge\rangle$.

This partial trace semantics can be expressed in a fixpoint form as well.

$$\Sigma^\star = \text{lfp}^\subseteq F :$$
$$F \in \Sigma^\star \to \Sigma^\star$$

$$F(X) \overset{\text{def}}{=} \{\sigma \xrightarrow{a'} \sigma' \in T \mid \sigma \in I\}\cup$$
$$\{\sigma_0 \xrightarrow{a_0} \dots \xrightarrow{a_{n-2}} \sigma_{n-1} \xrightarrow{a_{n-1}} \sigma_n \mid \sigma_0 \xrightarrow{a_0} \dots \xrightarrow{a_{n-2}} \sigma_{n-1} \in X \wedge \sigma_{n-1} \xrightarrow{a_{n-1}} \sigma_n \in T\}$$

Let $\langle \wp(\Sigma^\star), \subseteq, \emptyset, \Sigma^\star, \cap, \cup \rangle$ be a complete lattice of partial execution traces, where "$\subseteq$" is the classical subset relation, "$\cup$" is the set union and "$\cap$" the set intersection.

## 2.3    Abstract Domain: Pos

Among all the abstract domains which are used in abstract interpretation of logic programs, Pos has received considerable attention [2,11]. This domain is most commonly applied to the analysis of groundness dependencies for logic programs.

Let $\overline{V} = \{\overline{x}, \overline{y}, \overline{z}, \cdots\}$ be a countably infinite set of propositional variables and let $FP(\overline{V})$ be the set of all finite subsets of variables of $\overline{V}$. The set of propositional formulae containing variables in $\overline{V}$ and logical connectives in $\Gamma \subseteq \{\wedge, \vee, \rightarrow, \neg\}$ is denoted by $\Omega(\Gamma)$. Similarly, given $U \in FP(\overline{V})$, the set of propositional formulae containing variables in $U$ and connectives in $\Gamma$ is denoted by $\Omega_U(\Gamma)$.

A *truth-assignment* is a function $\overline{T} : \overline{V} \rightarrow \{T, F\}$ that assigns to each propositional variable the value true (T) or false (F). Given a formula $f \in \Omega(\Gamma)$, $\overline{T} \vDash f$ means that $\overline{T}$ satisfies $f$, and $f_1 \vDash f_2$ is a shorthand for "$\overline{T} \vDash f_1$ implies $\overline{T} \vDash f_2$". $\Omega(\Gamma)$ is ordered by $f_1 \trianglelefteq f_2 \Leftrightarrow f_1 \vDash f_2$. Two formulae $f_1$ and $f_2$ are logically equivalent, denoted $f_1 \equiv f_2$ iff $f_1 \trianglelefteq f_2$ and $f_2 \trianglelefteq f_1$.

The *unit assignment* $u$ is defined by $u(x) = T$ for all $\overline{x} \in \overline{V}$. We define the set of positive formulae by Pos $= \{f \in \Omega(\Gamma) \mid u \vDash f\}$. Some obvious examples are $T, x_1 \in$ Pos and $F, \neg x_1 \notin$ Pos.

We can consider the propositional formula $\psi$ as a conjunction of subformulae $(\zeta_0 \wedge \ldots \wedge \zeta_n)$. We denote the set of subformulae of $\psi$ as $Sub_\psi$. Let $\triangledown$ be the least upper bound operator on propositional formula defined by $\triangledown\{\psi_0, \ldots, \psi_n\} = \bigwedge\{Sub_{\psi_0}, \ldots, Sub_{\psi_n}\}$. (Pos, $\trianglelefteq, \triangledown$) forms a join semi lattice. Moreover, let $\ominus :$ Pos $\times$ Pos $\rightarrow$ Pos be a binary operator defined as "simplification" between two propositional formulae: $\psi_0 \ominus \psi_1 = \bigwedge(Sub_{\psi_0} \setminus Sub_{\psi_1})$. This "simplification" permits us to obtain all the implication in $\psi_0$ which are not contained in $\psi_1$.

## 2.4    Abstract Semantics

Our approach is based on the abstract domain of logic formulae representing dependency between variables (which tracks the propagation of sensitive/insensitive information). The detection of possible information leakages is performed by evaluating formulae on truth-assignment functions. In particular, the analysis involves the following steps:

- Constructs at each program point the propositional formula $\psi$ through a fixpoint algorithm which represents an over-approximation of variable's dependencies up to that program point.
- Partitions the variables into public and private privacy levels. Apply a truth-assignment function $\overline{T}$ that assigns to each propositional variable the value T (true) or the value F (false) if the corresponding variable is private or public,

respectively. If $\overline{\Upsilon}$ does not satisfy $\psi$ at all program points, then there could be some information leakages.

The logic formulae, obtained from program's instructions, are in the form:

$$\bigwedge_{0 \le i \le n \; 0 \le j \le m} \{\overline{x}_i \to \overline{y}_j\}$$

which means that the values of variable $\overline{y}_j$ could depend on the values of variable $\overline{x}_i$. For instance, the formula $\overline{y} \to \overline{x}$ represents variable dependency in assignment statement $x := y$; similarly, in case of conditional statement if$(x == 0)$ then $y := z$ we obtain the formula $(\overline{x} \to \overline{y}) \wedge (\overline{z} \to \overline{y})$. Notice that the propositional variable $\overline{v}$ corresponds to the program variable v.

Formally, an abstract state $\sigma^\sharp \in \Sigma^\sharp \stackrel{\text{def}}{=} L \times \mathsf{Pos}$ is a pair $\langle \ell, \phi \rangle$ where $\phi \in \mathsf{Pos}$ represents the dependencies occurred among program variables up to label $\ell \in L$. Given a pair $\sigma^\sharp = \langle \ell, \phi \rangle$, we define $l(\sigma^\sharp) = \ell$ and $r(\sigma^\sharp) = \phi$. Let $BV(c)$, defined in Table 9, be the set of bound variables in command c.

**Table 9.** $BV$ function

| |
|---|
| $BV(^\ell\mathsf{skip}) = \{\emptyset\}$ |
| $BV(^\ell v := \mathsf{exp}) = \{\overline{v}\}$ |
| $BV(c_0; c_1) = BV(c_0) \cup BV(c_1)$ |
| $BV(\text{if } ^\ell b \text{ then } c_0 \text{ else } c_1 \; ^{\ell'}\text{endif}) = BV(c_0) \cup BV(c_1)$ |
| $BV(\text{while } ^\ell b \text{ do } c \; ^{\ell'}\text{done}) = BV(c)$ |

**Table 10.** Abstract semantics

| |
|---|
| $\overline{T}[\![^\ell\mathsf{skip}^{\ell_1}]\!] = \{\langle \ell, \psi \rangle \to \langle \mathit{fin}[\![^\ell\mathsf{skip}^{\ell_1}]\!], \psi \rangle\}$ |
| $\overline{T}[\![^\ell v := \mathsf{exp}^{\ell_1}]\!] = \{\langle \ell, \psi \rangle \to \langle \mathit{fin}[\![^\ell v := \mathsf{exp}^{\ell_1}]\!], \psi_0 \rangle\}$ |
| $\overline{T}[\![c_0; c_1]\!] = \overline{T}[\![c_0]\!] \cup \overline{T}[\![c_1]\!]$ |
| $\overline{T}[\![\text{if } ^\ell b \text{ then } c_0 \text{ else } c_1 \; ^{\ell'}\text{endif}^{\ell_1}]\!] = \overline{T}[\![c_0]\!] \cup \overline{T}[\![c_1]\!] \cup$ |
| $\qquad \{\langle \ell, \psi \rangle \to \langle \mathit{in}[\![c_0]\!], \psi \rangle\} \cup \{\langle \ell, \psi \rangle \to \langle \mathit{in}[\![c_1]\!], \psi \rangle\} \cup$ |
| $\qquad \{\langle \ell', \psi \rangle \to \langle \mathit{fin}[\![\text{if } ^\ell b \text{ then } c_0 \text{ else } c_1 \; ^{\ell'}\text{endif}^{\ell_1}]\!], \psi_1 \rangle\}$ |
| $\qquad \{\langle \ell', \psi \rangle \to \langle \mathit{fin}[\![\text{if } ^\ell b \text{ then } c_0 \text{ else } c_1 \; ^{\ell'}\text{endif}^{\ell_1}]\!], \psi_2 \rangle\}$ |
| $\overline{T}[\![\text{while } ^\ell b \text{ do } c \; ^{\ell'}\text{done}^{\ell_1}]\!] = \overline{T}[\![c]\!] \cup \{\langle \ell, \psi \rangle \to \langle \mathit{in}[\![c]\!], \psi \rangle\} \cup$ |
| $\qquad \{\langle \ell', \psi \rangle \to \langle \mathit{fin}[\![\text{while } ^\ell b \text{ do } c \; ^{\ell'}\text{done}^{\ell_1}]\!], \psi_3 \rangle\}$ |
| **where** |
| $\psi_0 = \bigwedge \{\overline{y} \to \overline{x} \mid \overline{y} \in \overline{V}(\mathsf{exp}) \wedge \overline{y} \ne \overline{x}\}$ |
| $\qquad \bigwedge \{\overline{z} \to \overline{w} \mid \overline{z} \to \overline{x}, \overline{x} \to \overline{w} \in \psi\} \wedge (\psi \ominus \bigwedge \{\overline{y} \to \overline{x} \mid \overline{y} \in \overline{V} \wedge \overline{x} \notin \overline{V}[\![\mathsf{exp}]\!]\})$ |
| $\psi_1 = \bigwedge \{\overline{y} \to \overline{x} \mid \overline{y} \in \overline{V}(b) \wedge \overline{x} \in BV(c_0) \wedge \overline{y} \ne \overline{x}\} \wedge \psi$ |
| $\psi_2 = \bigwedge \{\overline{y} \to \overline{x} \mid \overline{y} \in \overline{V}(b) \wedge \overline{x} \in BV(c_1) \wedge \overline{y} \ne \overline{x}\} \wedge \psi$ |
| $\psi_3 = \bigwedge \{\overline{y} \to \overline{x} \mid \overline{y} \in \overline{V}(b) \wedge \overline{x} \in BV(c) \wedge \overline{y} \ne \overline{x}\} \wedge \psi$ |

The *abstract semantics* of a command c is defined by $\overline{T}[\![c]\!]$. Similar to the concrete domain, we denote the transition from $\sigma_1^\sharp$ to $\sigma_2^\sharp$ by $\sigma_1^\sharp \to \sigma_2^\sharp$. The abstract semantics in the domain of propositional formulae is defined in Table 10.

Consider two sets of abstract states $S_1$ and $S_2$ such that $S_1 = \{\langle \ell_0^1, \psi_0^1 \rangle, \ldots, \langle \ell_n^1, \psi_n^1 \rangle\}$ and $S_2 = \{\langle \ell_0^2, \psi_0^2 \rangle, \ldots, \langle \ell_m^2, \psi_m^2 \rangle\}$. The partial ordering is defined by $S_1 \sqsubseteq^\sharp S_2 \Leftrightarrow n \leq m | \forall i \in [0, n], \ell_i^1 = \ell_i^2 \wedge \forall i \in [0, n], \psi_i^1 \trianglelefteq \psi_i^2$. Let $S_0, \ldots S_n \in \wp(\Sigma^\sharp)$ be sets of abstract states. $\langle \wp(\Sigma^\sharp), \sqsubseteq^\sharp \rangle$ forms a poset since it is reflexive, antisymmetric, and transitive by basic properties of logic implication. The join operator $\sqcup^\sharp$ is defined by:

$$\sqcup^\sharp \{S_0, \ldots, S_n\} = \bigcup(S_0, \ldots, S_n)$$

$$\cup \{\langle \ell, \psi \rangle \mid \psi = \nabla\{\psi' \mid \langle \ell, \psi' \rangle \in \bigcup(S_0, \ldots, S_n)\}\}$$

$$\setminus \{\langle \ell, \psi \rangle \in \bigcup(S_0, \ldots, S_n) \mid \exists \langle \ell, \psi' \rangle \in \bigcup(S_0, \ldots, S_n) \wedge \psi \neq \psi'\}$$

and the meet operator $\sqcap^\sharp$ by:

$$\sqcap^\sharp \{S_0, \ldots, S_n\} = \{\langle \ell, \psi \rangle \in S' \mid S' \in \{S_0, \ldots, S_n\} \wedge$$

$$\forall i \in [0, n]. \exists \langle \ell, \psi_i' \rangle \in S_i \wedge \psi \trianglelefteq \psi_i'\}$$

Basically, the join operator consists in the union of all elements. When two elements have the same label but different formula, the join operator takes the biggest one. Instead, the meet operator considers only the abstract states, with the same label, which are in all elements. In case of different formulae, the meet operator takes the smallest one. By definition join and meet operator are defined for every subset of elements of our domain. Therefore, we can conclude that $\langle \wp(\Sigma^\sharp), \sqsubseteq^\sharp, \emptyset, \Sigma^\sharp, \sqcup^\sharp, \sqcap^\sharp \rangle$ forms a complete lattice.

Let $I^\sharp[\![\mathcal{P}]\!] = \{\langle in[\![\mathcal{P}]\!], \top \rangle\}$ be the set of possible initial abstract state of program $\mathcal{P}$. We define the *abstract semantics* as the set of all finite sets of abstract states, denoted by $\Sigma^{\star\sharp}$, reachable during one or more executions, in a finite time. For each element $S \in \Sigma^{\star\sharp}$ we can denote by $S^\dashv$ the set of terminal states, defined as $S^\dashv = \{\sigma_0^\sharp \mid \nexists \sigma_1^\sharp \in S.\sigma_0^\sharp \to \sigma_1^\sharp \in \overline{T}\}$ and by $\ell(S)$ all labels of S. Let $S_{\sigma_0^\sharp, \sigma_n^\sharp}$ denote a set of states, called *abstract sequence*, that contains a starting state $\sigma_0^\sharp$ and an ending state $\sigma_n^\sharp$ such that contains one or more traces from $\sigma_0^\sharp$ to $\sigma_n^\sharp$. We have that $S_{\sigma_0^\sharp, \sigma_n^\sharp}^\dashv = \{\sigma_n^\sharp\}$.

We express the abstract semantics in a fixpoint form.

$$\Sigma^{\star\sharp} = lfp^{\sqsubseteq} F^\sharp \text{ where } F^\sharp \in \Sigma^{\star\sharp} \to \Sigma^{\star\sharp}$$

$$F^\sharp(X) \stackrel{\text{def}}{=} \{\sigma^\sharp \mid \sigma^\sharp \in I^\sharp\} \cup \{S_{\sigma_0^\sharp, \sigma_n^\sharp} \mid n \geq 1 \wedge \sigma_0^\sharp \in I^\sharp \wedge S_{\sigma_0^\sharp, \sigma_{n-1}^\sharp} \in X$$

$$\wedge \sigma_{n-1}^\sharp \to \sigma_n^\sharp \in \overline{T}\} \cup \{\sqcup^\sharp \{S_{\sigma_0^\sharp, \sigma_n^\sharp} \mid S_{\sigma_0^\sharp, \sigma_n^\sharp} \in X\}\}$$

*Example 1.* In order to better understand how our dependency analysis works, consider the code in Fig. 1 and the program points 4, 5, 8, 10, 12 and 14. When we apply the steps defined above we obtain the propositional formulae in Table 11.

**Table 11.** Results of the analysis by Pos domain

| Label | Propositional formula |
|-------|----------------------|
| 4 | $\overline{x} \to \overline{y}$ |
| 5 | $\overline{p} \to \overline{sum}$ |
| 8 | $(\overline{x} \to \overline{y}) \wedge (\overline{p} \to \overline{sum}) \wedge (\overline{y} \to \overline{sum})$ |
| 10 | $(\overline{x} \to \overline{y}) \wedge (\overline{p} \to \overline{sum}) \wedge (\overline{x} \to \overline{sum})$ |
| 12 | $(\overline{x} \to \overline{y}) \wedge (\overline{p} \to \overline{sum}) \wedge (\overline{x} \to \overline{sum}) \wedge (\overline{y} \to \overline{sum})$ |
| 14 | $(\overline{x} \to \overline{y}) \wedge (\overline{p} \to \overline{sum}) \wedge (\overline{x} \to \overline{sum}) \wedge (\overline{y} \to \overline{sum}) \wedge (\overline{n} \to \overline{sum}) \wedge$ $(\overline{i} \to \overline{sum}) \wedge (\overline{i} \to \overline{n}) \wedge (\overline{k} \to \overline{sum}) \wedge (\overline{k} \to \overline{n})$ |

Through our analysis we tracked all the relation between variables. Suppose that variables $\{\overline{x}, \overline{p}\}$ are private, while all other variables are public. Formally, the correspondent truth-assignment function is defined by $\overline{\varUpsilon} = \{\overline{x}, \overline{p} \mapsto \mathsf{T}\} \cup \{\overline{v} \mapsto \mathsf{F} : \overline{v} \in V \setminus \{\overline{x}, \overline{p}\}\}$. $\overline{\varUpsilon}$ does not satisfy the propositional formulae since in all considered program points there are some public variables that depends on one or more private variables.

Notice that we detect several spurious relations, too. For instance, in contrast with the obtained result, the variable $\overline{sum}$ does not depend on $\overline{n}$. Indeed at the end of the both branches the variable $\overline{sum}$ has always the same value. In Sect. 3 we will refine the results through the domains combination.

## 2.5   An Instrumented Concrete Domain

To simplify the proof that our concrete and abstract domains from a Galois connection, we introduce another domain, isomorphic to the concrete domain. Let $\sigma^\diamond \in \Sigma^\diamond = \mathsf{L} \times \mathsf{A}$ be the set of states of this intermediate domain. A pair $\langle \ell, a \rangle \in \mathsf{L} \times \mathsf{A}$ represents an action $a$ which occurs at program label $\ell$. Consider the set $\Sigma^{\star\diamond}$ which contains all the possible traces of $\sigma^\diamond$ that can occur during a finite computation. Given $\varPi_0^\diamond, \varPi_1^\diamond \in \wp(\Sigma^{\star\diamond})$, we define that $\varPi_0^\diamond \sqsubseteq \varPi_1^\diamond$ if and only if for each $\pi_0^\diamond \in \varPi_0^\diamond$ there exists a $\pi_1^\diamond \in \varPi_1^\diamond$ such that $\pi_0^\diamond \preceq^\diamond \pi_1^\diamond$. We have that $\pi_0^\diamond \preceq^\diamond \pi_1^\diamond$ if and only if $\pi_0^\diamond$ is a subsequence of $\pi_1^\diamond$. Therefore $\langle \wp(\Sigma^{\star\diamond}), \subseteq, \emptyset, \Sigma^{\star\diamond}, \cap, \cup \rangle$ forms a lattice. Moreover, we denote by $\pi^{\diamond\dashv}$ the last state of the sequence. We can relate $\wp(\Sigma^\star)$ and $\wp(\Sigma^{\star\diamond})$ by an abstraction $\alpha^\diamond \in \wp(\Sigma^\star) \to \wp(\Sigma^{\star\diamond})$ and a concretization $\gamma^\diamond \in \wp(\Sigma^{\star\diamond}) \to \wp(\Sigma^\star)$ function.

Let $X = \{\pi_0, \ldots, \pi_n\} \in \wp(\Sigma^\star)$ be a set of partial traces and let $Y = \{\pi_0^\diamond, \ldots, \pi_n^\diamond\} \in \wp(\Sigma^{\star\diamond})$ be a set of sequences of $\sigma^\diamond$.

$$\alpha^\diamond(X) \equiv \{\langle \ell_0, a_0 \rangle \to \ldots \to \langle \ell_m, a_m \rangle \mid \sigma_0 \xrightarrow{\ell_0\, a_0} \ldots \xrightarrow{\ell_m\, a_m} \sigma_{m+1} \in X\}$$
$$\gamma^\diamond(Y) \equiv \{\pi \in \wp(\Sigma^\star) \mid \alpha^\diamond(\{\pi\}) \subseteq Y\}$$

**Lemma 1.** $\wp(\Sigma^\star) \xleftarrow[\alpha^\diamond]{\gamma^\diamond} \wp(\Sigma^{\star\diamond})$ *forms an isomorphism, that is,* $\gamma^\diamond \circ \alpha^\diamond = \alpha^\diamond \circ \gamma^\diamond = id$ *(where id is the identity function).*

*Proof.* We have to prove that $\gamma^\circ \circ \alpha^\circ = \alpha^\circ \circ \gamma^\circ = id$, where $id$ is the identity function. Let X and Y be elements of $\wp(\Sigma^{\star\circ})$ and $\wp(\Sigma^\star)$ respectively.

$$\alpha^\circ(\gamma^\circ(X)) = \{\langle \ell_0, a_0 \rangle \rightarrow \ldots \rightarrow \langle \ell_m, a_m \rangle \mid \sigma_0 \xrightarrow{\ell_0\, a_0} \ldots \xrightarrow{\ell_m\, a_m} \sigma_{m+1} \in \gamma^\circ(X)\}$$
$$\text{by definition of } \alpha^\circ$$
$$= \{\langle \ell_0, a_0 \rangle \rightarrow \ldots \rightarrow \langle \ell_m, a_m \rangle \mid \sigma_0 \xrightarrow{\ell_0\, a_0} \ldots \xrightarrow{\ell_m\, a_m} \sigma_{m+1}$$
$$\in \{\pi \mid \alpha^\circ(\{\pi\}) \subseteq X\}\} \text{by definition of } \gamma^\circ$$
$$= \{\langle \ell_0, a_0 \rangle \rightarrow \ldots \rightarrow \langle \ell_m, a_m \rangle \mid \langle \ell_0, a_0 \rangle \rightarrow \ldots \rightarrow \langle \ell_m, a_m \rangle \in X\}$$
$$= X$$

$$\gamma^\circ(\alpha^\circ(Y)) = \{\pi \in \wp(\Sigma^\star) \mid \alpha^\circ(\{\pi\}) \subseteq \alpha^\circ(Y)\}$$
$$\text{by definition of } \gamma^\circ$$
$$= \{\pi \in \wp(\Sigma^\star) \mid \alpha^\circ(\{\pi\}) \subseteq \{\alpha^\circ(\{\pi'\}) \mid \pi' \in Y\}\}$$
$$\text{by definition of } \alpha^\circ$$
$$= \{\pi \in \wp(\Sigma^\star) \mid \pi \in Y\}$$
$$= Y$$

$\square$

Now we define the relation between $\wp(\Sigma^{\star\circ})$ and $\wp(\Sigma^{\star\sharp})$ by $\alpha^\sharp$ and $\gamma^\sharp$. $\alpha^\sharp : \wp(\Sigma^{\star\circ}) \rightarrow \wp(\Sigma^{\star\sharp})$ is defined by $\alpha^\sharp(X) = \sqcup^\sharp\{\theta(\pi^\circ) \mid \pi^\circ \in X\}$, where $\theta : \Sigma^{\star\circ} \rightarrow \wp(\Sigma^{\star\sharp})$ is defined as follows.

$$\theta(X) = \{\langle \ell, \psi \rangle \mid \forall \pi \in X.\forall \pi' = \langle \ell_0, a_0 \rangle \rightarrow \langle \ell_m, a_m \rangle \preceq^\circ \pi :$$
$$m \geq 0 \wedge \ell = \ell_m \wedge \psi = f_0 \wedge \ldots \wedge f_n\}$$

such that:

1. $(\forall \langle \ell, v := exp \rangle \in \pi' : \forall \langle \ell', v := exp' \rangle \in \pi'.\ell' \leq \ell).\exists f_i = \bar{y} \rightarrow \bar{v} : \bar{y} \in \overline{V}(exp)$
2. $\forall((\langle \ell_i, b \rangle \rightarrow \ldots \rightarrow \langle \ell_j, endif \rangle) \vee (\langle \ell_i, not\, b \rangle \rightarrow \ldots \rightarrow \langle \ell_j, endif \rangle)) \preceq^\circ \pi^\circ$ which represents an if statement and $\forall \langle \ell_k, v := exp_k \rangle : i < k < j$ exists $f_h = \bar{y} \rightarrow \bar{v}$ such that $\bar{y} \in \overline{V}(b)$.
3. $\forall((\langle \ell_i, b \rangle \rightarrow \ldots \rightarrow \langle \ell_j, done \rangle) \vee (\langle \ell_i, not\, b \rangle \rightarrow \ldots \rightarrow \langle \ell_j, done \rangle)) \preceq^\circ \pi^\circ$ which represents a while statement and $\forall \langle \ell_k, v := exp_k \rangle : i < k < j$ exists $f_h = \bar{y} \rightarrow \bar{v}$ such that $\bar{y} \in \overline{V}(b)$.

Intuitively, the function $\theta$ transforms each action (or sequence of actions) in one or more propositional formulae. The easiest (case 1) applies when the action is an assignment statement ($v := exp$): we simply obtain the corresponding formula as defined in the transition semantics T. Instead, for if statements (case 2), we track all the assignment actions that are between if and endif. while statements are treated in a similar way (case 3).

Notice that $\langle \ell_i, b \rangle \rightarrow \ldots \rightarrow \langle \ell_j, endif \rangle$ (or $\langle \ell_i, not\, b \rangle \rightarrow \ldots \rightarrow \langle \ell_j, endif \rangle$) represents an if statement if and only if $\forall(\langle \ell_p, b \rangle \vee \langle \ell_p, not\, b \rangle) : i < p < j.\exists(\langle \ell_q, endif \rangle \vee \langle \ell_q, done \rangle) : p < q < j$ and $\forall(\langle \ell_q, endif \rangle \vee \langle \ell_q, done \rangle) : i < q < j.\exists(\langle \ell_p, b \rangle \vee \langle \ell_p, not\, b \rangle) : i < p < q$. Similarly for while statement.

Informally, the pair if and endif (or while and done) is an if (while) statement if and only if between these two actions, there are only assignments or other pairs if-endif or while-done which correspond to nested if and while statements. To better understand, consider the sequence $\cdots \langle \ell_0, b_0 \rangle \rightarrow \langle \ell_1, b_1 \rangle \rightarrow \langle \ell_2, v := exp \rangle \rightarrow \langle \ell_3, endif \rangle \cdots$: the pairs $\langle \ell_0, b_0 \rangle$ and $\langle \ell_3, endif \rangle$ are not an if statement because between these two actions there is $\langle \ell_1, b_1 \rangle$, which does not represent an assignment action neither an if statement.

The concretization function $\gamma^\sharp : \wp(\Sigma^{\star\sharp}) \rightarrow \wp(\Sigma^{\star\diamond})$ is defined by $\gamma^\sharp(Y) = \{\pi^\diamond \in \Sigma^{\star\diamond} \mid \theta(\pi^\diamond) \sqsubseteq^\sharp Y \wedge l(\pi^{\diamond\dashv}) \in \ell(Y^\dashv)\}$ where $Y \in \wp(\Sigma^{\star\sharp})$.

**Lemma 2.** $\theta : \Sigma^{\star\diamond} \rightarrow \wp(\Sigma^{\star\sharp})$ *is monotonic:* $x \preceq^\diamond y \Rightarrow \theta(x) \sqsubseteq^\sharp \theta(y)$

*Proof.* Let $x_0 = \{\sigma_0 \rightarrow \ldots \rightarrow \sigma_n\}$ and $x_1 = \{\sigma'_0 \rightarrow \ldots \rightarrow \sigma'_m\}$ be two elements of $\Sigma^{\star\diamond}$ such that $x_0 \preceq^\diamond x_1$ and consider $\theta(x_0) = \{\sigma^\sharp_0, \ldots, \sigma^\sharp_n\}$ and $\theta(x_1) = \{\sigma^{\sharp'}_0, \ldots, \sigma^{\sharp'}_m\}$.

By the definition of "$\preceq^\diamond$" we know that $n \leq m$, $\forall i \in [0, n].\sigma_i = \sigma'_i$. Therefore, by the definition of $\theta$, we have that $\forall i \in [0, n].\sigma^\sharp_i = \sigma^{\sharp'}_i$. Then, by definition of "$\sqsubseteq^\sharp$", $\theta(x_0) \sqsubseteq^\sharp \theta(x_1)$. $\qquad\square$

**Lemma 3.** $\alpha^\sharp : \wp(\Sigma^{\star\diamond}) \rightarrow \wp(\Sigma^{\star\sharp})$ *is monotonic:* $X \subseteq Y \Rightarrow \alpha^\sharp(X) \sqsubseteq^\sharp \alpha^\sharp(Y)$

*Proof.* Consider $X_0, X_1 \in \wp(\Sigma^{\star\diamond})$ such that $X_0 \subseteq X_1$, $\alpha^\sharp(X_0) = \sqcup^\sharp\{\theta(\pi^\diamond) \mid \pi^\diamond \in X_0\}$ and $\alpha^\sharp(X_1) = \sqcup^\sharp\{\theta(\pi^\diamond) \mid \pi^\diamond \in X_1\}$. By definition of "$\subseteq$", $\forall \pi^\diamond \in X_0, \exists \pi^\diamond \in X_1$. By Lemma 2, $\theta(\pi^\diamond_0) \sqsubseteq^\sharp \theta(\pi^\diamond_1)$ for all $\pi^\diamond_0 \in X_0$ and $\pi^\diamond_1 \in X_1$. Then we have $\alpha^\sharp(X_0) \sqsubseteq^\sharp \alpha^\sharp(X_1)$: $\alpha^\sharp(X_1)$ contains all the elements in $\alpha^\sharp(X_0)$. $\qquad\square$

**Lemma 4.** $\gamma^\sharp : \wp(\Sigma^{\star\sharp}) \rightarrow \wp(\Sigma^{\star\diamond})$ *is monotonic:* $X \sqsubseteq^\sharp Y \Rightarrow \gamma^\sharp(X) \subseteq \gamma^\sharp(Y)$

*Proof.* Consider $X_0, X_1 \in \wp(\Sigma^{\star\sharp})$ such that $X_0 \sqsubseteq^\sharp X_1$, $\gamma^\sharp(X_0) = \{\pi^\diamond \in \wp(\Sigma^{\star\diamond}) \mid \theta(\pi^\diamond) \sqsubseteq^\sharp X_0 \wedge l(\pi^\diamond) \in \ell(X_0^\dashv)\}$ and $\gamma^\sharp(X_1) = \{\pi^\diamond \in \wp(\Sigma^{\star\diamond}) \mid \theta(\pi^\diamond) \sqsubseteq^\sharp X_1 \wedge l(\pi^\diamond) \in \ell(X_1^\dashv)\}$. By definition of "$\sqsubseteq^\sharp$" and by Lemma 2, for all $\pi^\diamond_0 \in \gamma^\sharp(X_0)$ exists $\pi^\diamond_1 \in \gamma^\sharp(X_1)$. Therefore $\gamma^\sharp(X_0) \sqsubseteq^\sharp \gamma^\sharp(X_1)$. $\qquad\square$

**Lemma 5.** $\alpha^\sharp \circ \gamma^\sharp$ *is the identity:* $\alpha^\sharp(\gamma^\sharp(X)) = X$

*Proof.* Let $X$ be an element of $\wp(\Sigma^{\star\sharp})$. By definition of $\alpha^\sharp$, $\alpha^\sharp(\gamma^\sharp(X)) = \sqcup^\sharp\{\theta(\pi^\diamond) \mid \pi^\diamond \in \gamma^\sharp(X)\}$. By definition of $\gamma^\sharp$, $\alpha^\sharp(\gamma^\sharp(X)) = \sqcup^\sharp\{\theta(\pi^\diamond) \mid \theta(\pi^\diamond) \sqsubseteq^\sharp X \wedge l(\pi^\diamond) \in \ell(X^\dashv)\}$. Then, $\alpha^\sharp(\gamma^\sharp(X))$ contains the least upper bound of all the abstract traces that have the same last label of $X$ and that are less or equal than $X$. Therefore $\alpha^\sharp(\gamma^\sharp(X)) = X$. $\qquad\square$

**Lemma 6.** $\gamma^\sharp \circ \alpha^\sharp$ *is extensive:* $X \sqsubseteq^\sharp \gamma^\sharp(\alpha^\sharp(X))$

*Proof.* Consider $X \in \wp(\Sigma^{\star\diamond})$. By definition of $\gamma^\sharp$, $\gamma^\sharp(\alpha^\sharp(X)) = \{\pi^\diamond \in \wp(\Sigma^{\star\diamond}) \mid \theta(\pi^\diamond) \sqsubseteq^\sharp \alpha^\sharp(X) \wedge l(\pi^\diamond) \in \ell(\alpha^\sharp(X)^\dashv)\}$. By definition of $\alpha^\sharp$, $\gamma^\sharp(\alpha^\sharp(X)) = \{\pi^\diamond \in \wp(\Sigma^{\star\diamond}) \mid \theta(\pi^\diamond) \sqsubseteq^\sharp \sqcup^\sharp\{\theta(\pi^\diamond) \mid \pi^\diamond \in X\} \wedge l(\pi^\diamond) \in \ell(\alpha^\sharp(X)^\dashv)\}$. By definition of "$\sqcup^\sharp$", "$\sqsubseteq^\sharp$" and by Lemma 2, $X \sqsubseteq^\sharp \gamma^\sharp(\alpha^\sharp(X))$. $\qquad\square$

**Lemma 7.** $\wp(\Sigma^{\star\diamond}) \xrightleftharpoons[\alpha^\sharp]{\gamma^\sharp} \wp(\Sigma^{\star\sharp})$ *is a Galois insertion.*

*Proof.* $\wp(\Sigma^{\star\circ})$ and $\wp(\Sigma^{\star\sharp})$ are two complete lattices, $\gamma^{\sharp}$ and $\alpha^{\sharp}$ are monotonic (Lemmas 3 and 4), $\alpha^{\sharp} \circ \gamma^{\sharp}$ is the identity (Lemma 5) and $\gamma^{\sharp} \circ \alpha^{\sharp}$ is extensive (Lemma 6). Therefore $\wp(\Sigma^{\star\circ}) \xleftrightarrow[\alpha^{\sharp}]{\gamma^{\sharp}} \wp(\Sigma^{\star\sharp})$ is a Galois insertion. □

Finally, we can express the relation between $\wp(\Sigma^{\star})$ and $\wp(\Sigma^{\star\sharp})$ by the composition of above functions, $\alpha = \alpha^{\sharp} \circ \alpha^{\circ}$ and $\gamma = \gamma^{\circ} \circ \gamma^{\sharp}$.

Since the composition of an isomorphism and a Galois insertion is a Galois insertion, we can assert that $\wp(\Sigma^{\star}) \xleftrightarrow[\gamma^{\sharp}]{\alpha^{\sharp}} \wp(\Sigma^{\star\sharp})$ is a Galois insertion.

## 2.6 Properties

The aim of information flow analysis is to verify the confidentiality and the integrity of the information in computer programs. An information flow analysis can be carried out by considering different attacker abilities. In this context we consider two different scenarios: when the attacker can read public variables only at the beginning and at the end of the computation, and when the attacker can read public variables after each step of the computation. Note that the attacker, in both cases, knows the source code of the program.

Both the properties and the types of attacker are checked through the definition and the satisfiability of the propositional formulae (Pos) with respect to the truth-assignment function. Let $\overline{\Upsilon_{\mathcal{P}}} : \mathsf{V} \to \{\mathsf{T}, \mathsf{F}\}$ be a truth-assignment function associated with the program $\mathcal{P}$. The security properties are modeled by the function definition, while the attacker is modeled by the set of propositional formulae we consider for the satisfiability. For the first case, in which the attacker can read public variables only at the beginning and at the end of the computation, the set of states to consider involves only the terminal states of each sequence $(\{\mathsf{S} \in \Sigma^{\star\sharp} \mid \overline{\Upsilon_{\mathcal{P}}} \vDash r(\mathsf{S}^{\dashv})\})$. Whereas in the second case, when the attacker can read public variables at each step of the computation, the set of states to consider involves all the propositional formulae in the sequence $(\{\mathsf{S} \in \Sigma^{\star\sharp} \mid \forall\sigma^{\sharp} \in \mathsf{S} : \overline{\Upsilon_{\mathcal{P}}} \vDash r(\sigma^{\sharp})\})$.

**Confidentiality.** Confidentiality refers to limiting information access and disclosure to authorized users. For example, we require when we buy something online that our private data (e.g., credit card number) can be read only by the merchant.

Let $\Upsilon_{\mathcal{P}} : \mathsf{V} \to \{\mathsf{L}, \mathsf{H}\}$ be a function which assigns to each variable of program $\mathcal{P}$ a security class. $\mathcal{P}$ respects the confidentiality property, if and only if it does not contain any information leakage with respect to the function $\Upsilon_{\mathsf{P}}$, i.e., there is no information that moves from private to public variables. To verify this property, we define the corresponding truth-assignment function $\overline{\Upsilon_{\mathcal{P}}}$ as follows.

$$\overline{\Upsilon_{\mathcal{P}}}(\overline{\mathsf{x}}) = \begin{cases} \mathsf{T} & \text{if } \Upsilon_{\mathcal{P}}(\mathsf{x}) = \mathsf{H} \\ \mathsf{F} & \text{if } \Upsilon_{\mathcal{P}}(\mathsf{x}) = \mathsf{L} \end{cases}$$

**Integrity.** By integrity we mean that unauthorized people cannot modify a message.

Let $\Upsilon_{\mathcal{P}} : V \to \{L, H\}$ be a function which assigns to each variable of program $\mathcal{P}$ a security class. The integrity property is verified if and only if public variables do not modify private variables, i.e., there is no information leakage from public variables to private variables. The corresponding truth-assignment function $\overline{\Upsilon_{\mathcal{P}}}$, to check this property, is defined as follows.

$$\overline{\Upsilon_{\mathcal{P}}}(\overline{x}) = \begin{cases} T & \text{if } \Upsilon_{\mathcal{P}}(x) = L \\ F & \text{if } \Upsilon_{\mathcal{P}}(x) = H \end{cases}$$

Notice that it is exactly the opposite of the truth-assignment function for the confidentiality property.

## 3   Combination of Symbolic and Numerical Domains

In this Section, we combine the symbolic propositional formulae domain described above with a numerical domain through reduced product, yielding to a refinement of the results obtained by the dependency analysis. Our modular construction allows to tune efficiency and accuracy changing the numerical domain. For instance, if we use intervals, we will be less precise than by using polyhedra, but we will obtain a more efficient analysis.

Let us briefly recall the main features of some numerical domains already in the literature.

*Intervals.* Intervals approximate a set of integers by an interval enclosing all of them. Formally, a set $V \subseteq \mathbb{Z}$ is approximated with $[a, b]$ where $a = min\ V$ and $b = max\ V$. If it is not possible to know precisely the upper and lower bound of a set of integers $a$ and $b$ are $-\infty$ and $+\infty$, respectively. This domain is a lattice, and the ordering operator $\sqsubseteq$ is such that $[a, b] \sqsubseteq [c, d]$ if and only if the interval $[a, b]$ is contained by $[c, d]$. Therefore the top element is the interval $[-\infty, +\infty]$ and the bottom element is an interval such that $a > b$. This lattice has infinite height and contains infinite ascending chains. So it needs a widening operator. Intervals scale up, but in some cases they are too rough.

*Polyhedra.* Convex polyhedra are regions of some n-dimensional space that are bounded by a finite set of hyperplanes. A convex polyhedron in $\mathbb{R}^n$ describes a relation between $n$ quantities. P. Cousot and N. Halbwachs [14] applied the theory of abstract interpretation to the static determination of linear equalities and inequalities among program variables by introducing the use of convex polyhedra as an abstract domain.

We denote by $\mathbf{v} = (v_0, \ldots v_{n-1}) \in \mathbb{R}^n$ a n-tuple (vector) of real numbers; $\mathbf{v} \cdot \mathbf{w}$ denotes the scalar product of vectors $\mathbf{v}, \mathbf{w} \in \mathbb{R}^n$; the vector $\mathbf{0} \in \mathbb{R}$ has all components equal to zero. Let $\mathbf{x}$ be a n-tuple of distinct variables. Then $\beta = (\mathbf{a} \cdot \mathbf{x} \bowtie b)$ denotes a linear constraint, for each vector $\mathbf{a} \in \mathbb{R}^n$, where $\mathbf{a} \neq \mathbf{0}$, $b \in \mathbb{R}$ and $\bowtie = \{=, \geq, >\}$. A linear inequality constraint $\beta$ defines an affine half-space of $\mathbb{R}^n$, denoted by $con(\{\beta\})$.

A set $\mathcal{P} \in \mathbb{R}^n$ is a (convex) polyhedron if and only if $\mathcal{P}$ can be expressed as the intersection of a finite number of affine half-spaces of $\mathbb{R}^n$, i.e., as the solution of a finite set of linear inequality constraints. The set of all polyhedra on the vector space $\mathbb{R}^n$ is denoted as $\mathsf{P_n}$. Let $\langle \mathsf{P_n}, \subseteq, \emptyset, \mathbb{R}^n, \uplus, \cap \rangle$ be a lattice of convex polyhedra, where "$\subseteq$" is the set-inclusion, the empty set and $\mathbb{R}^n$ as the bottom and top elements, respectively. The binary meet operation returns the greatest polyhedron smaller than or equal to the two arguments, correspond to set intersection, and "$\uplus$" is the binary join operation and returns the least polyhedron greater than or equal to the two arguments. This abstract domain has exponential complexity, and it does not scale up in practice.

For more details about polyhedra, many works in literature define abstract domains based on polyhedra as Galois connection [6] and implement this domain [5, 26].

*Octagons.* A. Miné introduced Octagons [33] for static analysis by abstract interpretation. The author extended a former numerical domain based on Difference-Bound Matrices [32] and showed practical algorithms to represent and manipulate invariants of the form $\pm x \pm y \leq c$ (where x and y are program variables and c is a real constant) efficiently. Such invariants describe sets of point that are special kind of polyhedra called *octagons* because they feature at most eight edges in a two dimensional space.

The set of invariants which the analysis discovers is a subset of the ones discovered by Polyhedra, but it is quite efficient. In fact, it infers the invariants with a $\mathcal{O}(n^2)$ worst case memory complexity per abstract state and a $\mathcal{O}(n^3)$ worst case time complexity per abstract operation, where $n$ is the number of variables in the program.

## 3.1   The Reduced Product

The best way to combine the propositional formulae domain $\langle \wp(\Sigma^{\star\sharp}), \sqsubseteq^\sharp, \emptyset, \Sigma^\sharp, \sqcup^\sharp, \sqcap^\sharp \rangle$ and a numerical domain $\langle \aleph, \sqsubseteq^\aleph, \bot^\aleph, \top^\aleph, \sqcup^\aleph, \sqcap^\aleph \rangle$ is by using the reduced product operator [13].

Let $\wp(\Sigma^\star) \xrightleftharpoons[\gamma_0]{\alpha_0} \wp(\Sigma^{\star\sharp})$ and $\wp(\Sigma^\star) \xrightleftharpoons[\gamma_1]{\alpha_1} \aleph$ be two Galois connections and let $\varrho : \wp(\Sigma^{\star\sharp}) \times \aleph \to \wp(\Sigma^{\star\sharp}) \times \aleph$ be a reduce operator defined as follows: let $\mathsf{X} \in \wp(\Sigma^{\star\sharp})$ be a set of partial traces, and $\mathfrak{N} \in \aleph$ an element of the numerical domain (a set of intervals, an octagon or a polyhedron). Notice that whatever domain you choose, $\mathfrak{N}$ can be seen as a set of relations among variables value. The reduce operator $\varrho$ is defined as $\varrho(\langle \mathsf{X}, \mathfrak{N} \rangle) = \langle \mathsf{X}', \mathfrak{N} \rangle$ where

$$\mathsf{X}' = \{\sigma^\sharp{}_{new} \mid \forall \sigma^\sharp \in \mathsf{X}.l(\sigma^\sharp{}_{new}) = l(\sigma^\sharp)$$
$$\wedge \ r(\sigma^\sharp{}_{new}) = (r(\sigma^\sharp) \ominus \{\overline{x} \to \overline{y} \mid y = z \in \mathfrak{N}, z \in \overline{V} \cup \mathbb{Z} \wedge z \neq x\})\}$$

```
foo (){
      ⁰n = 0; ¹x = 1; ²i = 0; ³y = x−1; ⁴sum = p;
      while (⁵i<= k) do
             if (⁶n%2 == 0) then
                          ⁷sum = y + p; ⁸n = n +1;
             else
                          ⁹sum = x +(p−1); ¹⁰n = n+3;
             ¹¹endif
             ¹²i = i+1;
      ¹³done
}¹⁴
```

**Fig. 1.** Reduced product example

The reduced operator is aimed at excluding pointless dependencies for all variables which have the same value during the execution, without loosing purposeful relations (by the condition "$x \neq z$"). The reduce operator removes from the propositional formulae, contained in $X$, the implications which have at the right side a variable that has a constant value. In fact if the variable has a constant value, it cannot depend on other variables.

Then, the reduced product $D^{\natural}$ is defined as follows:

$$D^{\natural} = \{\varrho(\langle X, \mathfrak{N} \rangle) \mid X \in \wp(\Sigma^{*\natural}), \mathfrak{N} \in \aleph\}$$

Consider $X_0, X_1 \in \wp(\Sigma^{*\natural}), \mathfrak{N}_0, \mathfrak{N}_1 \in \aleph$ and $\langle X_0, \mathfrak{N}_0 \rangle, \langle X_1, \mathfrak{N}_1 \rangle \in D^{\natural}$. Then $\langle X_0, \mathfrak{N}_0 \rangle \sqsubseteq^{\natural} \langle X_1, \mathfrak{N}_1 \rangle$ if and only if $X_0 \sqsubseteq^{\natural} X_1$ and $\mathfrak{N}_0 \sqsubseteq^{\aleph} \mathfrak{N}_1$. We define the least upper bound and greatest lower bound operator by $\langle X_0, \mathfrak{N}_0 \rangle \sqcup^{\natural} \langle X_1, \mathfrak{N}_1 \rangle = \langle X_0 \sqcup^{\natural} X_1, \mathfrak{N}_0 \sqcup^{\aleph} \mathfrak{N}_1 \rangle$ and $\langle X_0, \mathfrak{N}_0 \rangle \sqcap^{\natural} \langle X_1, \mathfrak{N}_1 \rangle = \langle X_0 \sqcap^{\natural} X_1, \mathfrak{N}_0 \sqcap^{\aleph} \mathfrak{N}_1 \rangle$, respectively. $\langle D^{\natural}, \sqsubseteq^{\natural}, \emptyset, \varrho(\langle \Sigma^{*\natural}, \mathbb{R}^n \rangle), \sqcup^{\natural}, \sqcap^{\natural} \rangle$ forms a complete lattice. In order to better understand the improvements yielded by the combination of the two domains consider the following example.

*Example 2.* Consider the code we introduced in Fig. 1. We adopt polyhedra as numerical domain. Below we report the results of two analyses for some program points.

Polyhedra

$$
\begin{array}{r|l}
4 & n = 0; x - 1 = 0; i = 0; y = 0 \\
5 & -p + sum = 0; y = 0; x - 1 = 0; -i + n \geq 0; 3i - n \geq 0; \\
8 & -p + sum = 0; y = 0; x - 1 = 0; -i + n \geq 0; -i + k \geq 0; 3i - n \geq 0; \\
10 & -p + sum = 0; y = 0; x - 1 = 0; -i + n \geq 0; -i + k \geq 0; 3i - n \geq 0; \\
12 & -p + sum = 0; y = 0; x - 1 = 0; -i + n - 1 \geq 0; -i + k \geq 0; \\
& i \geq 0; 3i - n + 3 \geq 0; \\
14 & -p + sum = 0; y = 0; x - 1 = 0; -i + n \geq 0; -i + k - 1 \geq 0; 3i - n \geq 0;
\end{array}
$$

Propositional formula

$$
\begin{array}{c|l}
4 & x \to y \\
5 & p \to sum \\
8 & (x \to y) \land (p \to sum) \land (y \to sum) \\
10 & (x \to y) \land (p \to sum) \land (x \to sum) \\
12 & (x \to y) \land (p \to sum) \land (x \to sum) \land (y \to sum) \\
14 & (x \to y) \land (p \to sum) \land (x \to sum) \land (y \to sum) \land (n \to sum) \land \\
  & (i \to sum) \land (i \to n) \land (k \to sum) \land (k \to n)
\end{array}
$$

When we apply the reduce operator defined above we obtain the following propositional formulas:

$$
\begin{array}{c|l}
4 & \text{T} \\
5 & p \to sum \\
8 & p \to sum \\
10 & p \to sum \\
12 & p \to sum \\
14 & (p \to sum) \land (i \to n) \land (k \to n)
\end{array}
$$

By using the reduce operator we simplified the propositional formulas, removing some implications which could in fact generate false alarms when using the direct product of the domains instead of the reduced product. For instance, in Pos analysis we track the relation $y \to sum$. At the same time, in the numerical analysis, we detect that variable $sum$ is always equal to $p$ (namely it is constant). This means that $y \to sum$ is a false alarm, hence by the reduce product we may delete it. At the same time, we cannot remove the relation between $sum$ and $p$ because it is detected also by the numerical analysis.

## 4  An Extension to Database Query Languages

In this section, we extend the full power of the proposed model to the case of data-intensive applications embedding SQL statements, in order to identify possible leakage of sensitive database information as well. This is particular important as in fact unauthorized leakage often occurs while propagating through database applications accessing and processing them legitimately.

### 4.1  A Motivating Example

Consider the database of Table 12 where customer's personal information and journey-details are stored in tables "Customer" and "Travel" respectively. On booking a particular flight by a customer, the journey details are added to the table "Travel" and the source-destination distance is added to the corresponding entry in 'DistanceCovered' attribute of the table "Customer". Observe that 10 points on the journey each 100 Km are offered which is reflected in the attribute 'Points'. In addition, a boarding-priority value in the attribute 'BoardPriority' is assigned to each journey based on the points acquired by the passenger. This is depicted by procedure BookFlight() in program $\mathcal{P}$ in Fig. 2.

**Table 12.** Database $dB$

(a) Table "Customer"

| custID | custName | Address | Age | DistanceCovered | Points |
|--------|----------|---------|-----|-----------------|--------|
| 1 | Alberto | Athens | 56 | 650 | 60 |
| 2 | Matteo | Venice | 68 | 49 | 0 |
| 3 | Francesco | Washington | 38 | 972 | 90 |
| 4 | Smith | Paris | 42 | 185 | 10 |

(b) Table "Travel"

| custID | Source | Destination | FlightID | JourneyDate | BoardPriority |
|--------|--------|-------------|----------|-------------|---------------|
| 1 | A | B | F139 | 26-04-14 | 2 |
| 2 | C | D | F28 | 16-11-13 | 0 |
| 3 | A | B | F139 | 26-04-14 | 3 |
| 4 | A | B | F139 | 26-04-14 | 1 |

```
Function BookFlight()
1.   $flight=checkAvailability($source, $dest);
2.   if($flight ≠ NULL){
3.     $dist=computeDistance($source, $dest);
4.     UPDATE Customer SET DistanceCovered = DistanceCovered +
       $dist WHERE custID=$id;
5.     UPDATE Customer SET Points = Points + 10 ×
       FLOOR($dist/100) WHERE custID=$id;
6.     ResultSet rs = SELECT Points FROM Customer WHERE
       custID=$id;
7.     while(rs.next()){
8.       $point=rs.next().Points;
9.       $priority=getPriority($point);
10.      INSERT INTO Travel(userID, Source, Destination,
         FlightID, JourneyDate, BoardPriority) VALUES
         ($id,$source,$dest,$flight,$date,$priority);}}
End of Function BookFlight()

       ...
       ...

Function Upgrade()
15. ResultSet rs = SELECT custID, DistanceCovered, Points FROM
    Customer WHERE Points>50;
16. while(rs.next()){
17.   $id=rs.next().custID;
18.   $point=rs.next().Points;
19.   UPDATE Travel SET BoardPriority=BoardPriority +
      ($point-50)/10 WHERE custID=$id;}
End of Function Upgrade()
```

**Fig. 2.** Program $\mathcal{P}$

Assume that values of the attributes 'Address', 'Age', 'DistanceCovered' and 'Points' in table "Customer" are private, whereas the information in Table "Travel" is public. To distinguish from the database attributes, we prefix $ to the application variables in $\mathcal{P}$. Finally, suppose the company has decided to upgrade the customers having more than 50 'Points' to the status of 'BoardPriority'. This is expressed in $\mathcal{P}$ by the activation of the `Upgrade()` function.

It is clear from the code that the values of 'BoardPriority' in tuples where 'custID' are equal to '1' and '3' will be upgraded from 2 to 3 and from 3 and 7 respectively. Therefore, an attacker can easily deduce the exact values of sensitive attribute 'Points' in Table "Customer", by observing the change that occurred in the public attribute 'BoardPriority' in Table "Travel".

The example above clearly shows that sensitive database information may be leaked through database applications when public attribute values depend, directly or indirectly, on private attribute values or private application variable values in the program. For instance, in the given example, the leakage occurs due to the dependence "Points→ BoardPriority" at program label 19.

### 4.2   Labeled Syntax and Concrete Semantics

The labeled syntax description of the language, depicted in Table 13, includes imperative statements embedding SQL. We express an SQL statement by a tuple $\langle \mathtt{OP}, \phi \rangle$, where $\phi$ is a precondition following first-order logic which is used to identify a set of tuples in the database on which the appropriate operation $\mathtt{OP}$ (either select, or insert, or update, or delete) is performed. Each operation represents a set of actions, *e.g.* select operation includes `GROUP BY`, aggregate functions, `ORDER BY`, etc. Observe that applications embedding SQL statements involve two distinct sets of variables: application variables $\mathsf{V_a}$ and database variables $\mathsf{V_d}$. Variables from $\mathsf{V_d}$ appear only in the SQL statements, whereas variables in $\mathsf{V_a}$ may appear in all types of instructions (either SQL or imperative).

We define the action function $a$ and variable function $\mathsf{V}$ for the language in Tables 14 and 15 respectively.

Lets recall from [22] the notion of *environments* correspond to the variables in $\mathsf{V_a}$ and $\mathsf{V_d}$ respectively.

An *application environment* $\rho_a \in \mathcal{E}_a$ maps a variable $x \in dom(\rho_a) \subseteq \mathsf{V_a}$ to its value $\rho_a(x)$. So, $\mathcal{E}_a \triangleq \mathsf{V_a} \longmapsto \mathfrak{D}_\mho$ where $\mathfrak{D}_\mho$ is the semantic domain for $\mathsf{V_a}$.

Consider a database as a set of indexed tables $\{t_i \mid i \in I_x\}$ for a given set of indexes $I_x$. A *database environment* is defined by a function $\rho_d$ whose domain is $I_x$, such that for $i \in I_x$, $\rho_d(i) = t_i$.

Given a database environment $\rho_d$ and a table $t \in d$. Assume $attr(t) = \{a_1, a_2, ..., a_k\}$. So, $t \subseteq D_1 \times D_2 \times .... \times D_k$ where $a_i$ is the attribute corresponding to the typed domain $D_i$. A *table environment* $\rho_t$ for a table $t$ is defined as a function such that for any attribute $a_i \in attr(t)$, $\rho_t(a_i) = \langle \pi_i(l_j) \mid l_j \in t \rangle$, where $\pi$ is the projection operator and $\pi_i(l_j)$ represents $i^{th}$ element of the $l_j$-th row. In other words, $\rho_t$ maps $a_i$ to the ordered set of values over the rows of the table t.

A *state* $\sigma \in \Sigma \triangleq \mathsf{L} \times \mathcal{E}_d \times \mathcal{E}_a$ is denoted by a tuple $\langle \ell, \rho_d, \rho_a \rangle$ where $\ell \in \mathsf{L}$, $\rho_d \in \mathcal{E}_d$ and $\rho_a \in \mathcal{E}_a$ are the label of the statement to be executed, the database environment and the application environment respectively.

The set of *states* of a program $\mathcal{P}$ is, thus, defined as $\Sigma[\![\mathcal{P}]\!] \triangleq \mathsf{L}[\![\mathcal{P}]\!] \times \mathcal{E}_d[\![\mathcal{P}]\!] \times \mathcal{E}_a[\![\mathcal{P}]\!]$, where $\mathsf{L}[\![\mathcal{P}]\!]$ is the set of labels in $\mathcal{P}$, and $\mathcal{E}_d[\![\mathcal{P}]\!]$ and $\mathcal{E}_a[\![\mathcal{P}]\!]$ are the sets

**Table 13.** Syntax of labeled programs embedding SQL

| | |
|---|---|
| **Constants** | |
| $\quad k \in K$ | Set of Constants |
| $\quad k ::= n \mid s$ | |
| $\qquad$ where $n \in \mathbb{N}, s \in$ Strings | |
| **Variables** | |
| $\quad v_a \in V_a$ | Set of Application Variables |
| $\quad v_a ::= x \mid y \mid z \mid \ldots$ | |
| $\quad v_d \in V_d$ | Set of Database Attributes |
| $\quad v_d ::= a_1 \mid a_2 \mid a_3 \mid \ldots$ | |
| **Expressions** | |
| $\quad exp \in E$ | Set of Arithmetic Expressions |
| $\quad exp ::= k \mid v_d \mid v_a \mid exp_1 \oplus exp_2$ | |
| $\qquad$ where $\oplus \in \{+, -, *, /\}$ | |
| $\quad b \in B$ | Set of Boolean Expressions |
| $\quad b ::= true \mid false \mid exp_1 \oslash exp_2 \mid \neg b \mid b_1 \otimes b_2$ | |
| $\qquad$ where $\oslash \in \{\leq, \geq, ==, >, \neq, \ldots\}$ and $\otimes \in \{\vee, \wedge\}$ | |
| **SQL Preconditions** | |
| $\quad \tau \in T$ | Set of Terms |
| $\quad \tau ::= k \mid v_d \mid v_a \mid f_n(\tau_1, \tau_2, \ldots, \tau_n)$ | |
| $\qquad$ where $f_n$ is an n-ary function. | |
| $\quad a_f \in A_f$ | Set of Atomic Formulas |
| $\quad a_f ::= R_n(\tau_1, \tau_2, \ldots, \tau_n) \mid \tau_1 == \tau_2$ | |
| $\qquad$ where $R_n(\tau_1, \tau_2, \ldots, \tau_n) \in \{true, false\}$ | |
| $\quad \phi \in W$ | Set of Pre-conditions |
| $\quad \phi ::= a_f \mid \neg \phi \mid \phi_1 \otimes \phi_2 \mid \odot v\, \phi$ | |
| $\qquad$ where $\otimes \in \{\vee, \wedge\}$ and $\odot \in \{\forall, \exists\}$ and $v \in (V_a \cup V_d)$ | |
| **SQL Functions** | |
| $\quad g(\mathbf{exp}) ::= \texttt{GROUP BY(exp)} \mid id$ | |
| $\qquad$ where $\mathbf{exp} = \langle exp_1, \ldots, exp_n \mid exp_i \in E \rangle$ | |
| $\quad e ::= \texttt{DISTINCT} \mid \texttt{ALL}$ | |
| $\quad s ::= \texttt{AVG} \mid \texttt{SUM} \mid \texttt{MAX} \mid \texttt{MIN} \mid \texttt{COUNT}$ | |
| $\quad h(exp) ::= s \circ e(exp) \mid \texttt{DISTINCT}(exp) \mid id$ | |
| $\quad h(*) ::= \texttt{COUNT(*)}$ | |
| $\qquad$ where $*$ represents a list of database attributes denoted by $\mathbf{v_d}$ | |
| $\quad h(u) ::= \langle h_1(u_1), \ldots, h_n(u_n) \rangle$ | |
| $\qquad$ where $h = \langle h_1, \ldots, h_n \rangle$ and $u = \langle u_1, \ldots, u_n \mid u_i = exp \vee u_i = * \rangle$ | |
| $\quad f(\mathbf{exp}) ::= \texttt{ORDER BY ASC(exp)} \mid \texttt{ORDER BY DESC(exp)} \mid id$ | |
| **Labeled Commands** | |
| $\quad \ell \in L$ | Set of Labels |
| $\quad q \in Q$ | Set of Labeled SQL Statements |
| $\quad q ::= \texttt{SELECT} \mid \texttt{UPDATE} \mid \texttt{INSERT} \mid \texttt{DELETE}$ | |
| $\texttt{SELECT} ::= \langle {}^{\ell_5}assign(v_a), {}^{\ell_4}f(\mathbf{exp'}), {}^{\ell_3}e(h(u)), {}^{\ell_2}\phi', {}^{\ell_1}g(\mathbf{exp}), {}^{\ell_0}\phi \rangle$ | |
| $\texttt{UPDATE} ::= \langle {}^{\ell'} \mathbf{v_d} \overset{upd}{=} \mathbf{exp}, {}^{\ell}\phi \rangle$ | |
| $\texttt{INSERT} ::= \langle {}^{\ell'} \mathbf{v_d} \overset{new}{=} \mathbf{exp}, {}^{\ell}true \rangle$ | |
| $\texttt{DELETE} ::= \langle {}^{\ell'} del(\mathbf{v_d}), {}^{\ell}\phi \rangle$ | |
| $\quad c \in C$ | Set of Labeled Commands |
| $\quad c ::= {}^{\ell}skip \mid {}^{\ell}v_a = exp \mid q \mid c_1; c_2$ | |
| $\qquad \mid$ if ${}^{\ell}b$ then $c_1$ else $c_2$ ${}^{\ell'}$endif | |
| $\qquad \mid$ while ${}^{\ell}b$ do $c$ ${}^{\ell'}$done | |
| $\quad \mathcal{P} ::= c^{\ell}$ | Program that ends with label $\ell$. |

**Table 14.** Definition of action function $a$

$$a[\![\text{SELECT}]\!] \stackrel{def}{=} \{^{\ell_5}assign(\mathbf{v_a}),\ ^{\ell_4}f(\mathbf{exp'}),\ ^{\ell_3}e(h(\mathbf{u})),\ ^{\ell_2}\phi',\ ^{\ell_1}g(\mathbf{exp}),\ ^{\ell_0}\phi\}$$

$$a[\![\text{UPDATE}]\!] \stackrel{def}{=} \{^{\ell'}\mathbf{v_d} \stackrel{upd}{=} \mathbf{exp},\ ^{\ell}\phi\}$$

$$a[\![\text{INSERT}]\!] \stackrel{def}{=} \{^{\ell'}\mathbf{v_d} \stackrel{new}{=} \mathbf{exp}\}$$

$$a[\![\text{DELETE}]\!] \stackrel{def}{=} \{^{\ell'}del(\mathbf{v_d}),\ ^{\ell}\phi\}$$

**Table 15.** Definition of variables function $\mathsf{V}$

$$\mathsf{V}[\![c]\!] \stackrel{def}{=} \emptyset$$

$$\mathsf{V}[\![v]\!] \stackrel{def}{=} \{v\},\ \text{where } v \in (V_a \cup V_d)$$

$$\mathsf{V}[\![\mathbf{v}]\!] \stackrel{def}{=} \bigcup_{v_i \in \mathbf{v}} \mathsf{V}[\![v_i]\!]$$

$$\mathsf{V}[\![exp_1 \oplus exp_1]\!] \stackrel{def}{=} \mathsf{V}[\![exp_1]\!] \cup \mathsf{V}[\![exp_1]\!],\ \text{where } \oplus \in \{+, -, *, /\}$$

$$\mathsf{V}[\![\mathbf{exp}]\!] \stackrel{def}{=} \bigcup_{exp_i \in \mathbf{exp}} \mathsf{V}[\![exp_i]\!]$$

$$\mathsf{V}[\![\text{true}]\!] \stackrel{def}{=} \emptyset$$

$$\mathsf{V}[\![\text{false}]\!] \stackrel{def}{=} \emptyset$$

$$\mathsf{V}[\![exp_1 \oslash exp_2]\!] \stackrel{def}{=} \mathsf{V}[\![exp_1]\!] \cup \mathsf{V}[\![exp_2]\!],\ \text{where } \oslash \in \{\leq, \geq, ==, >, \neq, \dots\}$$

$$\mathsf{V}[\![\neg b]\!] \stackrel{def}{=} \mathsf{V}[\![b]\!]$$

$$\mathsf{V}[\![b_1 \otimes b_2]\!] \stackrel{def}{=} \mathsf{V}[\![b_1]\!] \cup \mathsf{V}[\![b_2]\!],\ \text{where } \otimes \in \{\vee, \wedge\}$$

$$\mathsf{V}[\![f_n(\tau_1, \dots, \tau_n)]\!] \stackrel{def}{=} \mathsf{V}[\![\tau_1]\!] \cup \dots \cup \mathsf{V}[\![\tau_n]\!],\ \text{where } f_n \text{ is an n-ary function.}$$

$$\mathsf{V}[\![R_n(\tau_1, \dots, \tau_n)]\!] \stackrel{def}{=} \mathsf{V}[\![\tau_1]\!] \cup \dots \cup \mathsf{V}[\![\tau_n]\!],\ \text{where } R_n(\tau_1, \tau_2, \dots, \tau_n) \in \{\text{true}, \text{false}\}$$

$$\mathsf{V}[\![\tau_1 = \tau_2)]\!] \stackrel{def}{=} \mathsf{V}[\![\tau_1]\!] \cup \mathsf{V}[\![\tau_2]\!]$$

$$\mathsf{V}[\![\neg\phi]\!] \stackrel{def}{=} \mathsf{V}[\![\phi]\!]$$

$$\mathsf{V}[\![\phi_1 \otimes \phi_2]\!] \stackrel{def}{=} \mathsf{V}[\![\phi_1]\!] \cup \mathsf{V}[\![\phi_2]\!],\ \text{where } \otimes \in \{\vee, \wedge\}$$

$$\mathsf{V}[\![\odot v\ \phi]\!] \stackrel{def}{=} \{v\} \cup \mathsf{V}[\![\phi]\!],\ \text{where } \odot \in \{\vee, \exists\}$$

$$\mathsf{V}[\![\text{SELECT}]\!] \stackrel{def}{=} \mathsf{V}[\![\mathbf{v_a}]\!] \cup \mathsf{V}[\![\mathbf{exp'}]\!] \cup \mathsf{V}[\![\mathbf{u}]\!] \cup \mathsf{V}[\![\phi']\!] \cup \mathsf{V}[\![\mathbf{exp}]\!] \cup \mathsf{V}[\![\phi]\!]$$

$$\mathsf{V}[\![\text{UPDATE}]\!] \stackrel{def}{=} \mathsf{V}[\![\mathbf{v_d}]\!] \cup \mathsf{V}[\![\mathbf{exp}]\!] \cup \mathsf{V}[\![\phi]\!]$$

$$\mathsf{V}[\![\text{INSERT}]\!] \stackrel{def}{=} \mathsf{V}[\![\mathbf{v_d}]\!] \cup \mathsf{V}[\![\mathbf{exp}]\!]$$

$$\mathsf{V}[\![\text{DELETE}]\!] \stackrel{def}{=} \mathsf{V}[\![\mathbf{v_d}]\!] \cup \mathsf{V}[\![\phi]\!]$$

of database and application environments whose domain is the set of database and application variables in $\mathcal{P}$ only.

The *labeled transition relation* $\mathsf{T} : \Sigma \times \mathsf{A} \longmapsto \wp(\Sigma)$ specifies which successor states $\sigma' = \langle \ell', \rho_{d'}, \rho_{a'} \rangle \in \Sigma$ can follow when an action $a \in \mathsf{A}$ executes on state $\sigma = \langle \ell, \rho_d, \rho_a \rangle \in \Sigma$. We denote a labeled transition by $\sigma \stackrel{a}{\to} \sigma'$ or by $\langle \ell, \rho_d, \rho_a \rangle \stackrel{a}{\to} \langle \ell', \rho_{d'}, \rho_{a'} \rangle$, or by $\langle \ell, \rho \rangle \stackrel{a}{\to} \langle \ell', \rho' \rangle$ where $\rho$ and $\rho'$ represent $(\rho_d, \rho_a)$ and $(\rho_{d'}, \rho_{a'})$ respectively.

The *labeled transition semantics* $\mathsf{T}[\![\mathcal{P}]\!] \in \wp(\Sigma[\![\mathcal{P}]\!] \times a[\![\mathcal{P}]\!] \longmapsto \wp(\Sigma[\![\mathcal{P}]\!]))$ of a program $\mathcal{P}$ restricts the transition relation to program actions, *i.e.*

$$\mathsf{T}[\![\mathcal{P}]\!]\sigma = \{\sigma' \mid \sigma \stackrel{a}{\to} \sigma' \wedge a \in a[\![\mathcal{P}]\!] \wedge \sigma, \sigma' \in \Sigma[\![\mathcal{P}]\!]\}$$

The *labeled transition semantics* of various commands in database applications can easily be defined from the semantic description reported in [22].

Given a program $\mathcal{P}$, let $\mathsf{I} = \{\langle in[\![\mathcal{P}]\!], \rho_d, \rho_a\rangle \mid \rho_a \in \mathcal{E}_a \wedge \rho_d \in \mathcal{E}_d\}$ be the set of initial states of $\mathcal{P}$. The *partial trace semantics* of $\mathcal{P}$ can be defined as

$$\mathsf{T}[\![\mathcal{P}]\!](\mathsf{I}) = \mathrm{lfp}_{\emptyset}^{\subseteq} F(\mathsf{I}) = \bigcup_{i \leq \omega} F^i(\mathsf{I})$$

where $F(\mathsf{I}_0) = \lambda X.\ \mathsf{I}_0 \cup \{\sigma_0 \xrightarrow{\mathsf{a}_0} \ldots \xrightarrow{\mathsf{a}_{n-1}} \sigma_n \xrightarrow{\mathsf{a}_n} \sigma_{n+1} \mid \sigma_0 \xrightarrow{\mathsf{a}_0} \ldots \xrightarrow{\mathsf{a}_{n-1}} \sigma_n \in X$

$\qquad\qquad\qquad \wedge \sigma_n \xrightarrow{\mathsf{a}_n} \sigma_{n+1} \in \mathsf{T}[\![\mathcal{P}]\!]\}$

### 4.3   Abstract Semantics

In case of applications embedding SQL statements, we need to consider two additional dependences, called *database-database* dependence and *program-database* dependence [23]. A *program-database* dependence arises between a database variable and an application variable, where values of the database variable depend on the value of the program variable or vice-versa. A *database-database* dependence arises between two database variables where the values of one depend on the values of the other.

*Example 3.* Consider the database of Table 12 in Sect. 4.1. Consider the following SELECT query:

$\mathsf{q}_1 = $ SELECT *Points*, AVG(*Age*) INTO $\mathsf{v}_a$ FROM *Customer* WHERE *Points* >=50
$\qquad$ GROUP BY *Points* HAVING SUM(*DistanceCovered*)>100 ORDER BY *Points*

Note that we use "INTO $\mathsf{v}_a$" in $\mathsf{q}_1$ to mention that the result of the query is finally assigned to $\mathsf{v}_a$, where $\mathsf{v}_a$ is a Record or ResultSet type application variable with fields $\boldsymbol{w} = \langle w_1, w_2 \rangle$. The type of $w_1$, $w_2$ are same as the return type of '*Points*', 'AVG(*Age*)' respectively. Recall from Table 13 that the syntax of SELECT statement is defined as:

$$\langle {}^{\ell_5}assign(\mathsf{v}_a),\ {}^{\ell_4}f(\mathbf{exp'}),\ {}^{\ell_3}e(\boldsymbol{h}(\boldsymbol{u})),\ {}^{\ell_2}\phi',\ {}^{\ell_1}g(\mathbf{exp}),\ {}^{\ell_0}\phi \rangle$$

According the syntax defined above, $\mathsf{q}_1$ can be formulated as:

$\mathsf{q}_1 = $ SELECT $e(\boldsymbol{h}(\boldsymbol{u}))$ INTO $\mathsf{v}_a(w)$ FROM *Customer* WHERE $\phi$ GROUP BY($\mathbf{exp}$) HAVING
$\qquad \phi'$ ORDER BY ASC($\mathbf{exp'}$)

where

- $\phi = Points \text{ >=}50$
- $\mathbf{exp} = \langle Points \rangle$
- $g(\mathbf{exp}) = $ GROUP BY($\langle Points \rangle$)
- $\phi' = $ (SUM∘ALL(*DistanceCovered*))>100
- $\boldsymbol{h} = \langle$ DISTINCT, AVG∘ALL $\rangle$
  $\boldsymbol{u} = \langle Points, Age \rangle$
  $\boldsymbol{h}(\boldsymbol{u}) = \langle$ DISTINCT(*Points*), AVG∘ALL(*Age*) $\rangle$
- $\mathbf{exp'} = \langle Points \rangle$
- $f(\mathbf{exp'}) = $ ORDER BY ASC($\langle Points \rangle$)

– $v_a$ = Record or ResultSet type application variable with fields $w = \langle w_1, w_2 \rangle$. The type of $w_1$ and $w_2$ are same as the return type of DISTINCT($Points$) and AVG∘ALL($Age$) respectively.

From $q_1$ we get the following set of logical formula representing variable dependences:

$$\overline{Points} \rightarrow \overline{v_a.w_1}, \qquad \overline{Age} \rightarrow \overline{v_a.w_2}, \qquad \overline{Points} \rightarrow \overline{v_a.w_2}$$
$$\overline{DistanceCovered} \rightarrow \overline{v_a.w_1}, \overline{DistanceCovered} \rightarrow \overline{v_a.w_2}$$

Below we depict variable dependences in other SQL commands.

$q_2$=UPDATE $Customer$ SET $DistanceCovered$ = $\$y + 150$ WHERE $custID$=2
/* where $\$y$ is an application variable. */

The logical formula obtained from $q_2$ are: $\overline{custID} \rightarrow \overline{DistanceCovered}, \overline{\$y} \rightarrow \overline{DistanceCovered}$.

$q_3$ = INSERT INTO        $Travel(custID, Source, Destination, FlightID,$
        $JourneyDate, BoardPriority)$ VALUES $(5, "D", "E", "F34", \$y, \$z)$
/* where $\$y$ and $\$z$ are application variables. */

The logical formula obtained from $q_3$ are: $\overline{\$y} \rightarrow \overline{JourneyDate}, \overline{\$z} \rightarrow \overline{BoardPriority}$.

$q_4$ = DELETE FROM $Customer$ WHERE $Age$ >60

The logical formula obtained from $q_4$ are:

$$\overline{Age} \rightarrow \overline{custID}, \overline{Age} \rightarrow \overline{custName}, \qquad \overline{Age} \rightarrow \overline{Address}$$
$$\overline{Age} \rightarrow \overline{Age}, \qquad \overline{Age} \rightarrow \overline{DistanceCovered}, \overline{Age} \rightarrow \overline{Points}$$

The dependences above indicate explicit-flow of information. An example of implicit-flow that may occur in case of our application is, for instance, when manipulation of any public database information is performed under the control statements involving high variables.

Table 16 depicts abstract labeled transition semantics of various statements in database applications. The abstract semantics of the program is obtained by fix-point computation over the abstract domain.

## 4.4   Enhancing the Analysis

The dependences that we considered so far are syntax-based, and may yield false positives in the analysis. For instance, let us consider the database in Table 17 and the query $q_5$.

$q_5$ = SELECT $Type$ INTO $v_a$ FROM $Emp, Job$ WHERE $Sal$ = $BASIC+(BASIC *$
        $(DA/100))+(BASIC * (HRA/100))$

**Table 16.** Definition of abstract transition function $\overline{\mathsf{T}}$

$$
\begin{aligned}
&\overline{\mathsf{T}}[\![\text{SELECT}]\!] \\
&\overset{def}{=} \overline{\mathsf{T}}[\![\langle {}^{\ell_5}assign(\mathsf{v_a}),\ {}^{\ell_4}f(\textbf{exp'}),\ {}^{\ell_3}e(h(u)),\ {}^{\ell_2}\phi',\ {}^{\ell_1}g(\textbf{exp}),\ {}^{\ell_0}\phi\rangle]\!] \\
&\overset{def}{=} \{\langle \ell_0, \psi\rangle \xrightarrow{\text{SELECT}} \langle fin[\![\text{SELECT}]\!], \psi'\rangle\} \\
&\text{where } \psi' = \bigwedge\{\bar{v} \to \overline{\mathsf{v_a}.w_i} \mid \bar{v} \in (\overline{V}[\![\phi]\!] \cup \overline{V}[\![\textbf{exp}]\!] \cup \overline{V}[\![\phi']\!] \cup \overline{V}[\![\textbf{exp'}]\!]) \wedge \overline{\mathsf{v_a}.w_i} \in \overline{\mathsf{v_a}.w} \wedge \bar{v} \neq \overline{\mathsf{v_a}.w_i}\} \wedge \\
&\qquad \bigwedge\{\bar{v_i} \to \overline{\mathsf{v_a}.w_i} \mid \bar{v_i} \in \overline{V}[\![u_i]\!] \wedge u_i \in u \wedge \overline{\mathsf{v_a}.w_i} \in \overline{\mathsf{v_a}.w}\} \wedge (\psi \ominus \bigwedge\{\bar{v} \to \overline{\mathsf{v_a}.w_i} \mid \bar{v} \in \overline{V} \wedge \overline{\mathsf{v_a}.w_i} \in \overline{\mathsf{v_a}.w}\}) \\[4pt]
&\overline{\mathsf{T}}[\![\text{UPDATE}]\!] \\
&\overset{def}{=} \overline{\mathsf{T}}[\![\langle {}^{\ell'} \mathsf{v_d} \overset{upd}{=} \textbf{exp},\ {}^{\ell}\phi\rangle]\!] \\
&\overset{def}{=} \{\langle \ell, \psi\rangle \xrightarrow{\text{UPDATE}} \langle fin[\![\text{UPDATE}]\!], \psi'\rangle\} \\
&\qquad\qquad\qquad\qquad\qquad \text{where } \psi' = \bigwedge\{\bar{v_1} \to \bar{v_2} \mid \bar{v_1} \in \overline{V}[\![\phi]\!] \wedge \bar{v_2} \in \overline{\mathsf{v_d}}\} \wedge \\
&\qquad\qquad\qquad\qquad\qquad \bigwedge\{\bar{v_i} \to \bar{v_j} \mid \bar{v_i} \in \overline{V}[\![exp_i]\!] \wedge exp_i \in \textbf{exp} \wedge \bar{v_j} \in \overline{\mathsf{v_d}}\} \wedge \psi \\[4pt]
&\overline{\mathsf{T}}[\![\text{INSERT}]\!] \\
&\overset{def}{=} \overline{\mathsf{T}}[\![\langle {}^{\ell'} \mathsf{v_d} \overset{new}{=} \textbf{exp},\ {}^{\ell}\text{true}\rangle]\!] \\
&\overset{def}{=} \{\langle \ell, \psi\rangle \xrightarrow{\text{INSERT}} \langle fin[\![\text{INSERT}]\!], \psi'\rangle\} \\
&\qquad\qquad\qquad \text{where } \psi' = \bigwedge\{\bar{v_i} \to \bar{v_j} \mid \bar{v_i} \in \overline{V}[\![exp_i]\!] \wedge exp_i \in \textbf{exp} \wedge \bar{v_j} \in \overline{\mathsf{v_d}}\} \wedge \psi \\[4pt]
&\overline{\mathsf{T}}[\![\text{DELETE}]\!] \\
&\overset{def}{=} \overline{\mathsf{T}}[\![\langle {}^{\ell'} del(\mathsf{v_d}),\ {}^{\ell}\phi\rangle]\!] \\
&\overset{def}{=} \{\langle \ell, \psi\rangle \xrightarrow{\text{DELETE}} \langle fin[\![\text{DELETE}]\!], \psi'\rangle\} \\
&\qquad\qquad\qquad\qquad \text{where } \psi' = \bigwedge\{\bar{v_1} \to \bar{v_2} \mid \bar{v_1} \in \overline{V}[\![\phi]\!] \wedge \bar{v_2} \in \overline{\mathsf{v_d}}\} \wedge \psi
\end{aligned}
$$

**Table 17.** Database $dB$

(a) Table *"Emp"*

| ID | Name | Sal |
|----|----------|------|
| 1 | Alberto | 1110 |
| 2 | Matteo | 1638 |
| 3 | Francesco | 2255 |
| 4 | Smith | 1840 |

(b) Table *"Job"*

| Type | Rank | BASIC | HRA | DA |
|-----------|------|-------|-----|----|
| Security | S1 | 800 | 20 | 65 |
| Security | S2 | 600 | 20 | 65 |
| Security | S3 | 520 | 15 | 65 |
| Technical | T1 | 1000 | 25 | 75 |
| Technical | T2 | 920 | 25 | 75 |
| Technical | T3 | 880 | 20 | 75 |
| Technical | T4 | 840 | 20 | 75 |
| Admin | A1 | 1240 | 25 | 80 |
| Admin | A2 | 1100 | 25 | 80 |

The following logical formulae representing PD-dependences exist in $q_5$:

$$\psi_5 = \overline{Sal} \to \overline{\mathsf{v_a}.w_1},\ \overline{BASIC} \to \overline{\mathsf{v_a}.w_1},\ \overline{DA} \to \overline{\mathsf{v_a}.w_1},\ \overline{HRA} \to \overline{\mathsf{v_a}.w_1},$$
$$\overline{Type} \to \overline{\mathsf{v_a}.w_1}$$

Assuming '$Sal$', '$BASIC$', '$HRA$', '$DA$' are private and at least one employee in each job-type must exist, we see that although syntactic PD-dependences above indicating the presence of information leakage, but in practice nothing about these secrets is leaked through $\mathsf{v_a}.w_1$.

Here is an another example of PD-dependence that is indicating false alarm on leakage: consider the code $\{\$x = 4 * \$w * log\ 2;\ \text{UPDATE}\ t\ \text{SET}\ a = a + \$x;\}$. Assuming $\$x$ is private and $\$w$, $a$ are public, we see that the dependence $\overline{\$x} \to \overline{a}$ generates false alarm as because $\$x$ is always equal to 0.

**Table 18.** Database $dB^{\sharp}$

(a) Table "$Emp^{\sharp}$"

| $ID^{\sharp}$ | $Name^{\sharp}$ | $Sal^{\sharp}$ |
|------|---------|-----------|
| 1 | Alberto | [1110, 1110] |
| 2 | Matteo | [1638, 1638] |
| 3 | Francesco | [2255, 2255] |
| 4 | Smith | [1840, 1840] |

(b) Table "$Job^{\sharp}$"

| $Type^{\sharp}$ | $Rank^{\sharp}$ | $BASIC^{\sharp}$ | $HRA^{\sharp}$ | $DA^{\sharp}$ |
|-----------|-----------|-------------|-----------|-----------|
| Security | [S1, S3] | [520, 800] | [15, 20] | [65, 65] |
| Technical | [T1, T4] | [840, 1000] | [20, 25] | [75, 75] |
| Admin | [A1, A2] | [1100, 1240] | [25, 25] | [80, 80] |

To remove all such false alarms and to increase the accuracy of the analysis, we analyze programs by using the semantic-based abstract interpretation framework.

Consider an abstract domain $\aleph$ where numerical attributes and numerical application variables are abstracted by the *domain of intervals*[4]. The abstraction yields an abstract query $q_6{}^{\sharp}$ corresponding to $q_6$ and an abstract database depicted in Table 18.

$$q_6{}^{\sharp} = \mathsf{SELECT}^{\sharp} \quad Type^{\sharp} \quad \mathsf{INTO}^{\sharp} \quad v_a{}^{\sharp} \quad \mathsf{FROM}^{\sharp} \quad Emp^{\sharp},$$
$$Job^{\sharp} \quad \mathsf{WHERE}^{\sharp} \quad Sal^{\sharp} \quad =^{\sharp} \quad BASIC^{\sharp}+(BASIC^{\sharp} \ *$$
$$(DA^{\sharp}/[100, 100]))+(BASIC^{\sharp} * (HRA^{\sharp}/[100, 100]))$$

The right-hand side expression of the condition in $\mathsf{WHERE}^{\sharp}$ is evaluated to abstract values $[936, 1480]$, $[1638, 2000]$, and $[2255, 2542]$ respectively corresponding to the three abstract tuples in "$Job^{\sharp}$". Observe that, according to the assumption that at least one employee must exist in each job-type, there exist at least one '$Sal^{\sharp}$' in "$Emp^{\sharp}$" for which "$Sal^{\sharp} =^{\sharp} [936, 1480]$" is true, according to the following:

$$[l_i, h_i] =^{\sharp} [l_j, h_j] \triangleq \begin{cases} \text{true} & \text{if } (l_i \geq l_j \wedge h_i \leq h_j) \\ \text{false} & \text{if } h_i < l_j \vee l_i > h_j \\ \top & \text{otherwise} \end{cases}$$

Similar for "$Sal^{\sharp} =^{\sharp} [1638, 2000]$" and "$Sal^{\sharp} =^{\sharp} [2255, 2542]$". Therefore, the evaluation of $q_6$ on $dB$ always gives the same result *w.r.t.* the property $\aleph$, irrespective of the states of "$Emp$".

We can perform similar analysis of the code $\{\$x = 4 * \$w * \log 2;\ \mathsf{UPDATE}\ t$ $\mathsf{SET}\ a = a + \$x;\}$ in the *domain of intervals*, yielding to "*no update*" of the values in public attribute $a$.

The interaction of the logical and numerical domains can be formalized by using the reduced Product $D^{\natural}$ as follows:

$$D^{\natural} = \{\varrho(\langle X, \mathfrak{N}\rangle) \mid X \in \wp(\Sigma^{\star\sharp}), \mathfrak{N} \in \aleph\}$$

where $\varrho(\langle X, \mathfrak{N}\rangle) = \{\langle \ell_i, \psi_k\rangle \mid \langle \ell_i, \psi_j\rangle \in X \wedge \psi_k = (\psi_j \ominus \{\overline{v}_1 \rightarrow \overline{v}_2 \mid y \in \gamma(\mathfrak{N})\})\}$.

In the example above, by analyzing $q_6$ in the abstract domain $\aleph$ where numerical variables are abstracted by the *domain of intervals*, we see that the value of $v_a.w_1$ generated by $q_6$ is always constant throughout the program execution

---

[4] For other type of variables, the abstraction function represents identity function.

*w.r.t.* $\aleph$. As $\psi_6 \in \mathsf{Pos}$ and $\mathsf{v_a}.w_1 \in \aleph$, the reduced product operator $\varrho$ removes from $\psi_6$ all dependences in the form "$x \to \mathsf{v_a}.w_1$" (that are representing false alarms), and makes the analysis more accurate and efficient.

## 5   Implementing the Analysis in Sails

In this section, we present Sails. The tool is an instance of the generic analyzer Sample. This is why we discuss the main issues we have to solve in order to deal with information leakage analysis within Sample.

### 5.1   Sample

Sample (Static Analyzer of Multiple Programming LanguagEs) is a generic analyzer based on the abstract interpretation theory. Relying on compositional analyses, Sample can be plugged with different heap abstractions, approximations of other semantic information (e.g., numeric domains or information flow), properties of interest, and languages. Several heap analyses, semantic and numerical domains have been already plugged. The analyzer works on an intermediate language called Simple. Up to now, Sample supports the compilation of Scala and Java bytecode to Simple.

Figure 3 depicts the overall structure of Sample. Source code programs are compiled to Simple. A fixpoint engine receives a heap analysis, a semantic domain, and a control flow graph (whose blocks are composed by a sequence of Simple statements), and it produces an abstract result over the control flow graph of each method. This result is passed to a property checker that produces some output (e.g., warnings) to the user. The integration of an analysis in Sample allows one to take advantage of all aspects not strictly related to the analysis but that can improve its final precision (e.g., heap or numerical abstractions). For instance, Sample is interfaced with the Apron library [27] and contains a heap analysis based of TVLA [37].

### 5.2   Heap Abstraction

In Sample heap locations are approximated by abstract heap identifiers. While the identifiers of program variables are fixed and represent exactly one concrete variable, the abstract heap identifiers may represent several concrete heap locations (e.g., if they summarize a potentially unbounded list), and they can be merged and split during the analysis. In particular we have to support (i) assignments on summary heap identifiers, and (ii) renaming of identifiers.

In order to preserve the soundness of Sails, we have to perform weak assignments on summary heap identifiers. Since a summary abstract identifier may represent several concrete heap locations and only one of them would be assigned in one particular execution, we have to take the upper bound between the assigned value, and the old one.

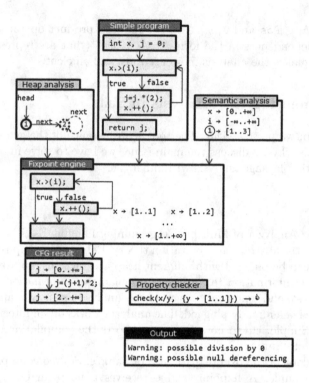

**Fig. 3.** The structure of Sample

The heap abstraction could require to rename, summarize or split existing identifiers. This information is passed through a replacement function $rep : \wp(\mathsf{Id}) \to \wp(\mathsf{Id})$, where $\mathsf{Id}$ is the set containing all heap identifiers. For instance, in TVLA two abstract nodes represented by identifiers $a_1$ and $a_2$ may be merged to a summary node $a_3$, or a summary abstract node $b_1$ may be splitted to $b_2$ and $b_3$. Our heap analysis will pass $\{a_1, a_2\} \mapsto \{a_3\}$ and $\{b_1\} \mapsto \{b_2, b_3\}$ to Sails in these cases, respectively. Given a single replacement $S_1 \mapsto S_2$, Sails removes all subformulae dealing with some of the variables in $S_1$, and for each removed subformula $s$ it inserts a new subformula $s'$ renaming each of the variables in $S_1$ to each of the variables in $S_2$. Formally:

$$rename : (\mathsf{Pos} \times (\wp(\mathsf{Id}) \to \wp(\mathsf{Id}))) \to \mathsf{Pos}$$
$$rename(\sigma^\sharp, rep) = \{(i'_1, i'_2) : (i_1, i_2) \in \sigma^\sharp \wedge$$
$$i'_1 = \begin{cases} i_1 & \text{if } \nexists R_1 \in dom(rep) : i_1 \in R_1 \\ k_1 & \text{if } \exists R_1 \in dom(rep) : i_1 \in R_1 \wedge k_1 \in rep(R_1) \end{cases},$$
$$i'_2 = \begin{cases} i_2 & \text{if } \nexists R_2 \in dom(rep) : i_2 \in R_2 \\ k_2 & \text{if } \exists R_2 \in dom(rep) : i_2 \in R_2 \wedge k_2 \in rep(R_2) \end{cases}\}$$

## 5.3  Propositional Formulae

We have to introduce some slight modifications on the domain for information leakage analysis described in Sect. 2 to work with object oriented languages. We can consider a propositional formula $\phi$ as a conjunction of subformulae ($\zeta_0 \wedge \ldots \wedge \zeta_n$). In the implementation, each subformula is an implication between two identifiers. Then we represent a subformula as a pair of identifiers and a formula as a set of subformulae. Consider the statement if$(x > 0)$ y = z;. The formula obtained after the analysis of this statement is represented by the set $\{(\overline{y}, \overline{z}), (\overline{x}, \overline{y})\}$, where we denote the identifier of the variable u by $\overline{u}$. The order relation "$\trianglelefteq$" is defined by the subset relation ($\phi_0 \trianglelefteq \phi_1 \Leftrightarrow \phi_0 \subseteq \phi_1$).

Consequently, in the implementation the set of propositional variables $\overline{V}$ consists in the set of identifier Id, a single propositional formula is represented by $\wp(\text{Id} \times \text{Id})$ and an abstract state $\sigma^{\sharp} \in \Sigma^{\sharp}$ is a conjunction of propositional formulae represented by $\wp(\wp(\text{Id} \times \text{Id}))$.

## 5.4  Implicit Flow Detection

An implicit information flow occurs when there is an information leakage from a variable in a condition to a variable assigned inside a block dependent on that condition. For instance, in if$(x > 0)$ y = z; there is an explicit flow from z to y, and an implicit flow from x to y. To record these relations we relate the variables in the conditions to the variables that have been assigned in the block. When we join two blocks coming from the same condition, we discharge all implicit flows on the abstract state. Observe that Sails does not support all cfgs that can be represented in Sample but only the ones coming from structured programs, i.e., that corresponds to programs with if and while statements and not with arbitrary jumps like goto.

## 5.5  Property

An information flow analysis can be carried out by considering different attacker abilities. We implemented two scenarios: when the attacker can read public variables only at the beginning and at the end of the computation, and when the attacker can read public variables after each step of the computation[5]. Moreover, we implemented two security properties for each attacker: secrecy (i.e., information leakage analysis) and integrity.

The verification of these properties happens after the computation of the analysis and the declaration of private variables (at run time, by a text files writing the variables name or by a graphical user interface selecting the variables in a list).

---

[5] Notice that, as in [45], we assume that the attacker, in both cases, knows the source code of the program.

## 5.6    Numerical Analysis

The information flow analysis is based on the reduced product of a dependency and a numerical analysis. Thanks to the compositional structure of Sample, we can plug Sails with different numerical domains. In particular, Sample supports the Apron library. In this way, we can combine Sails with all numerical domains contained in Apron (namely, Polka, the Parma Polyhedra Library, Octagons, and a deep implementation of Intervals).

In addition, we can apply different heap abstractions. For instance, if we are not interested to the heap structure, we can use a less accurate domain that approximates all heap locations with one unique summary node, as we will do in Sect. 6.2.

## 5.7    Complexity of the Analysis

The complexity of variables dependency analysis showed in Sect. 2 is strictly correlated to the complexity of propositional formulae. Logical domains, in literature, are widely treated and generally, the logical equivalence of two boolean expression is a co-NP-complete problem. However, this complexity issue may not matter much in practice because the size of the set of variables appearing in the program is reasonably small. Hence, on the one hand, work with propositional formulae requires the solving of a co-NP-complete problem, while on the other hand, in many frameworks (included our system), Pos only deal with the variables appearing in the programs, reducing in this way the complexity. Generally, it is possible to increase the efficiency of the computation using the *binary decision diagrams* (BDDs) for the implementation of propositional formulae. For more information about binary decision diagrams see [1].

The simplification adopted in the implementation, i.e. the definition of "$\trianglelefteq$" by the subset relation ($\phi_0 \trianglelefteq \phi_1 \Leftrightarrow \phi_0 \subseteq \phi_1$), permits to decrease the complexity. In fact, decreasing the precision of the analysis, we can compare two propositional formulae in polynomial time.

About polyhedra analysis, the complexity is well and completely treated in many works [5] and heavily depends on its implementation. For example many implementations, e.g. Polylib and New Polka, use matrices of coefficients, that cannot grow dynamically, and the worst case space complexity of the methods employed is exponential. In PPL library, instead, all data structures are fully dynamic and automatically expanded (in amortized constant time) ensuring the best use of available memory. Comparing the efficiency of polyhedra libraries is not a simple task, because the pay-off depends on the targeted applications: in [5] the authors presented many test results about it.

The complexity of reduced product, and more precisely of reduction operator presented in Sect. 3.1, is strictly connected with the complexity of the operations on the domains we combine.

# 6    Experimental Results

In this section, we present the experimental results of Sails. First of all, we present the results in terms of precision when we analyze a case study involving recursive data structures. Then, we present the results obtained when applying Sails to the SecuriBench-micro suite.

## 6.1    Case Study

Consider the Java code in Fig. 4. Class ListWorkers models a list of workers of an enterprise. Each node contains the salary earned by the worker, and some other data (e.g., name and surname of the person). Method updateSalaries is defined as well. It receives a list of employees and a list of managers. These two lists are supposed to be disjoint. First method updateSalaries computes the maximal salary of an employee. Then it traverses the list of managers updating their salary to the maximal salary of employees if manager's salary is less than that.

Usually managers would not like to leak information about their salary to employees (secrecy property). This property could be expressed in Sails specifying that we do not want to have a flow of information *from* managers *to* employees. More precisely, we want to prove the absence of information leakage from the content of field salary of any node reachable from managers to any node reachable from employees.

```java
class ListWorkers {
    int salary;
    ListWorkers next;
    ...
}

public void updateSalaries
(ListWorkers employees, ListWorkers managers){
    int maxSalary = 0;
    ListWorkers it=employees;
    while(it!=null) {
        if(it.salary>maxSalary)
            maxSalary=it.salary;
        it=it.next;
    }
    it=managers;
    while(it!=null) {
        if(it.salary < maxSalary)
            it.salary=maxSalary;
        it=it.next;
    }
}
```

Fig. 4. A motivating example

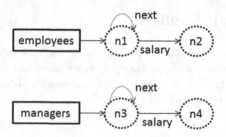

**Fig. 5.** The initial state of the heap abstraction

We combine Sails with a heap analysis that approximates all objects created by a program point with a single abstract node [19]. We start the analysis of method updateSalaries with an abstract heap in which lists managers and employees are abstracted with a summary node and they are disjoint. Figure 5 depicts the initial state, where n2 and n4 contains the salary values of the ListWorkers n1 and n3, respectively. In the graphic representation we adopt dotted circles to represent summary nodes, rectangles to represent local variables, and edges between nodes to represent what is pointed by local variables or fields of objects. Note that the structure of these two lists does not change during the analysis of the program, since method updateSalaries does not modify the heap structure.

Sails infers that, after the first while loop at line 15, there is a flow of information from n2 to maxSalary. This happens because variable it points to n1 before the loop (because of the assignment at line 9), and it iterates following field next (obtaining always the summary node n1) perhaps assigning the content of it.salary (that is, node n2) to maxSalary. Therefore, at line 15 we have the propositional formula n2 $\rightarrow$ maxSalary.

Then updateSalaries traverses the managers list. For each node, it could assign maxSalary to it.salary. Similarly to what happened in the previous loop, variable it points to n3 before and inside the loop, since field next always points to the summary node n3. Therefore the assignment at line 18 could potentially affects only node n4. For this reason, Sails discovers a flow of information from maxSalary to n4, represented by the propositional formula maxSalary $\rightarrow$ n4.

At the end of the analysis, Sails soundly computes that (n2 $\rightarrow$ maxSalary) $\land$ (maxSalary $\rightarrow$ n4). By the transitive property, we know that there could be a flow of information from n2 to n4, that is, from employees to managers. This flow is allowed by our security policy. On the other hand, we also discovered that there is no information leakage from list managers to list employees, since Sails does not contain any propositional formula with this flow. Therefore Sails proves that this program is safe.

"Noninterference of programs essentially means that a *variable* of confidential (high) input does not cause a variation of public (low) output" [36]. Thanks to the combination between a heap abstraction and an abstract domain tracking information flow, Sails deals directly with the structure of the heap, extending the concept of noninterference from variables to portions of the heap represented by abstract nodes. This opens a new scenario since we can prove that a whole data structure does not interfere with another one, as we have done in this example. As far as we know, Sails is the only tool that performs a noninterference analysis over a heap abstraction, and therefore it can prove properties like "there is no information flow from the nodes reachable from $v_1$ to the nodes reachable from $v_2$".

## 6.2 Benchmarks

A well-established way of studying the precision and the efficiency of information flow analyses is the SecuriBench-micro suite [43]. We applied Sails to this test suite; the description and the results of these benchmarks are reported in Table 19. Column fa reports if the analysis did not produce any false alarm. We combined Sails with a really rough heap abstraction that approximates all

Table 19. SecuriBench-micro suite

| Name | Description | fa |
|------|-------------|----|
| Aliasing1 | Simple aliasing | ✓ |
| Aliasing2 | Aliasing false positive | ✓ |
| Basic1 | Very simple XSS | ✓ |
| Basic2 | XSS combined with a conditional | ✓ |
| Basic3 | Simple derived integer test | ✓ |
| Basic5 | Test of derived integer | ✓ |
| Basic6 | Complex test of derived integer | ✓ |
| Basic8 | Test of complex conditionals | ✓ |
| Basic9 | Chains of value assignments | ✓ |
| Basic10 | Chains of value assignments | ✓ |
| Basic11 | A simple false positive | ✓ |
| Basic12 | A simple conditional | ✓ |
| Basic18 | Protect agains simple loop unrolling | ✓ |
| Basic28 | Complicated control flow | ✓ |
| Pred1 | Simple if(false) test | ✗ |
| Pred2 | Simple correlated tests | ✓ |
| Pred3 | Simple correlated tests | ✓ |
| Pred4 | Test with an integer variable | ✓ |
| Pred5 | Test with a complex conditional | ✓ |
| Pred6 | Test with addition | ✗ |
| Pred7 | Test with multiple variables | ✗ |

Table 20. Jif case studies

| Name | Description | fa |
|---|---|---|
| A | Simple explicit flow test | ✓ |
| Account | Simple explicit flow test | ✓ |
| ConditionalLeak | Explicit flow in if statement | ✓ |
| Do | Implicit flow in the loop | ✓ |
| Do2 | Implicit flow if and loop | ✓ |
| Do3 | Implicit flow loop and if | ✓ |
| Do4 | Implicit flow loop and if | ✓ |
| Do5 | Implicit flow loop and if | ✓ |
| If1 | Simple implicit flow | ✓ |
| Implicit | Simple implicit flow | ✓ |

concrete heap locations with one abstract node. Sails detected all information leakages in all tests, but in three cases (Pred1, Pred6 and Pred7) it produced false alarms. This happens because Sails abstracts away the information produced when testing to true or false boolean conditions in if or while statements.

Since these benchmarks cover only problems with explicit flows, we performed further experiments using some Jif [34] case studies. The results are reported in Table 20: we discovered all flows without producing any false alarm.

These results allow us to conclude that Sails is precise, since in 90% of the cases (28 out of 31 programs) it does not produce any false alarm.

About the performances, the analysis of all case studies takes 1.092 s (0.035 s per method in average) without combining it with a numerical domain. When we combine it with Intervals it takes 3.015 s, whereas it takes 6.130 s in combination with Polka. All tests are performed using a MacBook Pro Intel Core 2 Duo 2.53 GHz with 4 GB of RAM memory. Therefore the experimental results underline the efficiency of Sails as well.

## 7    Related Work

In a security-typed language Volpano et al. [44] were the first ones to develop a type system to enforce information flow policies, where a type is inductively associated at compile-time with program statements in such a way that well-typed programs satisfy the non-interference property. The authors formulated the certification conditions of Denning's analysis [17] as a simple type system for a deterministic language: basically, a formal system of type inference rules for making judgments about programs. More generally, type-based approaches are designed such that well-typed programs do not leak secrets. A type is inductively associated at compile-time with program statements in such a way that any statement showing a potential low disclosing secrets is rejected. Type systems that enforce secure information flow have been designed for various languages and they have been used in different applications. Some of these approaches are, for example, applied to specific programs, e.g., written in VHDL [42], where the analysis of information flow is closely related to the context. Moreover, the secure information flow problem was also handled in different situation, for example with multi-threaded programs [40] or with programs that employ explicit cryptographic operations [3,20].

A different approach is the use of standard control flow analysis to detect information leakage, e.g., [9,28,29]. The idea, of this technique, is to conservatively find the program paths through which data may flow. Generally, the data flow analysis approach to secure information flow as a translation from a given program that captures and facilitates reasoning about the possible flows. For example, Leino and Joshi [28] showed an application based on semantics, deriving a first-order predicate whose validity implies that an attacker cannot deduce any secure information from observing the public inputs, outputs and termination behavior of the program.

The use of abstract interpretation in language-based security is not new, even though there aren't many works that use the lattice of abstract interpretations for evaluating the security of programs (for example [47]).

Probably, the main work about information flow analysis by abstract interpretation was done by Giacobazzi and Mastroeni [21] that generalizes the notion of non-interference making it parametric relatively to what an attacker can observe, and using it to model attackers as abstractions. A program semantics was characterized as an abstract interpretation of its maximal trace semantics in the corresponding transition system. The authors gave a method for checking abstract non-interference and they proved that checking abstract non-interference is a standard static program analysis problem. This method allows both to compare attackers and program secrecy by comparing the corresponding abstractions in the lattice of abstract interpretations, and to design automatic program certification tools for language-based security.

There are not so many implementations of secure information flow. In early 2000, some works began the control of sensitive information in realistic languages [7,35]. Jif [4] and Flow CAML [38] are, as far as we know, the two main implementations about information flow analysis. Notice that, in the last years other language-based tools are developed for some specific language, e.g., Fabric [30] for distributed computing, the LIO library in haskell [41] and FlowFox [15] a tool for JavaScript.

According to [39], it seems be helpful to distinguish between two different application scenarios: *developing secure software* and *stopping malicious software*. The first scenario is based on to secure information flow analysis to help the development of software that satisfies some security properties. In this case, the analysis serves as a program development tool. The static analysis tool would alert the programmer to potential leaks and the developer could rewriting the code as necessary. An example of this scenario can be found in [4], where Askarov and Sabelfeld discusses the implementation of a "mental poker" protocol in Jif. The second scenario, instead, the secure information flow analysis is used as a kind of filter to stop malicious software. In this case, we might imagine analyzing a piece of untrusted code before executing it, with the goal of guaranteeing its safety. This is much more challenging than first scenario: probably we would not have access to the source code and we would need to analyze the binary code. Analyzing binaries is more difficult than analyzing source code and has not received much attention in the literature (a Java bytecodes analysis is performed, for instance, by Barthe and Rezk in [8]).

Given this overall context, the approach adopted in Sails is quite different from existing tools that deal with information flow analysis. Jif, for example, is a security-typed programming language that extends Java with support for information flow and access control, enforced at compile time and it is an ad hoc analysis that requires to annotate the code with some type information. If on the one hand Jif is more efficient than Sails, on the other hand Sails does not require any manual annotation, and it takes all advantages of compositional analyzers (e.g., we can combine Sails with a TVLA-based heap abstraction).

Our approach does not require to change the programming language, since it infers the flow of information directly on the original program, and it asks what are the private data that have not to be leaked to the user during the analysis execution.

## 8    Conclusions

In this paper we presented an information flow analysis through abstract interpretation based on a new domain that combines a variable dependency analysis and a numerical domain. We then introduced Sails that applies and implements this analysis on object-oriented programs. Sails is an extension of Sample, therefore it is modular with respect to the heap abstraction, and it can verify noninterference over recursive data structures using simple and efficient heap analyses. The experimental results underline the effectiveness of the analysis, since Sails is in position to analyze several benchmarks in few milliseconds per program without producing false alarms in more than 90% of the programs. Moreover, our tool does not require to modify the original language, since it works with mainstream languages like Java, and it does not require any manual annotation.

**Acknowledgments.** This work has been partially supported by CINI Cybersecurity National Laboratory within the project "FilieraSicura: Securing the Supply Chain of Domestic Critical Infrastructures from Cyber Attacks" funded by CISCO Systems Inc. and Leonardo SpA, and by MIUR-MAE within the Project "Formal Specification for Secured Software System", under the Indo-Italian Executive Programme of Cooperation in Scientific and Technological Cooperation Project number IN17MO07.

# References

1. Andersen, H.R.: An introduction to binary decision diagrams. Technical report, Course Notes on the WWW (1997)
2. Armstrong, T., Marriott, K., Schachte, P., Søndergaard, H.: Two classes of boolean functions for dependency analysis. Sci. Comput. Program. **31**, 3–45 (1998)
3. Askarov, A., Hedin, D., Sabelfeld, A.: Cryptographically-masked flows. Theor. Comput. Sci. **402**, 82–101 (2008)
4. Askarov, A., Sabelfeld, A.: Security-typed languages for implementation of cryptographic protocols: a case study. In: di Vimercati, S.C., Syverson, P., Gollmann, D. (eds.) ESORICS 2005. LNCS, vol. 3679, pp. 197–221. Springer, Heidelberg (2005). https://doi.org/10.1007/11555827_12
5. Bagnara, R., Hill, P.M., Zaffanella, E.: The parma polyhedra library: toward a complete set of numerical abstractions for the analysis and verification of hardware and software systems. Sci. Comput. Program. **72**, 3–21 (2008)
6. Bagnara, R., Hill, P.M., Zaffanella, E.: Applications of polyhedral computations to the analysis and verification of hardware and software systems. Theor. Comput. Sci. **410**, 4672–4691 (2009)
7. Banerjee, A., Naumann, D.A.: Secure information flow and pointer confinement in a Java-like language. In: Proceedings of the 15th IEEE Workshop on Computer Security Foundations, CSFW 2002. IEEE Computer Society, Washington, DC (2002)
8. Barthe, G., Rezk, T.: Non-interference for a JVM-like language. In: Proceedings of the 2005 ACM SIGPLAN International Workshop on Types in Languages Design and Implementation, TLDI 2005, pp. 103–112. ACM, New York (2005)
9. Bodei, C., Degano, P., Nielson, F., Nielson, H.R.: Static analysis for secrecy and non-interference in networks of processes. In: Malyshkin, V. (ed.) PaCT 2001. LNCS, vol. 2127, pp. 27–41. Springer, Heidelberg (2001). https://doi.org/10.1007/3-540-44743-1_3
10. Clause, J., Li, W., Orso, A.: Dytan: a generic dynamic taint analysis framework. In: Proceedings of the 2007 International Symposium on Software Testing and Analysis, ISSTA 2007, pp. 196–206. ACM, New York (2007)
11. Cortesi, A., Filé, G., Winsborough, W.H.: Prop revisited: propositional formula as abstract domain for groundness analysis. In: LICS, pp. 322–327 (1991)
12. Costantini, G., Ferrara, P., Cortesi, A.: Static analysis of string values. In: Qin, S., Qiu, Z. (eds.) ICFEM 2011. LNCS, vol. 6991, pp. 505–521. Springer, Heidelberg (2011). https://doi.org/10.1007/978-3-642-24559-6_34
13. Cousot, P., Cousot, R.: Systematic design of program analysis frameworks. In: Proceedings of the 6th ACM SIGACT-SIGPLAN Symposium on Principles of Programming Languages, POPL 1979, pp. 269–282. ACM, New York (1979)
14. Cousot, P., Halbwachs, N.: Automatic discovery of linear restraints among variables of a program. In: Proceedings of the 5th ACM SIGACT-SIGPLAN Symposium on Principles of Programming Languages, POPL 1978, pp. 84–96. ACM, New York (1978)
15. De Groef, W., Devriese, D., Nikiforakis, N., Piessens, F.: FlowFox: a web browser with flexible and precise information flow control. In: Proceedings of the 19th ACM Conference on Computer and Communications Security (CCS 2012). ACM (2012)
16. Denning, D.E.: A lattice model of secure information flow. Commun. ACM **19**, 236–243 (1976)

17. Denning, D.E., Denning, P.J.: Certification of programs for secure information flow. Commun. ACM **20**, 504–513 (1977)
18. Ferrara, P.: Static type analysis of pattern matching by abstract interpretation. In: Hatcliff, J., Zucca, E. (eds.) FMOODS/FORTE-2010. LNCS, vol. 6117, pp. 186–200. Springer, Heidelberg (2010). https://doi.org/10.1007/978-3-642-13464-7_15
19. Ferrara, P.: A fast and precise alias analysis for data race detection. In: Proceedings of the Third Workshop on Bytecode Semantics, Verification, Analysis and Transformation (Bytecode 2008), Electronic Notes in Theoretical Computer Science. Elsevier, April 2008
20. Focardi, R., Centenaro, M.: Information flow security of multi-threaded distributed programs. In: Proceedings of the third ACM SIGPLAN Workshop on Programming Languages and Analysis for Security, PLAS 2008, pp. 113–124. ACM, New York (2008)
21. Giacobazzi, R., Mastroeni, I.: Abstract non-interference: parameterizing non-interference by abstract interpretation. In: Proceedings of the 31st ACM SIGPLAN-SIGACT Symposium on Principles of Programming Languages, POPL 2004, pp. 186–197. ACM, New York (2004)
22. Halder, R., Cortesi, A.: Abstract interpretation of database query languages. Comput. Lang. Syst. Struct. **38**, 123–157 (2012)
23. Halder, R., Cortesi, A.: Abstract program slicing of database query languages. In: Proceedings of the 28th Annual ACM Symposium on Applied Computing, Coimbra, Portugal, pp. 838–845. ACM Press (2013)
24. Halder, R., Zanioli, M., Cortesi, A.: Information leakage analysis of database query languages. In: Proceedings of the 29th Annual ACM Symposium on Applied Computing, Gyeongju, Korea, pp. 813–820. ACM Press, 24–28 March 2014
25. Hennessy, M.: The Semantics of Programming Languages: An Elementary Introduction Using Structural Operational Semantics. Wiley, New York (1990)
26. Jeannet, B.: Convex polyhedra library, March 2002. Documentation of the "New Polka" library. http://www.irisa.fr/prive/Bertrand.Jeannet/newpolka.html
27. Jeannet, B., Miné, A.: APRON: a library of numerical abstract domains for static analysis. In: Bouajjani, A., Maler, O. (eds.) CAV 2009. LNCS, vol. 5643, pp. 661–667. Springer, Heidelberg (2009). https://doi.org/10.1007/978-3-642-02658-4_52
28. Joshi, R., Rustan, K., Leino, M.: A semantic approach to secure information flow. Sci. Comput. Program. **37**, 113–138 (2000)
29. Laud, P.: Semantics and program analysis of computationally secure information flow. In: Sands, D. (ed.) ESOP 2001. LNCS, vol. 2028, pp. 77–91. Springer, Heidelberg (2001). https://doi.org/10.1007/3-540-45309-1_6
30. Liu, J.D., George, M.D., Vikram, K., Qi, X., Waye, L., Myers, A.C.: Fabric: a platform for secure distributed computation and storage. In: Proceedings of the ACM SIGOPS 22nd Symposium on Operating Systems Principles, SOSP 2009, pp. 321–334. ACM, New York (2009)
31. Liu, Y., Milanova, A.: Static information flow analysis with handling of implicit flows and a study on effects of implicit flows vs explicit flows. In: Proceedings of the 2010 14th European Conference on Software Maintenance and Reengineering, CSMR 2010, pp. 146–155. IEEE Computer Society, Washington, DC (2010)
32. Miné, A.: A new numerical abstract domain based on difference-bound matrices. In: Danvy, O., Filinski, A. (eds.) PADO 2001. LNCS, vol. 2053, pp. 155–172. Springer, Heidelberg (2001). https://doi.org/10.1007/3-540-44978-7_10

33. Miné, A.: The octagon abstract domain. In: Proceedings of the Workshop on Analysis, Slicing, and Transformation (AST 2001), pp. 310–319. IEEE CS Press, October 2001
34. Myers, A.C., Zheng, L., Zdancewic, S., Chong, S., Nystrom, N.: JIF: Java information flow. Software release, July 2001–2004
35. Pottier, F., Simonet, V.: Information flow inference for ML. ACM Trans. Program. Lang. Syst. **25**, 117–158 (2003)
36. Sabelfeld, A., Myers, A.C.: Language-based information-flow security. IEEE J. Sel. Areas Commun. **21**(1), 5–19 (2003)
37. Sagiv, M., Reps, T., Wilhelm, R.: Parametric shape analysis via 3-valued logic. ACM Trans. Program. Lang. Syst. **24**, 217–298 (2002)
38. Simonet, V.: The flow Caml System: documentation and user's manual. Technical report 0282, Institut National de Recherche en Informatique et en Automatique (INRIA), July 2003
39. Smith, G.: Principles of secure information flow analysis. In: Malware Detection, pp. 297–307 (2007)
40. Smith, G., Volpano, D.: Secure information flow in a multi-threaded imperative language. In: Proceedings of the 25th ACM SIGPLAN-SIGACT Symposium on Principles of Programming Languages, POPL 1998, pp. 355–364. ACM, New York (1998)
41. Stefan, D., Russo, A., Mitchell, J.C., Mazières, D.: Flexible dynamic information flow control in Haskell. SIGPLAN Not. **46**(12), 95–106 (2011)
42. Tolstrup, T.K., Nielson, F., Nielson, H.R.: Information flow analysis for VHDL. In: Malyshkin, V. (ed.) PaCT 2005. LNCS, vol. 3606, pp. 79–98. Springer, Heidelberg (2005). https://doi.org/10.1007/11535294_8
43. Stanford University. Stanford SecuriBench Micro. http://suif.stanford.edu/~livshits/work/securibench-micro/
44. Volpano, D., Irvine, C., Smith, G.: A sound type system for secure flow analysis. J. Comput. Secur. **4**, 167–187 (1996)
45. Zanioli, M., Cortesi, A.: Information leakage analysis by abstract interpretation. In: Černá, I., Gyimóthy, T., Hromkovič, J., Jefferey, K., Králović, R., Vukolić, M., Wolf, S. (eds.) SOFSEM 2011. LNCS, vol. 6543, pp. 545–557. Springer, Heidelberg (2011). https://doi.org/10.1007/978-3-642-18381-2_45
46. Zanioli, M., Ferrara, P., Cortesi, A.: Sails: static analysis of information leakage with sample. In: Proceedings of the 2012 ACM Symposium on Applied Computing, pp. 1308–1313. ACM Press (2012)
47. Zanotti, M.: Security typings by abstract interpretation. In: Hermenegildo, M.V., Puebla, G. (eds.) SAS 2002. LNCS, vol. 2477, pp. 360–375. Springer, Heidelberg (2002). https://doi.org/10.1007/3-540-45789-5_26

# Minimizing Aliasing Effects Using Faster Super Resolution Technique on Text Images

Soma Datta[1(✉)], Nabendu Chaki[1], and Khalid Saeed[2]

[1] Department of Computer Science and Engineering, University of Calcutta,
JD Block, Sector III, Saltlake, Kolkata, India
sdcse_rs@caluniv.ac.in, nabendu@ieee.org
[2] Bialystok University of Technology, Bialystok, Poland
khalids@wp.pl

**Abstract.** Image quality improvement is not bounded within the application of different types of filtering. Resolution improvement is also essential and it solely depends on the estimation of the unknown pixel value that involves a lot of computation. Here a resolution enhancement technique is proposed to reduce the aliasing effects from the text documented image with a reduced amount of computational time. The proposed hybrid method provides better resolution at most informative regions. Here, the unknown pixel value is estimated based on their local informative region. This technique finds the most informative areas, discontinuity at the edges and less informative areas separately. The foreground regions are segmented at the first phase. The unknown pixels values of the foreground regions are calculated in the second step. All-of-these separated images are combined together to construct the high-resolution image at the third phase. The proposed method is mainly verified on aliasing affected text documented images. A distinct advantage of the proposed method over other conventional approaches is that it requires lower computational time to construct a high-resolution image from a single low-resolution one.

**Keywords:** Single image super resolution · Aliasing · Clustering
K nearest neighbour · Feature similarity index metrics

## 1 Introduction

Document image analysis is a technique that converts the document images into a computer readable format. This result comes from the definition of image analysis – it gives a rather digital form as a result of image thinning (pixel number reduction [1]) and segmentation. The latter divides the image into two or more regions, usually, but not necessarily, a main part (foreground) and its background. One of the segmentation techniques is through image binarization [2]. Document image analysis is different from conventional image processing techniques due to its contents, layout structure etc. [3]. Because of some technical

M. L. Gavrilova et al. (Eds.): Trans. on Comput. Sci. XXXI, LNCS 10730, pp. 136–153, 2018.
https://doi.org/10.1007/978-3-662-56499-8_7

limitations in the imaging devices and systems, poor quality images are produced [4]. These include:

1. Lens blurriness, presence of optical distortion.
2. Improper sensor sampling density.
3. Motion blurriness due to low shutter speed.

Scanned documented image contains not only different types of noises but aliasing artifacts as well [5]. Some of the renowned de-noising techniques often fail to generate high quality image. As for example, a low pass filter could uniform the whole image but, it also blurs the significant information of the image. Table 1 shows the general limitations of some well-known text image de-noising methods [6–9]. Aliasing of an image is basically nuisance, it occurs when an image does not contain enough sampling points to represent high frequencies. A sample signal is aliased when sampling frequency is less than twice of the maximum signal frequency [10]. Moreover, in aliasing image, high frequency components are folded into low frequency component. This results in broken edges or artificial pattern of the image. Aliasing effect is increased when image size is increased by simple zooming. Figure 1 shows the aliasing signal and normal signal and Fig. 2 shows few aliasing affected text images. Two different approaches could be followed to get alias free images: either by using anti-aliasing filter or using the super resolution techniques.

**Table 1.** Limitations of some well known de-noising techniques

| Method name | Type of noise | Limitations |
| --- | --- | --- |
| Mathematical morphology | Impulsive noise or salt and pepper noise | Drastically reduce the sharpness of the text and graphical components in the image |
| Vertical and horizontal projection | Clutter noise | Unfortunately, any text attached to the border has been removed |
| Mean and Wiener filter | Gaussian noise | Destruction of lines, blurring of edges and fine details |
| Projection profile based method | Border noise | Can't handle document image with large degree of skew/curl |

Sometimes, anti-aliasing filters are used to minimize the aliasing effects. The concept behind these filters is that it reduces the bandwidth of the original image. Some common anti-aliasing filters are Gaussian low pass filter, Butterworth low pass filter, Median filter, etc. However, these anti-aliasing filters have some common limitation as given below [5, 11].

1. Unable to remove diagonal aliasing effects.
2. Real sub-pixel features and sub-pixel motion are not properly handled.

3. Original shape of the object is distorted, mostly the sharp corners, edges etc.
4. At sub-pixel level, shading aliasing is not completely removed.
5. Computational time is high.

On the other hand, super resolution is an image reconstruction technique that de-aliasing the under sampled images to get the alias free image and increase the resolution of the given input image. This plays a vital role in the last two decades in different fields like, satellite imaging, video surveillance, medical imaging, astronomy etc. Naturally the question comes into our mind that why super resolution is so important in the field of removing aliasing effects. The reason behind that, super resolution (SR) is used to sharpen the smooth and rough edges and to reconstruct the missing texture in the image. SR provides better visualization and interpretations of low resolution image [12].

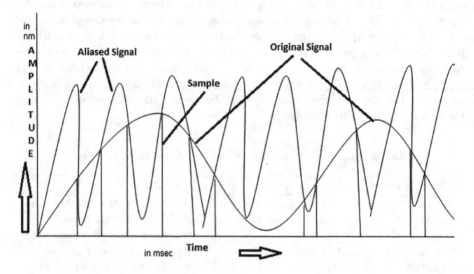

**Fig. 1.** The basic pixel mapping concept in SR

Moreover, in the normal de-noising technique the input, output image sizes are same. Only the quality of the output image gets improved. Whereas, SR techniques aim to increase the number of pixel size per unit area along with the resolution improvement. The high-resolution document image not only yields a clearer image, but also provides additional information that is significant for further analysis.

Figure 3 shows the mapping between given low resolution input image (a) and output image (b). Input image consists of four pixels and the corresponding output image consists of sixteen pixels. Then how the intermediate pixels (marked as "?") are getting the proper intensity value? That is done by different types of SR techniques [13]. In this paper, we have mainly addressed to remove the aliasing effect of the given text documented image. The proposed method

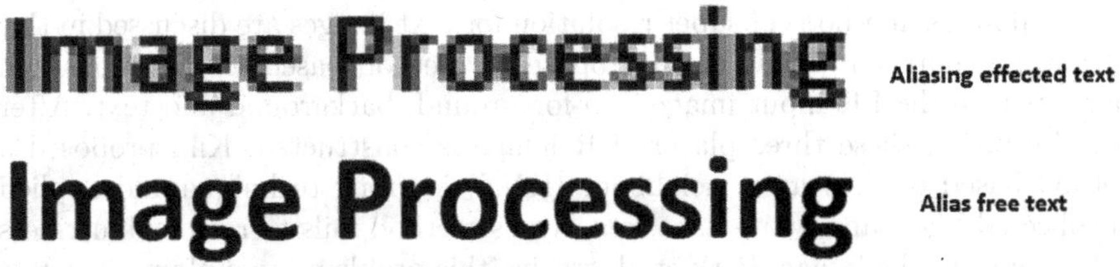

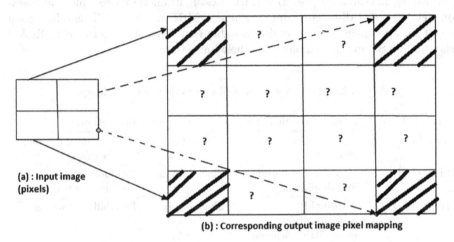

Fig. 2. Aliased and non-aliased text images

Fig. 3. Pixel mapping before and after super resolution

is based on the selected region approach so that the total computational time is less. This method also reduces the effects of noise in produced high resolution image. The rest of the paper is organised in three more sections. Section 2 introduces the technical details of the whole system. Section 3 describes the performance analysis and result. Section 4 is about the conclusions and finally the references.

## 1.1 Related Work

Resolution improvement from poor quality image has become hot research topic. Super resolution method for text image aliasing removal is broadly categorized as [13,14].

1. Non-training based resolution enhancement approach that produces HR image from LR image by performing some deduction without using any training dataset.
2. Training based resolution enhancement approach depending on some machine learning technique that finds some relationships between LR and HR images based on the extracted features of training sample data.

Few popular methods of super resolution for text images are discussed in this section in a nutshell. Zheng et al. proposed a method based on decomposition that separate the LR input image into foreground, background and text. After that, by fusing these three players HR image is constructed. Kim proposed a method based on K-nearest neighbour (KNN) learning technique and applied on collected black and white data sets. Kim's method fails to remove blurriness and noise from the image. Park et al. resolve this problem by applying iterative Bayesian framework. In this method, some prior knowledge has been collected by performing maximum a posterior (MAP) estimation. Banerjee's method based on iterative edge directed framework and a MRF modelling. This offers good result for the images that contains variable font, size, style, script etc. Table 2 shows some SR methods along with their limitations [15–19].

**Table 2.** Limitations of some well known de-noising techniques.

| Proposed by | Name of the methods | Processing unit | Limitations |
|---|---|---|---|
| Thouin et al. | Optimization of scoring function | Block of pixels | Can't remove the rough edge artifacts |
| Shan et al. | Iterative up-sampling and de-blurring | Block of pixels | Produces ringing artifacts for text image |
| Ho et al. | Threshold decomposition and curve fitting scheme | Block of pixels | Possibility of wrong clustering |
| Kim's method | KNN learning | Block of pixels | Not able to handle gray scale images where blur and noise relative to the imaging sensor are explicitly present |
| Xin Li's method | Edge directed interpolation based on bilinear and covariance adaptive approach | Pixel | Computational complexity is very high. Not well suited for hand written documented image |
| Park et al. | Iterative Bayesian framework and MRF model | Block of pixels | Does not offers good result if training samples contains different font, size and style in the text or graphics |
| Kyuha Choi | Learning patch pairs of low and high-resolution images | Pixel | The one to multiple mapping of an LR patch to HR patches those results in image quality degradation |

The above-mentioned SR methods may not always offer good result for the text documented images due to the following reasons:

1. There exist very little differences between some text characters like l (small L) and I (capital i).
2. Complex documented text image contains huge components like edges, corners, line segments among its characters.
3. Contextual information could be lost if the resolution is very poor.
4. There may continuity of lines with same frequencies.
5. Computational time is very high for text documented images. In our method, we have tried to resolve points 3, 4 and 5 for aliasing affected text documented images.

We have tried to resolve points 3, 4 and 5 for aliasing affected text documented images.

## 2  Design of the New Super Resolution Technique

Aliasing is most essential at the time when, improving the resolution in text documented image. There are lots of computation techniques to reduce aliasing effects. However, those techniques consume a considerable time to compute. A hybrid approach is described to reduce computation time during the improvement of resolution for a documented text image. Figure 4 shows the block diagram of the whole system. In this approach, an estimation based improvement algorithm is proposed. It is applied on the selected foreground of the text regions. The distinction between foreground and background regions is determined by combining two separated techniques as pre-processing 1 and pre-processing 2. Here, input image is pre-processed in three independent pre-processing stages. Pre-processing 1 efficiently detects the text locations and the boundary of the contours from the entire image. However, it is unable to determine the text regions. Besides that, pre-processing 2 selects text region along with some background noises. The combination of pre-processing 1 and pre-processing 2 provides much better result. After completion of pre-processing 1 and pre-processing 2, the both output matrix are merged together to determine the foreground regions. It is used as a mask in next phase. In the third independent enhancement phase, the contrast is enhanced and overall noises have been removed from the whole image. Finally, this enhanced image is combined with the previously calculated foreground regions for constructing the higher resolution image. The block diagram is explained in the next sub sections.

### 2.1  Image Acquisition

USI_SIPI [20] and Ghega [21] datasets are used here. USI_SIPI database contains various sizes of data as $256 * 256$ pixels, $512 * 512$ pixels and $1024 * 1024$ pixels. The size of black and white image is 8 bits/pixels. The 24 bit/pixels are used for colour images. The Ghega dataset contains two groups of documents, 110 data-sheets of electronic components and 136 patents. Each .png image is about 300 dpi.

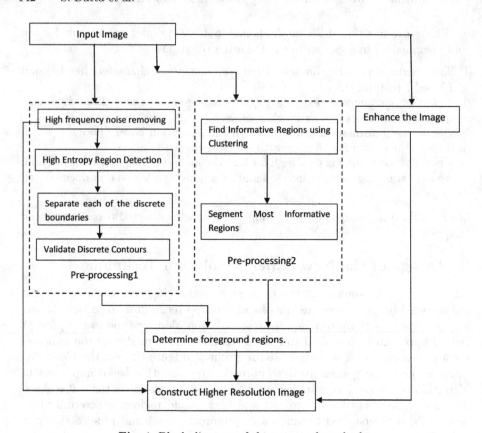

**Fig. 4.** Block diagram of the proposed method

## 2.2    Enhancement

Document image quality degrades due to poor storage condition, environmental effects, usage manual scanning error etc. Document image enhancement is vital to recover the damage character, minimize shadow through effects, removing unwanted border and finally to eliminate the noisy background area and highlight the text regions. Some of the input image does not have sharp boundary in the documented text image characters. Second order derivatives are useful for sharpening the boundary. From the experimental result, it is observed that: Laplacian operator [20] works much better than Prewitt, Sobel [21] etc. to determine the boundary. Since, Laplacian operator is a second order derivative mask and the others are first order derivative mask. The second order derivative with respect to x and y is calculated as:

$$\frac{\delta^2 f}{\delta x^2} = f(x+1,y) - 2*f(x,y) + f(x-1,y) \qquad (1)$$

and

$$\frac{\delta^2 f}{\delta y^2} = f(x,y+1) - 2*f(x,y) + f(x,y-1) \qquad (2)$$

Hence the Laplacian results,

$$\Delta^2 f(x,y) = f(x+1,y) - 4 * f(x,y) + f(x-1,y) + f(x,y-1) \qquad (3)$$

Laplacian filter highlights grey level discontinuities in an image. It de-emphasizes regions with slowly changing grey levels and increments of greyish edge lines, other discontinuities on a dark background. These sharpened images would be used later during higher resolution image construction. Figure 5 shows the noiseless output image.

 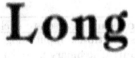

**Fig. 5.** Effects of using filter on noisy document

## 2.3  Pre-processing 1

Pre-processing 1 is a sequence of process that is applied upon the input image to locate the position of texts information rather than the entire regions. The sequences for the entire operations are already illustrated in Fig. 4.

**High Frequency Noise Removal.** Most of the documented image has light coloured background that contains spots due to dust, oil etc. Low pass filter efficiently removes such spots; because the spots are not as dark as text. The main idea behind low pass filter is that it passes the low frequency signals while blocking the high frequency signal. Here, Butterworth low pass filter [9] is used to remove unwanted spots or patches. The first $2*n-1$ derivatives for the power function with respect to frequency are zero. It is formulated as follows:

$$|H(j\omega)| = \frac{1}{\sqrt{1 + (\frac{\omega}{\omega_c})^{2*n}}} \qquad (4)$$

where presents transfer function at angular frequency $\omega$. $\omega$ is angular frequency and is equal to $2\pi f$. $\omega_o$ is the cut off frequency expressed as an angular value and is equal to $2\pi f_o$. After applying this filter, the spots and other high frequencies noises are removed. However, it blurs the whole image.

**Boundary Detection.** After removing the high frequency noises, text regions need to be extracted. It is observed that the entropy is high in transit regions between text and background. Hence gradient operator [22] is suitable to detect boundary region. Mathematically, for an image function f(x, y), the gradient magnitude g(x, y) and the gradient direction $\theta(x,y)$ are computed as

$$\theta(x,y) \cong \tan \frac{\Delta y}{\Delta x} \quad \text{and} \quad g(x,y) \cong (\Delta x^2 + \Delta y^2)^{1/2} \qquad (5)$$

where $\triangle x = f(x+n,y) - f(x-n,y)$ and $\triangle y = f(x,y+n) - f(x,y-n)$ and n is a small integer.

**Separate Each of the Discrete Boundaries.** In the previous workflow the boundary has been detected, now main remaining task is to separate individual contour region for further analysis. Procedure 1 explains this contour separation process. It accepts the binary matrix obtained from previous section as input and separates each of the contours.

---

**Procedure 1.** Isolate each of the contours

**Assumptions:** Input image should be in gray scale.
**Input:** The binary matrix i.e., B-Edge-Matrix containing out layer of text regions.
**Output:** Segment individual regions.
**Step**
 1: Consider any arbitrary point, from B-Edge-Matrix, with a value 1.
 2: Push this point into stack.
 3: Pop a point from a stack.
 4: Change the corresponding status of popped point into B-Edge-Matrix as T.
 5: Store the popped point into an array A. Find all other points from B-Edge-Matrix which has a value 1 and adjacent with popped point.
 6: Push all the points obtained in step 6 into the stack.
 7: Repeat step 3 to step 7 until stack is empty.
 8: Fetch all the points from array A, and send them into algorithm 2 for validation.
 9: Clear the array A and repeat step 1 to step 9 until no more point is available in B-Edge-Matrix.
10: End

---

Procedure 1 segments each individual region and send them for validation. In this procedure stack and queue data structures are used. Stack is used to accumulate connected components of a contour. 8-connectivity [21] is used to find the components that are discussed in Step 6. Queue is used for temporary storage that stores the points of contour. Next section describes the contour validation process.

**Validation of Individual Contours.** In this section each individual contour patterns are examined. Procedure 2 will explain the validation process. It takes the co-ordinates of contour points as an input and returns the decision whether it is valid or not a valid text region.

In Procedure 2, number of sample point is 1/3 of total points. This actually reduces the influence of the pattern. Otherwise local variation pattern will dilute the overall contour pattern. In step 3 the values of "Val" vector varies in wide ranges of decimal points. Hence they need to be fitted in the scale. Nearest neighbour technique is used to map them in a scale of $0°, 15°, 30°, 35°$ etc. After determining the validation of contour points, they are sent to the "Determining text region; Sect. 2.5" where documented text regions are extracted.

**Procedure 2.** Determine the Validation of Individual Contours

**Assumptions:** Individual contour points.

**Input:** Individual contour points.

**Output:** Return the result regarding the validation of each individual contours.

**Step**

1: Find the number of connected points in the contour and store the value in P variable.

2: Find $P/3$ sample points from contour points.

3: Find the angle between two consecutive points in clock wise direction using Eq. 5.

$$Value = \tan^{-1} \frac{y_2 - y_1}{x_2 - x_1} \tag{6}$$

Val[i] is the ith element of array value.

4: Calculate histogram of Val array using an approximation 15° and the ranges are 0, 15, 30, 45, ..... store the results in angle vector. Apply a binary classifier upon P and angle vector to classify whether it is a valid contour or not. The number of tree is 7. The binary classifier is trained with preloaded data. End

## 2.4 Pre-processing 2

The advantage of this approach over pre-processing 1 is that it determines the text region more accurately. It is observed that text region has high gray scale variation rather than background region. Hence texture information is suitable to detect most informative region. As it works upon the texture information, hence it is independent on gray scale intensity variation. Partially supervised clustering technique [23] is suitable to determine most informative region. Procedure 3 will describe the technique to find most informative regions. The output of Procedure 3 is mostly important during increment of resolution.

This is a partially supervised clustering technique. In Procedure 3, Step 1 to Step 5 is used to calculate the smoothness factor of the input image. Step 6 to Step 11 describes the technique to categorize the image pixels into foreground and background. $C_1$, $C_2$, $C_3$ are the initial cluster centres. The initial value is chosen on the basis of experimental results.

## 2.5 Determine Text Region

Pre-processing 2 finds most informative regions on the basis of texture variation. Hence pre-processing 2 is not able to distinguish between gray scale variations caused by text region like high frequency noises. However pre-processing 1 is not good to detect the total text regions. Procedure 4 is used to combine pre-processing 1 and pre-processing 2.

Procedure 4 combines the two independent pre-processing methods and finalized the foreground text regions where estimation is required during up gradation of resolution.

## Procedure 3. Find most informative region.

**Assumptions:** Let $E = \{e1, e2, e3..., en\}$ is the set of entropy values in entropy matrix. $C = \{C1, C2, C3\}$ is the set of initial cluster centers.

**Input:** The input Image.

**Output:** The most informative region's mask

**Step**

1: r=total-row-input-image; c=total-columns-input-image
2: Repeat Step 3 to Step 6 for row=n/2 to r−n/2
3: Repeat Step 4 to Step 6 for col=n/2 to c−n/2
4: Crop the sub image Sub-image = input-image(row−n/2 to row+n/2, col−n/2 to col+n/2)
5: Compute smoothness S for the sub image

$$S = 1 - \frac{1}{1 + \sigma^2} \tag{7}$$

Where $\sigma$ is the standard deviation the sub images.

6: Region(row,col)=S
7: // Clustering method Assume the number of clusters to be made, that is, C, where $2 \leq C \leq N$. Choose an appropriate level of cluster fuzziness $f > 1$. In this case $C = 3$. $C_1$ is the initial cluster centre of most informative region. $C_2$ is comparative less informative cluster region and $C_3$ is the less informative region. These cluster centres are considered as initial cluster centres.
8: Initialize the $N * C * M$ sized membership matrix U, at random, such that $U_{ijm} \in [0, 1]$ and

$$\sum_{j=1}^{C} U_{ijm} = 1 \tag{8}$$

for each i and a fixed value of m.

9: for $j^{th}$ cluster and its $m^{th}$ dimension, calculate cluster centers $CC^{jm}$ by using the expression given below

$$C_{ij} = \frac{\sum_{j=1}^{N} U_{ijm}^{f} * X_{im}}{\sum_{j=1}^{N} U_{ijm}^{f}} \tag{9}$$

10: Find the Euclidean distance between $i^{th}$ data point and $j^{th}$ cluster centre with respect to, $m^{th}$ dimension as:

$$D_{ijm} = |(X_{ij} - C_{jm})| \tag{10}$$

Update fuzzy membership matrix U according to $D_{ijm}$. If $D_{ijm} > 0$, then

$$U_{ijm} = \frac{1}{\sum_{c=1}^{C} \frac{D_{ijm}}{D_{icm}}^{\frac{2}{f-1}}} \tag{11}$$

If $D_{ijm} = 0$, then the data point coincides with the corresponding data point of $j^{th}$ cluster centre $CC_{jm}$ and it has the full membership value, that is, $U_{ijm} = 1$.

11: Repeat from Step 6 to Step 11 until the changes in $U \leq \varrho$, where $\varrho$ is a pre-specified termination criterion.
12: Find all the regions that belongs to cluster $Z_1$ whose cluster centre is denoted by $C_1$
13: The regions supplied by the previous Steps are considered as most informative region and returned the coordinates of most informative regions.
14: Stop

**Procedure 4.** Find actual text regions from a documented text image

**Input:** Two output matrixes, $M_1$ and $M_2$ provided by Procedure 2 and Procedure 3 respectively.

**Output:** A binary matrix (BM) that contains the mask of actual text region.

**Step**

1: i=1
2: Choose any arbitrary point from $M_2$ where value is 1.
3: Push the coordinate of that point into stack. Change the value of the point of $M_2$ with i.
4: Pop a coordinate point from stack.
5: Pop a coordinate point from stack.
6: Find all other points adjacent to the coordinates with a value 1 from $M_2$ with i.
7: Push that coordinates into stack and change the value of the points of $M_2$ with i.
8: Repeat step 4 to step 6 until stack in empty.
9: i=i+1.
10: Repeat step 2 to step 3 until there is no more element in $M_2$ with value 1.
11: j=2.
12: Find the coordinates of the points from $M_2$ where value is j. Store the coordinates in C vector and number of points in P variable.
13: If the number of points (P) obtained in step 11 is 0 the GOTO step 18
14: Find the number of points from $M_1$ matrix whose coordinates are in C and value is 1. Store the result in count1 variable.
15: Calculate the ratio $R = C/P$ If R is greater than a predetermine threshold then the region is a valid text region.
16: Update corresponding values BM as 1; $BM(P) = 1$.
17: j=j+1
18: GOTO step 11
19: Stop

## 2.6    Constructing the Higher Resolution Image

The final stage is to construct higher resolution image from the intermediate image. Lots of techniques exist to construct higher resolution image from single low-resolution image. However, those methods take much more computational time to generate the output image. Background is not important in documented text image. Hence computational time for background processing should be avoided. Procedure 5 is a technique to construct a higher resolution anti-aliased foreground image.

## 3    Experimental Results

The proposed method has been evaluated with images from USI_SIPI [24] and Ghega [25] dataset. Results are evaluated both visually and quantitatively on the said database and compared with other existing super resolution approaches for text documented image analysis. The performance of the proposed method is evaluated based on some quality metrics and computational time. The quality

---

**Procedure 5.** Construct higher resolution image

---

**Input:** Enhanced image $E_1$ obtained from 2.1 sections, Low pass image $L_1$ supplied
from Sect. 2.2.2 Binary matrix (mask) obtained from Procedure 4 to determine
foreground region. Zoom is the resolution scaling factor.

**Output:** High resolution image new-matrix

**Step**

1: row and col variable represent the sizes of the input image.

2: Repeat Step 3 for all row and the index is i-row.

3: Repeat Step 4 to Step 15 for all col and the index is denoted as i-col.

4: Check the coordinate (i-row, i-col) that belongs to foreground or background from
$M_2$ matrix. If it is background pixel then no need to estimate the intermediate
values and GOTO Step 12.

5: For foreground pixels intermediate values need to be estimate. A=$E_1(i_row, i_col)$
B=$E_1(i - row + 1, j)$ C=$E_1(i + 1, j + 1)$ D=$E_1(i, j + 1)$
Start-row-value=A Row-value-diff-ratio=(B-A)/zoom End-row-value=D End-
row-value-diff-ratio=(C-D)/zoom Count1=0

6: Repeat Step 7 to Step 11 for ((i-row-1 * zoom+1) to (((i-1)*zoom+1)+zoom) and
in each time new index will be stored i-frac.

7: new-matrix(i-frac, ((j-1)*zoom+1)) = start-row-value + count1 * row-value-diff-
ratio

8: new-matrix(i-frac,      (((j-1)*zoom+1)+zoom))=end-row-value+count1*end-row-
value-diff-ratio $count1 = count1 + 1$

9: A-dss=$new - matrix(i - frac, ((j - 1) * zoom + 1))$ D-daa=$new - matrix(i - frac, (((j - 1) * zoom + 1) + zoom))$ col-value-difference-ratio=$(D - daa - A - dss)/zoom$ count2 =0

10: Repeat Step 11 for the interval ((j-1)*zoom+1) to (((j-1)*zoom+1)+zoom) and
store the index into j-frac.

11: new-matrix(i-frac,   j-frac)=A-dss+count2*col-value-difference-ratio    count2   =
count2 +1; GOTO Step 15. Repeat Step 13 for the interval ((i-1)*zoom+1) to
(((i-1)*zoom+1)+zoom) and in each iteration new index value is stored in i-frac

12: Repeat Step 14 for the interval ((j-1)*zoom+1) to (((j-1)*zoom+1)+zoom) and in
each iteration new index value is stored in i-frac

13: new-matrix(i-frac, j-fractor)=High-Pass(i-row, j-col)

14: Print i and j

15: Stop

---

metrics are Peak Signal to Noise Ratio (PSNR), Structure Similarity Index Measurement (SSIM), Feature Similarity Index Measurement (FSIM), Root Mean
Square Error (RMSE) and Smoothness [26–28]. All of these metrics need reference images.

The metrics are compared with the output image and the corresponding
reference images. USI_SIPI and Ghega datasets does not contain any reference
images. We have prepared low-resolution images from the said databases and
performed all the operation on the generated low-resolution images. Here the
original USI_SIPI and Ghega datasets are used as the corresponding reference
image. This method follows two phases. First, one has to segment the only textual
informative region and remove the non-informative region, i.e., the background.

This independently increases resolution at the cost of additional computation. Assume the computational time to complete this phase is T1. In phase 2, super resolution is to be applied on the newly segmented informative regions. This also independently lowers the computational time. Let the computational time to complete phase two is T2. Hence the total computational time for our approach is T = T1 + T2. Table 3 and Fig. 6 shows the total computational time and graphical representation for different methods respectively.

**Table 3.** Computational time calculation

| Method name | Name of the database | Total computational time | Computational time for increase resolution of the informative region $T = (T1 + T2)$ |
|---|---|---|---|
| Xin's "NEDI" method | USI-SIPI | 28.1283 s | NA |
| | Ghega | 77.1743 s | NA |
| Bicubic interpolation | USI-SIPI | 54.9589 s | NA |
| | Ghega | 128.96660 s | NA |
| Yun Zheng's method | USI-SIPI | 205.3261 s | NA |
| | Ghega | 83.5737 s | NA |
| Proposed method | USI-SIPI | 10.9548 s | T1 = 6.9548 s, T2 = 4.0 s |
| | Ghega | 12.52074 s | T1 = 8.20 s, T2 = 4.32 s |

Here, the proposed method takes considerably less amount of time for images taken from both the databases. "NEDI" method uses bilinear interpolation and covariance-based adaptive interpolation. Due to these two steps, it takes 28.1283 s for USI_SIPI and 77.1743 s for Ghega database. On the other hand, only "bicubic interpolation" takes 54.9589 s and 128.9666 s respectively. Table 4 summarizes the value of metrics for USI_SIPI database and Table 5 illustrates value of metrics for Ghega database. Smoothness of our proposed method is much higher than the other methods for both the databases. SSIM is very near

**Table 4.** Metrics measurement for Ghega Database.

| Metrics name/Measurement | Xin's "NEDI" method | Bicubic interpolation | Yun Zheng's method | Our method |
|---|---|---|---|---|
| PSNR | 4.2689 | 4.5291 | 9.7086 | 5.3521 |
| SSIM | .9154 | .9301 | .8928 | .9038 |
| FSIM | .6471 | .5234 | .6105 | .6028 |
| RMSE | 155.9888 | 151.3852 | 83.3889 | 137.7009 |
| Smoothness | .1650 | .6131 | .1233 | .1684 |

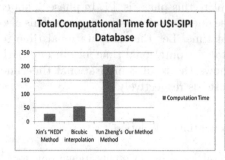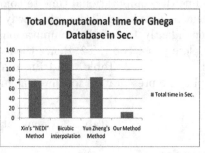

**Fig. 6.** Total computational time for different methods.

| Ground Truth Image | Bicubic (a) | Xin's "NEDI" Method (b) | Yun Zheng's Method (c) | Proposed Method (d) |
|---|---|---|---|---|
| Dr. | Dr. | Dr. | Dr. | Dr. |
| CLL4729A THRU CLL4764A  1.0W ZENER DIODE 5% TOLERANCE | CLL4729A THRU CLL4764A  1.0W ZENER DIODE 5% TOLERANCE | CLL4729A THRU CLL4764A  1.0W ZENER DIODE 5% TOLERANCE | CLL4729A THRU CLL4764A  1.0W ZENER DIODE 5% TOLERANCE | CLL4729A THRU CLL4764A  1.0W ZENER DIODE 5% TOLERANCE |
| Aa | Aa | Aa | Aa | Aa |
| A myth | A myth | A myth | A myth | A myth |
| super | super | super | super | super |

**Fig. 7.** An output image produced by (a) Bicubic, (b) NEDI method, (c) Zheng's method and (d) Proposed method

**Table 5.** Metrics measurement for USI-SIPI Database

| Metrics name/Measurement | Xin's "NEDI" method | Bicubic interpolation | Yun Zheng's method | Our method |
|---|---|---|---|---|
| PSNR | 6.11 | 7.7102 | 6.0141 | 7.5826 |
| SSIM | .8312 | .9449 | .8030 | .9494 |
| FSIM | .5551 | .4281 | .5041 | .4218 |
| RMSE | 126.1046 | 104.9619 | 127.5961 | 106.5154 |
| Smoothness | .1027 | .0524 | .0981 | .4218 |

to 1 for Ghega database. These metrics values reflects the good quality of images and minimizing of aliasing effects. Experiments were done on the test images for magnification factor 5. Figure 7 shows the optical effects on some selected input images for Bicubic interpolation [29], Xin's "NEDI" super-resolution method [30], Yun Zheng's method [31] and the proposed method respectively.

## 4   Conclusion

In this paper, we have proposed a new hybrid anti-aliasing technique that improves the resolution for text document images. Experiments with different standard databases demonstrate that the proposed method provides good result in terms of some metrics besides having significantly lower computational time. One limitation for our method is that it does not provide good result if the document contains dark spot or patches. In such cases, experimental results show that RMSE value is going to be higher than the other methods. However, the main contribution of the proposed method is to remove aliasing effects in lower processing time. Text aliasing reflects in the eventual smoothness of the target image. Higher smoothness value means smaller amount of aliasing effects. The proposed method offers much better smoothness value than the other existing methods, for images taken from both USI_SIPI and Ghega databases. Our next goal is to remove aliasing effects, dark patches, and spots of oils and to increase the resolution of the whole image as well.

**Acknowledgement.** I would like to acknowledge Visvesvaraya PhD Scheme for Electronics and IT. I am also thankful to Department of Computer Science and Engineering, University of Calcutta for infrastructural supports.

## References

1. Tabedzki, M., Saeed, K., Szczepański, A.: A modified K3M thinning algorithm. Int. J. Appl. Math. Comput. Sci. **26**(2), 439–450 (2016)
2. Buczkowski, M., Saeed, K.: Fusion-based noisy image segmentation method. In: Chaki, R., Cortesi, A., Saeed, K., Chaki, N. (eds.) Advanced Computing and Systems for Security. AISC, vol. 396, pp. 21–35. Springer, New Delhi (2016). https://doi.org/10.1007/978-81-322-2653-6_2

3. Fujisawa, H.: Forty years of research in character and document recognition—an industrial perspective. Pattern Recogn. **41**(8), 2435–2446 (2008)
4. Yuan, L., Sun, J., Quan, L., Shum, H.Y.: Image deblurring with blurred/noisy image pairs. ACM Trans. Graph. (TOG) **26**, 1 (2007). ACM
5. Jimenez, J., Echevarria, J.I., Sousa, T., Gutierrez, D.: SMAA: enhanced subpixel morphological antialiasing. Comput. Graph. Forum **31**, 355–364 (2012). Wiley Online Library
6. Papandreou, A., Gatos, B.: A novel skew detection technique based on vertical projections. In: 2011 International Conference on Document Analysis and Recognition (ICDAR), pp. 384–388. IEEE (2011)
7. LatifoğLu, F.: A novel approach to speckle noise filtering based on artificial bee colony algorithm: an ultrasound image application. Comput. Methods Programs Biomed. **111**(3), 561–569 (2013)
8. Chen, J., Benesty, J., Huang, Y., Doclo, S.: New insights into the noise reduction Wiener filter. IEEE Trans. Audio Speech Lang. Process. **14**(4), 1218–1234 (2006)
9. Fan, K.C., Wang, Y.K., Lay, T.R.: Marginal noise removal of document images. Pattern Recogn. **35**(11), 2593–2611 (2002)
10. Nyquist, H.: Certain topics in telegraph transmission theory. Proc. IEEE **90**(2), 280–305 (2002)
11. Kaur, J., Kaur, M., Kaur, P., Kaur, M.: Comparative analysis of image denoising techniques. Int. J. Emerg. Technol. Adv. Eng. **2**(6), 296–298 (2012)
12. Park, S.C., Park, M.K., Kang, M.G.: Super-resolution image reconstruction: a technical overview. IEEE Signal Process. Mag. **20**(3), 21–36 (2003)
13. Nasrollahi, K., Moeslund, T.B.: Super-resolution: a comprehensive survey. Mach. Vis. Appl. **25**(6), 1423–1468 (2014)
14. Li, X., Lam, K.M., Qiu, G., Shen, L., Wang, S.: Example-based image super-resolution with class-specific predictors. J. Vis. Commun. Image Represent. **20**(5), 312–322 (2009)
15. Thouin, P.D., Chang, C.I.: A method for restoration of low-resolution document images. Int. J. Doc. Anal. Recogn. **2**(4), 200–210 (2000)
16. Park, J., Kwon, Y., Kim, J.H.: An example-based prior model for text image super-resolution. In: Proceedings of the Eighth International Conference on Document Analysis and Recognition, pp. 374–378. IEEE (2005)
17. Kim, H.Y.: Binary operator design by k-nearest neighbor learning with application to image resolution increasing. Int. J. Imaging Syst. Technol. **11**(5), 331–339 (2000)
18. Ho, T.C., Zeng, B.: Super-resolution image by curve fitting in the threshold decomposition domain. In: IEEE Asia Pacific Conference on Circuits and Systems, APC-CAS 2008, pp. 332–335. IEEE (2008)
19. Shan, Q., Li, Z., Jia, J., Tang, C.K.: Fast image/video upsampling. ACM Trans. Graph. (TOG) **27**(5), 153 (2008)
20. Datta, S., Chaki, N., Choudhury, S.: Information density based image binarization for text document containing graphics. In: Saeed, K., Homenda, W. (eds.) CISIM 2016. LNCS, vol. 9842, pp. 105–115. Springer, Cham (2016). https://doi.org/10.1007/978-3-319-45378-1_10
21. Gonzalez, R.C., Woods, R.E.: Image processing. In: Digital Image Processing, vol. 2 (2007)
22. Ando, S.: Consistent gradient operators. IEEE Trans. Pattern Anal. Mach. Intell. **22**(3), 252–265 (2000)
23. Ghosh, P., Bhattacharjee, D., Nasipuri, M.: Blood smear analyzer for white blood cell counting: a hybrid microscopic image analyzing technique. Appl. Soft Comput. **46**, 629–638 (2016)

24. Southern California: USC-SIPI image database. University of Southern California. http://sipi.usc.edu/database/
25. von Ghega, C.R.: Ghega-dataset: a dataset for document understanding and classification. http://machinelearning.inginf.units.it/data-and-tools/ghega-dataset
26. Jagalingam, P., Hegde, A.V.: A review of quality metrics for fused image. Aquat. Procedia **4**, 133–142 (2015)
27. Zhang, L., Zhang, L., Mou, X., Zhang, D.: FSIM: a feature similarity index for image quality assessment. IEEE Trans. Image Process. **20**(8), 2378–2386 (2011)
28. Hanhart, P., Bernardo, M.V., Pereira, M., Pinheiro, A.M., Ebrahimi, T.: Benchmarking of objective quality metrics for HDR image quality assessment. EURASIP J. Image Video Process. **2015**(1), 39 (2015)
29. Keys, R.: Cubic convolution interpolation for digital image processing. IEEE Trans. Acoust. Speech Signal Process. **29**(6), 1153–1160 (1981)
30. Li, X., Orchard, M.T.: New edge-directed interpolation. IEEE Trans. Image Process. **10**(10), 1521–1527 (2001)
31. Zheng, Y., Kang, X., Li, S., He, Y., Sun, J.: Real-time document image superresolution by fast matting. In: 2014 11th IAPR International Workshop on Document Analysis Systems (DAS), pp. 232–236. IEEE (2014)

# Author Index

Printed in the United States
By Bookmasters